T0246295

Also by Julie Sedivy

Memory Speaks:
On Losing and Reclaiming Language and Self

Language in Mind:
An Introduction to Psycholinguistics

Sold on Language:
How Advertisers Talk to You and What This
Says About You (coauthor)

Linguaphile

Linguaphile

A Life of Language Love

Julie Sedivy

Farrar, Straus and Giroux

New York

Farrar, Straus and Giroux
120 Broadway, New York 10271

Copyright © 2024 by Julie Sedivy
All rights reserved
Printed in the United States of America
First edition, 2024

Library of Congress Cataloging-in-Publication Data
Names: Sedivy, Julie, author.
Title: Linguaphile : a life of language love / Julie Sedivy.
Description: First edition. | New York : Farrar, Straus and Giroux, 2024. |
   Includes bibliographical references. |
Identifiers: LCCN 2024008758 | ISBN 9780374601836 (hardcover)
Subjects: LCSH: Language and languages. | Psycholinguistics.
Classification: LCC P107 .S43 2024 | DDC 401/.9—dc23/eng/20240523
LC record available at https://lccn.loc.gov/2024008758

Designed by Patrice Sheridan

Our books may be purchased in bulk for promotional, educational, or business
use. Please contact your local bookseller or the Macmillan Corporate and
Premium Sales Department at 1-800-221-7945, extension 5442, or by email at
MacmillanSpecialMarkets@macmillan.com.

www.fsgbooks.com
Follow us on social media at @fsgbooks

1   3   5   7   9   10   8   6   4   2

For my brother Vac, the bello biondo *among us:*
I remember you as the silver moon
floating over darkened fields, leading us all home

In the language of love, words are our soul.
We are language—these ruins, our palaces.

—NIZAMI GANJAVI (D. 1209), *TREASURY OF MYSTERIES*,
TRANSLATED BY AQSA IJAZ

Contents

PART I: Childhood

Before meaning   3

Minds, meeting and parting   22

Feral polyglot   48

Prosthesis   66

Crevasses   79

PART II: Maturity

The rectilinear movement of time   105

Resolving ambiguities   143

How to be a success!   162

Pleasure hunts   177

PART III: Loss

Missing words   213

Limits   230

Silence   252

Notes   277

Acknowledgments   319

PART I

Childhood

Before meaning

Do you want to see our rabbits? asked Maura, my new friend, who at four years of age outpaced me by a year. She was speaking Italian, which I did not speak. I nodded. She brought me to a pen outside the barn with a mass of rabbits at its center. Looking closely, I could make out a few individuals, small clumps of fur huddled against the rabbit pile.

Do you want to see some bigger rabbits? she asked, still in Italian. Again, I nodded. In a nearby pen, much larger this time, were dozens of meaty rabbits flexing their legs, lurching around in the cage, hopping over each other, ignoring all the other animals including me and Maura.

Do you want to see *bigger* rabbits? asked Maura. I nodded vigorously. She led me to the barn, and we stepped into the sweet, stinking darkness. I could make out two enormous shapes, bigger than horses. I fled.

When Maura persuaded me the next day to reenter the barn, I could see, after I let my eyes adjust to the darkness, that the two animals were oxen, not gargantuan rabbits. Perhaps she had never said "rabbits" after all. Who knows what she had said? At that time, Italian was to me a bewitching confusion, boiling and streaming in all directions. Its connection to the actual world was tenuous and constantly shifting. It was only now and then that I caught a word with my mind; words were like fish, solid things making sudden, unexpected appearances, flashes of substance and meaning in the liquidity of language flowing all around me. You had to be quick to snatch them before they were lost in the fast-moving stream.

My childhood was defined by repeated immersions in unfamiliar languages. By the age of five, due to my family's winding trajectory through Europe and eventually to Canada, five languages had seeped into my brain to various degrees: Czech, the language of my parents and of my birth country; German, spoken by the orderly and temperate Viennese, who frowned with disapproval when my siblings and I spilled out to play on the grass of the city parks; Italian, the language in which I roamed with the wild Maura over a farm near the Dolomites, the language of a freedom bought by the harried neglect of parents far too preoccupied with the business of survival to keep track of my proximity to the well, where I was most drawn to play; French, learned in the back alleys of East Montreal, where we organized footraces and games, relying on the *lingua francophona* shared by the various immigrant kids there.

Then English—the language of authority and aspiration. I first properly encountered it at school, in strangely formal interactions with a pretty kindergarten teacher who spoke an English seasoned with a French-Canadian accent and who lavished approval on my ever-more-successful attempts to emulate this official language.

English would come to dominate all the others, jostling its way to the front of everything, like the big, loud, entitled sibling whose demands leave its peers cowed and in a state of ongoing disequilibrium. Languages can coexist in the human mind, but they are fated to live out an endless power struggle; languages that garner the favors and attentions of their host brain grow ever stronger at the expense of their fellows. And in the brain of an Eastern European immigrant kid growing up in Montreal before the enactment of language laws to protect French, the contest was nothing if not rigged.

But English also began as liquid. In my first weeks in that serene kindergarten room with its stenciled alphabet and cushion-strewn rug, English sounded like this:

taktheblicksenoffazinzerlappingwentheyfostedfringilybu-
talmofaid. Okay?

By kindergarten, I had experienced an infant's state of in-comprehension not once, twice, three, or four times, but five. Many adults have no memory of ever being in such a state. For me it was a prolonged, recurring condition.

By the time a newborn emerges into the cool air, its mind flares with recognition when it hears the language that flowed outside the flesh walls that cradled it. Scientists can measure this: they place pacifiers in the mouths of newborns, wired to record the vigor of their sucking, and note that infants suck more eagerly when they hear their mother tongue—even if spoken by strangers over a loudspeaker—than when a foreign language is emitted from the speaker. In the womb, they have absorbed the click-clack of the rhythms of their language, its cadences and rising-falling motifs, its predilections for herding consonants together or for spacing them out as sparse counterpoints to the airiness of vowels.

It is then, and in the months that follow, that an infant and her native language come to possess each other—before naming, before meaning, before there is even a notion that sound bears the burden of meaning. Something like love is there in the depth of familiarity that has settled into the infant's neurons. It can be measured by pacifiers connected to electrical devices.

It can also be measured like this: in my daughter's first minutes of life in open air, as she was held by a nurse, I spoke; her head turned in my direction; she was profoundly silent, her still dark eyes seeking out the voice that rang out clear and known to her amid the boiling sea of sound into which she'd been plunged. Perhaps an infant's love for her native language is something like this searching love for a mother's voice.

I can also describe it this way: it's like the jolt of pleasure you feel in the milliseconds before you recognize your lover in a crowd at the train station. Before the brain has identified him, before it can drive his name toward your lips, it has registered and leaped with joy at the sight of his unique lope, cadence of limbs, precise angle of shoulder meeting collarbone, the click-clack of his step.

This love I have felt for a language not once, twice, three, or four times, but five. In those months with Maura, there was little of Italian that I understood. Nevertheless, I belonged to it, and it to me, in a familial way that had nothing to do with reason or with wanting or with deciding. I felt entitled to it, as one might feel to a birthright; it was mine by virtue of the warm flush of familiarity that precedes comprehension.

In high school, I decided to add Spanish to my store of languages. It did not flow in a boiling stream around me. It was doled out to us piecemeal by an aging nun who had spent a year or two at a mission in Guatemala. Simple templates of sentences, with units that could be predictably swapped in and out: *Me llamo Julie. Me llamo Teresa. Me llamo Andrea.* Lists pairing Spanish words with their English doppelgängers, always with the masculine or feminine tag—*el* or *la*—preceding the Spanish word, tags that we were instructed to commit to memory, because confusing them would cause Spanish speakers to wince. Tables of verb conjugations, in orderly rows and columns. It was only after we had properly digested each serving that Sister Mooney dished out the next one.

Those who create language courses seem to believe that a language must be carefully titrated, that it needs to be controlled as a slow drip into learners' minds, lest they be flooded with the magnitude of the new language, overwhelmed by a glimpse of its horizonless ocean, or drowned in the fast-moving current of sound not yet congealed into meaning.

Students, unlike newborns, are judged capable of the patient, deliberate labor of learning, so they are corralled onto the dry land of curriculum. They are not left to bob about in the liquidity of language; they are handed solid bricks of it and encouraged to build things, things that are useful and that conform to building codes. Sitting at my desk, in my designated spot—third from last in the row closest to the windows—I learned to build questions, salutations, instructions, useful assertions about where I was from, how many and which rooms there were in my home, what I liked to do in my spare time. These were called conversations.

But this way of learning makes you cautious. It is the opposite of reckless, ignorant, infantile language love. You size up each incoming syllable to see what piece of the world it is hitched to, and when you speak, you plot the shape of the sounds that will trail after your verb stem, you consult the grammatical building codes, and when you blunder, instead of plunging on with abandon, you walk yourself back and try to cover your tracks.

What I wonder is this: Having learned Spanish in this way, would I have *ever* followed a Spanish-speaking stranger into a dark barn, thinking I was going to see very large rabbits, or something else I thought they had promised to show me, without really being at all sure of what it was I was being promised?

No one, not even an infant, can fall in love with utter chaos.

A newborn's vocation is to find order in a world that advertises itself as a random assault on the senses. There is no curriculum. No prefabricated bricks of structure. But the baby is equipped with a dogged faith that language, indeed reality itself, *does* have order and structure, that it *wants* to settle and arrange itself into patterns and motifs. This faith is amply rewarded.

In the child's mind, what separates the beloved language from foreign burble is the order stitching it together. The infant intuits structure from beneath every surface of language. Under the very noses of adults who have no idea of the scholarship taking place in their presence, their child begins a secret, analytical love affair with the patterns discerned in language's sounds.

Order begins at the pulsing center of language, as if a fetus were somehow conditioned, by nearness to its mother's heart, to seek out the regularity of rhythm that propels speech forward. Each language has something that sounds like a heartbeat, but its fundamental principles can vary. In some languages, like French and Italian, units of timing are syllables, each allotted an egalitarian space in perceptual time. In other languages, like English and German, the meter of speech is heard as tapped out not by syllables themselves but by the stress laid over syllables at intervals, with multiple syllables sometimes mashed into a single beat. Yet others, like Japanese, seem to organize their time signatures around particles of speech finer than the syllable, so that more complex syllables, composed of long vowels or ending in a consonant, occupy two beats instead of the one apportioned to a simple syllable. Even newborns can hear the rhythmic differences between these languages, whether or not they have heard them before, and they group together languages that operate on similar principles: an infant carried within a Japanese womb registers a shift from an unfamiliar stress-timed language (German) to a foreign syllable-timed one (French)—here is something different!— but does not seem to notice that French and Italian diverge from each other.

Patterns build upon patterns. In the first half year of her born life, a Czech infant may grasp—without knowing that she has grasped—that stress falls on the first syllable of every word, but that the loudness of stress is not twinned with the length of a vowel. This permits words like the name of the Czech composer Janáček, in which stress bears down on the first vowel even though it's the second vowel that sprawls. An English child of the same age may intuit that most (but not all) words of English begin with a stressed syllable, and both babies will prefer to listen to invented words that mark stress on the first syllable. But unlike the Czech child, an English baby (and perhaps you yourself) can't conceive of a long vowel that does not also bear stress. In English, vowels that lack the privilege of stress are never long; they tend to shrivel into barely pronounced slips of sound, as happens to the robust, round shape of the stressed first vowel in "photograph" when that word is absorbed into "photographer" and the stress hops over onto the next vowel. If that English child grows up to be a radio announcer, she may be fated to mispronounce the name of the Czech composer Janáček, placing stress on the long second syllable.

But how do these infants intuit the shapes of words, immersed as they are in language in its liquid form? The particles of one meaningless word flow in an uninterrupted stream with the particles of other meaningless words. Without being handed bricks of words, how does the child extract solid objects from this torrent?

The order in language ripples throughout all its layers, from the solid crust of meaning down into its meaningless, boiling substrate of sound. The very existence of words has mathematical consequences: syllables that are part of the same word occur together in speech more often than syllables that belong to different words. Tell an uncomprehending infant, "We'regoingtovisitgrampa," and she may recognize that the syllables "vi-sit" form a unified clump of . . . *something*. She may know this only because these two syllables have appeared next to each other many times before, seemingly bonded to each other whenever they run the river of sound; the syllables "sit-gram," however, have bobbed and floated apart more often than not, despite being linked together in this particular sentence.

If you invent a new language with fabricated, meaningless words repeated over and over in various combinations, and play it continuously for a few minutes, a child of about eight months will come to distinguish sequences of sounds that form "words" from combinations that do not. Thus, babies intuit the pure mathematics of sound before they have tethered these sounds to meanings, perhaps even before they know for certain that they have meanings.

Unlike adults, infants inhabit a liminal space of language, perceiving order that runs on its own plane of existence, detached from meaning. These patterns have great importance, and babies labor to reproduce them. They babble alone in their cribs like ardent believers touched by the gift of tongues, and though their babble has no meaning, it becomes a closer and closer imitation of the structured sounds of the mother tongue.

Over time, language becomes less fluid as more and more clumps of sound solidify. These offer themselves as vessels for meaning, and the strands of sound and meaning begin to braid together. But there was a time in each of our lives when we experienced language as sheer music. We felt its rhythms in our bodies, we recognized its patterns and motifs, we could be soothed by its repetition, then surprised by its departure from pattern. But we did not understand it.

What would our lives be like, if we continued to live in this state? If, like the baby babbling alone in his crib, we devoted precious time to becoming virtuosos of language sounds that had no referents or signifiers? If this language music, meaningless as it was, still acted as a glue that bound us to each other?

We might live, I think, much as birds do.

One of nature's puzzles is how little we have in common with our primate kin in the domain of language. The calls, hoots, and shrieks of monkeys and apes have some sort of meaning, to be sure. But they lack the structure threaded into our language-music. And even the most articulate of apes fail tragically in their efforts to shape the sounds of speech. In the wild, their vocalizations spring from instinct—like human laughter or yelps of fear—more than from deliberate intent. Even under human tutelage, when it comes to speech, apes don't do much aping; they can mimic much of our behavior, gestures, even signed words, but they are terrible at mimicking speech.

This has led us to believe that we live alone in the house of language.

But among songbirds, we find our kindred patternmakers and imitators of sound. Just as we do with language, songbirds build elaborate structures of sound. They fashion syllables, motifs, and phrases out of notes—not in random combinations, but according to the templates of the music of their species. The more we listen to birds and their songs, the more echoes of language we hear.

Although birds' *calls* are much like the innate cries of primates (which, like human laughter or cries of pain, need no practice), their songs are different in kind. Songs come from culture, not biology alone. They must be rehearsed, like the babbled sounds of human babies, and a young bird's warbling only gradually takes on the shape of its parents' songs. A songbird raised in isolation produces poor, distorted versions of its native songs. If raised by foster parents of another species, many birds can learn their parents' foreign songs (whereas honeybees, following the dictates of their genes, can only dance the dance of their biological parents).

For birds, as for children, love is an accelerant for learning. Fostered birds can learn the alien songs of their nurturing adoptive parents, but if the same songs are piped in over a loudspeaker, the birds do not learn to sing them any more than a child learns to speak a language from television.

Like human language, birdsong selects its own society. Some scientists have raised young female European starlings in a sparse community composed only of adult males and other young females. Preferring the company of their peers, the young birds copied the songs of their less adept friends rather than the virtuosic songs of the adult males—a result poignantly familiar to some fathers of adolescent girls.

And, as with humans and their language, time is cruel to the musical brain of a bird. Quick to absorb the patterns of song in youth, a bird's talent for learning songs erodes with age. Older birds hearing birdsong for the first time are like adults who come to a new country, knowing they will never speak its language as flawlessly as their children will.

Perhaps we are so enraptured by birdsong because we recognize its connection to us. In our evolutionary family tree, we're like the black-sheep musician descended from a long line of tone-deaf ancestors who are baffled by our obsession with rearranging sound. We feel ourselves unique, out of place, misaligned with our heritage. But then we discover that one of our very, *very* distant cousins is also a musician. Somewhere back in deepest time, a shared ancestor provided the genetic material for our musical life, our language love—genes that have lain dormant in many of our relatives but that have flowered on a few select branches.

Like human infants, birds recognize the songs of their own species from birth. Scientists can measure this by the quickening tempo of nestlings' hearts and the urgency of their begging upon hearing a shift from foreign songs to native ones. But unlike us, our bird cousins live in language's liminal, meaningless space throughout their lives. Their strand of language-music never intertwines with meaning.

As far as we know, even birds that can sing hundreds of different songs do not sing to offer advice, enact laws, make promises, protest their leaders, admonish their young, or do anything resembling the conversion of symbol into sound. Yet, unlike most of our mammalian relatives, they do not dismiss song as useless. All this intricate, rehearsed arrangement of sound exists for the sole purpose of revealing themselves. Birds use song much as mammals use the more primitive signal of scent. From the complexity of their songs, prospective mates and rivals can discern the singers' health, their intelligence, the reach of their territory, even how well they have kept parasites at bay. They sing: Here I am. Know me.

At the public library, a man is blaring music from his computer. A staff member walks over and asks him to turn it down. He erupts: Why do *I* need to turn it down? *I'm* only playing my music to drown out the sound of all these *people* in here yammering in all these *languages*. Why don't you tell them to turn down all their *languages*?

It seems to me I've watched this scene before. A man I know suspects that the people speaking Chinese on the bus are talking about the other (non-Chinese) people on the bus, with impunity. His suspicion is fueled by the fact that a Chinese person he knows once admitted that sometimes Chinese people *do* talk about those around them, confident they won't be understood. This strikes him as offensive.

Other versions of this scene: My sister admits to feeling annoyed by the language of poetry, which strikes her as nonsensical and therefore vaguely offensive. A young student of poetry writes, "Whenever I read a modern poem, it's like my brother has his foot on the back of my neck in the swimming pool."

It seems that once we've plaited the sounds of language together with messages and intentions, we can no longer live in language's liquid, musical state. We can't tolerate it when meaning is withheld from us.

As infants, we're able to float underwater without drawing water into our lungs, but when we outgrow the bradycardic reflex, being tossed into water leaves us sputtering, gasping, feeling that we're drowning. This is the sputtering I see in the man in the library, in my sister's hostility toward poetry. The need to shake off the foot on the back of the neck.

There are psychologists who study the threat we feel at the unraveling of meaning. A threat to meaning, they say, can come at us from any direction: nonsensical strings of words; a surreal painting that bends the laws of reality; a reminder of our own mortality. Any of these can leave us feeling unsettled and disoriented. These scholars say we are driven to maintain meaning at all costs; when meaning frays, we use whatever is at hand to restore a sense of order. Sometimes, we reach for traditions and codes of conduct, or take refuge in what we presume is a shared identity. (Reading a story by Kafka, for example, has made some study volunteers more willing to punish a woman charged with illegal prostitution; thinking about death has provoked others to support nationalist groups.)

Perhaps our language teachers are right to control the drip of a foreign language. Maybe it's true that we would drown in a fast-moving current of meaningless sound.

But it occurs to me that incomprehensible language carries within itself the seeds of its own restoration. When meaning frays, there is always that other thread that runs, intact and orderly, through language. It's there in the rhythms and regularities of syllables, stressed or unstressed, and in the rules of the tango between vowels and consonants. We can feel these rhythms in our bodies, recognize their patterns and motifs, repetition and departure. In poetry, these cadences are mastered and shaped by the most skillful of human songbirds. The poets among us are the ones who know the most songs and who sing the most intricate melodies. If we listen to their poems as birds might, relieved of our preoccupation with message, we may hear the beloved music of our language on display, intensified, toyed with, subverted, stretched taut to its quivering point. Poetry is what makes the language sing: Here I am. Know me.

Perhaps my repeated immersion into new languages, which extended into conscious memory, tamed for me the threats of meaningless language. As a child, I listened to Czech, then German and Italian, then French and its bossy sibling, English, with ear cocked like a little bird learning the songs of its relatives, whether adoptive or not. On the kindergarten rug, I remember belting out songs whose words had not yet clumped into solid shapes, but this made the songs no less joyful to sing. Back then, language offered itself as laden with astonishments, discoveries not yet made. Some of these discoveries were as unsettling as gargantuan rabbits. But they came cradled on the rhythms of a familiar, beloved language-music, and this felt like protection enough.

I still seek out this sensation of language.

In my life right now, there is a family from Syria I have come to love. Their Arabic speech is a boiling stream around me. Occasionally, I consult a program on my computer to retrieve useful bricks of their language. But mostly, I want to prolong this feeling of bobbing around in Arabic, letting my ear become attuned to its patterns. I want Arabic to be poetry before it becomes weighed down with meaning.

In its rhythms and melodies, Arabic moves much more like English than Italian does. A newborn might not be able to tell them apart. Like English, Arabic is a stress-timed language; if English and Arabic speakers recite their language to a metronome's beat, they will align the stressed syllables with the clicks and clacks of the machine. In Arabic these beats almost always fall on the last heavy syllable of a word, ending in a consonant or a lengthened vowel. In English, more often than not, the first syllable is stressed, but far from always, and words are allowed to choose for themselves where the stress will fall. English has a larger collection of vowels; Arabic has more consonants, which serve as a rigid spine for its words. Arabic has more restrictive laws governing the shapes of words: a word, for example, is forbidden to begin with a tight cluster of consonants.

Of course, I perceive these patterns long before I'm aware I know them. Gradually, the sounds of Arabic begin to leap out at me on crowded trains in the same way a dear friend's face sharpens into focus against the blur of a multitude. I know that I'm on my way to belonging to this language when, one day, a young man visits my Syrian friends and I hear something off-kilter in his Arabic, the linguistic equivalent of someone taking a photograph of his face and running it through a program to make him resemble, subtly, someone else. I exclaim: You speak Arabic with an English accent! My friends say: Yes, he does. I can detect that his Arabic has a tint of English, but I still do not understand the meaning of any of the words he has uttered.

Such experiences of language fill me with pleasure. But more than that, they are for me a way to defuse the threats of a world that often seems to be so filled with chaos that surely not even a newborn could love it. They remind me that I once passed through worlds more meaningless than the one I'm in now and I did not die. I've learned that it's worth having a dogged faith in the existence of order and that we perceive more of it than we're aware we know. I know to listen for lucid particles of sound that float on the surface of roiling absurdity. If I'm patient, if I keep listening to the music, meaning may once again coagulate into rabbits, big and small.

Minds, meeting and parting

―――――――――

I. Convergences

I have no memory of the first time I understood that clumps of sound could contain the thoughts of others. But I have watched meaning's sunrise on the faces of my own babies as I held them and pointed out the essential components of their world: "rabbit," "Daddy," "shoe," "milk," "toes," "nose." Their heads swiveling to follow mine, their mouths stone-still with concentration. And I'm sure that it was like this for me too, sitting on your knee, Mother, and scanning your face, following your gaze like the searchlight that it was. My most important work then was to merge my mind and attention with yours.

As we grow older, we forget the intimacy of these first lessons in meaning. We come to believe that the meanings of words rest, consecrated, between the covers of a dictionary. We take these entries to be like the commandments handed down to Moses on the mountain, the urgings and prohibitions pre-chiseled into the slabs of rock he was made to haul all the way down on his arthritic shoulders. We understand them as setting the legal borders that contain words and their meanings. Like all sacred texts, dictionaries are not so much read as consulted for their authority: to learn the correct way to behave or speak, you thumb your way to a certain page.

But as a very small child, I knew nothing of stone tablets or dictionaries, sacred or otherwise. I understood that meanings were valuable secrets held under guard inside the minds of others. If I peered inside very intently, I might catch a glimpse of what was hidden behind the barricades. And if I stood by the gates at the precise moment when they swung open, I might be allowed to venture in.

Children are famously self-absorbed. Like miniature autocrats, they try to bend others to their will with their displays of rage and determination. Still, they are not so egocentric as to assume that when others speak, their words are describing the child's own experiences or observations. If a toddler's gaze is held by a pink stuffed rabbit, and she hears a disembodied word spoken over loudspeakers, she does not fall under the delusion that some omniscient consciousness is echoing her own fascination with the toy. She does not baptize the object of her attention with the word she has just heard reverberating through the room. Nor does she presume, if an adult next to her happens to speak just at the moment when she is intently examining that rabbit, that the adult's speech relates to the focus of her own attention. Instead, she looks up and searches the speaker's face, laboring to glean some insight about the contents of that other, foreign mind. If the adult's gaze is fixed on a different object while uttering a word, the child shifts her own attention to align with that of her interlocutor. And she eagerly attaches the word not to the focus of her own fascination but to whatever it was that captivated the other. She understands, without being taught, that words describe the mental landscape of the speaker and not that of the hearer.

And so, as children, we readily entered the minds of others. Language was the invitation. Through words, we were given hints that some things were especially worthy of attention. We began to look more intently, trying to discern what it was our articulate elders could see. A name assigned to an object conferred special status, a reason to separate *this* thing from the background clutter. When various objects, creatures, or people were all anointed with the same word, we understood this naming to mean that these things all had some essence in common: some essence of redness, perhaps, or of dogness, or of childness, or of instigating a singular pleasure in the mouth, or of the need for wariness. Language taught us to look closely for such essences. To observe, group, distinguish, compare, divide, and describe everything in our orbit. Words were the *X*s on treasure maps that led to an orderly understanding of this world, an understanding that we sensed already existed, buried deep inside the minds of others.

There would have been times, too, when the gates to your mind swung open less freely, leaving me stranded outside. I imagine there were times, Mother, when you—like all adults who have mastered language so that it resembles breath—

unspooled great reels of speech that pointed only inward, to your own private thoughts of past or future objects or events, untethered to anything I could see or touch. "This afternoon, we'll go visit Grandma, and I'm sure she'll let you have a delicious cookie," says a parent absently while rifling through a pile of clothing in search of a clean shirt. How is the child to glean from this stream of sound, released at this particular moment, what is meant by "cookie," when there is no sweet, crumbly thing to jam into her mouth? "Do you remember how she made those snickerdoodles you loved last week? I bet she's already in the kitchen, mixing up the dough, ready to pop them into the oven for us." A lovely music, but the words themselves—"snickerdoodles," "week," "kitchen," "dough," "oven"—are disembodied wisps. There is nothing in the here and now to which they can be anchored.

It is tempting to credit children with miraculous powers of language learning, to believe them to have direct access to meaning simply by sitting in language's Presence. But children can't enter into meaning unless an opening is provided. Unless there is some way for minds to converge. Psychologists have devised a simple test to simulate the task at hand. They re-create for adults the experience of a child who is beginning to learn what words mean. The laboratory re-creation goes like this: The adult subject is shown a video recording of a parent addressing a child, but with the speech silenced. This is meant to remove the crutch of meaningful speech, a thing that is not yet of any use to the wordless child, while still preserving all nonverbal cues that might help the child infer meaning—the visual setting and the parent's movements, gestures, and facial expressions. At the precise moment when the word of inter-est was originally uttered by the parent, a beep is spliced in instead, and the adult subject is asked to guess what word the parent might have uttered at that moment.

Can the adults-as-infants intuit the word's meaning from the actions of the speaker, from the parent's orientation to the physical world? Sometimes they can, but at other times they cannot. A clear thread between the internal and the external worlds of the speaker is required: if the speaker's attention visibly alights on a crucial object that is physically present, whether by pointing or touching, or by gaze alone, and if this occurs within a certain amount of time of the utterance of the targeted word (heard as a beep by the adults-as-infants), then a tentative connection between word and meaning is made.

Children deploy the same tactics as their adult imperson-ators. Meaning is penetrated most readily by children whose parents understand—perhaps only by sheer instinct—the na-ture of the task facing the child. Attuned to their children's need for clues that bind speech to thoughts, these parents take care to speak so that many threads are cast, linking the internal world to the external one. "Oho, what have we here?" teases Father. "It's a hat!" He produces the hat with a theatri-cal flourish. "What a pretty hat," he murmurs while caressing it, exhibiting it on his own head ("Let me try this hat"), then plucking it away and arranging it on the child's ("Now you wear the hat"). In this way, parents make a flamboyant dis-play of their thoughts. The fortunate children of parents who excel at such displays find it easier to collect words and their meanings; over the first few years of their lives, their vocabularies grow more quickly than the word collections of children whose parents provide fewer openings into meaning.

I have never suffered a shortage of words relative to my peers, so you (along with my father) must have provided many openings into meaning. And in my first years, when I had so few words of my own but was driven by faith that language was the lamplight by which one made sense of the murk and chaos of the world, I would have been eager to explore the organized wisdom of your mind. Like all children, I would have intuited that words were the keys to a pedagogy of love and survival. I wish I could bring into purposeful recall some of those moments when a new word sparked a form of perfect communion between us; I wish I could remember what it was like for our eyes and minds to seek and hold each other. You giving and me receiving meaning. But I can merely infer, and not remember, those most intimate of moments I shared with you in my first year or two, how I monitored your face, eyes, and posture, waiting for the unlatching of the gate when my mind would swoop in to meet yours.

I think often of Helen Keller, whose deafness and blindness hindered her awareness of language, thereby postponing these intimate epiphanies until she was of an age when they could solidify into memories. She was seven years old by the time her teacher Anne Sullivan (who understood that language resided not just in mouths and ears but also in hands) shaped words into the little girl's palm, over and over, forming the signs that spelled "w-a-t-e-r" into the hand over which the thing itself poured, the cool liquid that bore the name occupying the same place on Helen's body as Anne's fingers drumming the word out on her palm, again and again.

As an adult, Helen claims to recall how this moment, when she grasped the link between the thing and the word, illuminated the reality in which she lived. The fully grown Helen writes of this moment,

> I left the well-house eager to learn. Everything had a name, and each name gave birth to a new thought. As we returned to the house, every object that I touched seemed to quiver with life. This was because I saw everything with that strange new sight that had come to me. On entering the door I remembered the doll I had broken. I went to the hearth and picked up the pieces. I tried vainly to put them together. Then my eyes filled with tears; I realized what I had done, and for the first time I felt repentance and sorrow.

As Helen describes it, that instant split her life into the before and after. That brief miracle of joining minds with her teacher, as they stood at the pump with water flowing over both of their hands, would repeat itself over and over in many forms, until the very end of Anne's life. No doubt Helen's memory of the precise moment when she first received the gift of language was a durable thread woven throughout her relationship with her teacher. I suspect she returned to that moment again and again in her mind. Perhaps her memory of it bound Helen to her teacher in much the same way as I would feel bound to a person who has thrown himself into a frothing river to save me from being smashed upon its rocks; the relationship springs whole from that one life-altering instant, and everything that follows is an elaboration of that instant.

But for me, as for almost all children, the miracle of language did not come as a joyous, mind-splitting flash within an already-conscious self. It came more as a languid dawn that brightened gradually, almost imperceptibly, over many months. To unearth my own first attempts to knit together speech and meaning, I have to reach very far back—before I was able to form lasting memories, before the wobble of my first steps toward you, before my efforts to propel myself by any means possible across the speckled kitchen linoleum, back even before I could sit by myself without toppling over. I have no hope of excavating these life-altering moments through the force of my own memory or even through the stories you might tell about me, because they are too subtle to have caught the notice of either you or my father; I have to rely on the meticulous observations and manipulations of scientists who have devoted their lives to understanding how we learn to achieve communion with each other through language.

At about three months of age, apparently, I was already scanning speech for any clues it might offer as to how to read the world around me. There was little to hold on to. Speech was still a river; its sounds had yet to cluster into words. But I had the sense, perhaps inherited, that this river of sound would unveil some secrets about the roiling world into which I'd been plunged. At this age, if infants hear someone speaking as they watch a procession of related things—a dog, a horse, a sheep—they press their attention closely against these things, and under the weight of this attention they notice the ways in which the things are similar. There is an impression of heads and legs and tails attached to some mass of body. If they then see a new thing that bears some similarity to this impression, perhaps a cow, they inspect this unfamiliar object with interest, perhaps absorbing this new thing into some new, wider category that is taking shape in their minds; a wholly unrelated thing, such as an airplane, provokes no special concentration.

In the presence of language, even though they do not yet understand the words that have been uttered, the infants have learned something about the properties that are common to dogs, horses, and sheep, and they recognize that cows also belong to this family of things but that airplanes do not. But if the same process is repeated with sequences of musical notes instead of speech, the infants appear to have learned nothing. Unlike language, the presence of music does not stir them to notice the bonds that link cows to dogs and horses but exclude airplanes.

It turns out, however, that human language is not unique in provoking this sort of learning among three-month-old infants. The calls of lemurs or macaques have the same effect. Perhaps we human primates share with our close animal kin an instinct that elevates certain sounds above the din of others. Words, but also calls and cries, and exclamations, guffaws, and other vocal ejections—we know in our bone marrow that these are meant to send a signal from one mind to another. Something has captured the attention of one being. Its owner squawks. Others in the vicinity crane their necks to see what's happening. Is this the knowledge that rumbles beneath Helen's crackle of insight on that fateful day at the pump?

Nonetheless, the distance from lemur cry to a child's first words is like the gap between the solitary note of a flute and the heaving music of a symphony. Over the span of a child's first year, various instruments are tuned and slowly converge upon a coordinated music, each instrument gradually learning to obey the same melodic themes and rhythmic patterns.

Tentatively, the child undertakes her own cataloging of the world and its objects. Sometimes at the prompting of speech, and sometimes driven by her own curiosity, she begins to elaborate her theories about the nature of objects and their effects upon each other. She investigates: strokes, pats, grasps, tastes, pulls, rolls, and throws, all in synchrony with her increasing powers of movement. She notes similarities and distinctions, means of grouping objects into useful categories, and she has the mounting suspicion that the music coming from her parents' mouths is intimately linked with these observations and many others that have escaped her notice thus far.

With time, the river of speech, like the world, also loses some of its formlessness. Certain clusters of sounds recur, in recognized combinations with certain other familiar clusters. This alerts the child to the fact that speech contains its own objects. No small task, still, to align the objects of speech with objects that populate the world and with their many properties, causes, and relations. This is where the child becomes a reader of minds.

It has not escaped her attention that the behavior of other

humans is also not formless; it obeys hidden laws. Other humans, like herself, must be acting in accordance with secret thoughts, desires, and goals. These, she learns, are not always the same as her own. She searches vigilantly for clues that might disclose the unseen contents of the other's mind. At three months, her own gaze flits in the direction of another person's, but it is not until the second half of her first year that she can lock her gaze on a nearby object that has captivated the attention of another pair of eyes. She will have eaten her first slice of her own birthday cake before she can follow her parent's gaze well enough to find an object hidden behind her back or otherwise out of her own sight.

She continues to observe and to refine her theories of other minds. She speculates about hidden intentions. If an adult overturns a glass of water and exclaims, "Oops!" the child looks on in sympathy and perhaps offers up a washcloth. If the same adult commits the same action, but instead leans back with an air of satisfaction and says, "There!" the child's impulse is to emulate the adult and knock over her own glass of water.

A sentence uttered by someone is most decidedly a deliberate act, not an accidental one requiring a washcloth or any other remedy, and a year-old child is perfectly capable of recognizing it as such. But what sort of act, precisely? Is the adult requesting? Warning? Instructing? Informing? To decipher the act, she searches the face of the speaker, sizes up the world around her, leans on her knowledge of the objects of speech, and ventures a guess.

Her guesses become more and more finely tuned. As she discovers that the objects of speech can be sorted into various grammatical categories, language guides her attention more precisely. If Father holds up a plush pink rabbit, saying, "This is Blick," she understands that he has christened this particular object and no other; "This is a blick" hints at the existence of other, unseen objects of its kind that bear the same name; upon hearing "This is blickish," she inspects the object's plushness, its pinkness, guessing that the word describes some property that is apparent; and when Father announces, "Now I'm going to blick," just before he rubs the rabbit's nose with his own, the child does the same, inspired by witnessing an action worthy of being named.

With time, language vaults a child to a plane of knowledge that would be impossible if she lived in a wordless state of solitary confinement; some thoughts remain nebulous until they are fixed with language. It was only from your speech, for example, that I learned the difference between knowing and believing, what duty is, how rain is made, why illness ransacks the body, that all the people I loved would someday cease to exist, of the unbounded nature of God. None of these were things I could see or stroke, pat, grasp, taste, pull, or roll, but hearing about them caused very specific feelings in my body and bulldozed the landscape of my own mind into new formations.

Helen, too, writes of how it was through words that she learned from Anne that there was such a thing as love, and that this word referred to the "invisible lines stretched between my spirit and the spirits of others."

This is also the definition of language.

For most children, it is impossible to locate a single mystical moment when speech becomes infused with meaning. At six months of age, a baby may have a dim suspicion about the meaning of a particular word; another six months later, the suspicion has brightened into near certainty. There is no shattering instant, only a slow entanglement of speech and meaning. But for Helen, the instrument of speech was entirely silent despite her growing ability to comprehend her physical and social worlds. When it finally made its entrance, not as gestures of the tongue but as movements of hands, these gestures were fused to a seven-year-old's understanding of the world, and the transformation was a miracle.

But what exactly was Helen remembering when she recalled that numinous moment at the pump? It wasn't simply the fastening of one mind by another to the same thought. As Helen writes in her memoir, she had long been using hand signs to make her wishes known to others. Hands cupped together, for example, to show that she wanted to go hunting for the eggs of guinea fowl hidden in nests in the grass near her home. A motion of slicing to show that she wanted bread. A pantomime of shivering to indicate her desire for ice cream. And when her mother made a sign into her hand, Helen understood which object she wished her to fetch from upstairs. Though she sensed that these signs were not enough to bridge the gulf she felt between herself and others, such moments of connection were not unknown to her. What, then, was the nature of the miracle that Anne wrought?

It seems, from Helen's writing, that the miracle lay not in understanding that Anne wished to direct her attention to the flowing water but in the realization that the handshapes her teacher was forming—which themselves bore no resemblance to the water itself—stood as a *name* for water. But what is a name, and what gives it such power? A name is a thing that can be made from thin air (with the help of one's own body) to represent an object that exists in the world or a thought that exists in the mind. Unlike Helen's cupped hands or gestures of slicing, it is not in itself a request. It can, however, be used to request. Also to warn, inquire, suggest, observe, reassure, condemn, beg, deceive, insinuate, affirm, deny, praise, proclaim. A name is a thing that can be picked up and manipulated, pressed into service when it is needed in order to carry out any one of the many purposes a human being might have in mind at one time or another when encountering another human being. It is a tool, not a fleeting moment of connection.

Perhaps it was the very fact that water's name bore no physical similarity to the thing itself that hinted at its potent, symbolic nature, its ability to be used for many purposes not yet dreamed of. I imagine it was this insight that gave birth to the possibility in Helen's mind that if water had a name, then perhaps everything else of importance might also have a name, a vehicle by which the thought of a thing could be carried from one mind to another. What stirred Helen was not just *this* moment of connection with Anne but the promise of countless others.

And perhaps something else shimmered at the edges of Helen's awareness: if a name is a tool that can be retrieved and wielded on many occasions—and not merely a performance that is improvised in the spur of the moment—then it can also be passed from hand to hand to hand. There is, perhaps, an entire guild of people already adept at its use. Her teacher Anne was proposing an apprenticeship, the possibility of joining such a guild. All around, future intimacies were multiplying, as if Helen were standing at the center of a kaleidoscope in full bloom.

II. Divergences

If language (or is it love?) is the invisible line stretched between our spirits and the spirits of others, then early on we learn that this line can fray. Perhaps I harbor a fantasy for a Helen Keller moment—for some miraculous memory of being tethered to you with language/love—precisely because the memories of you and me that surface all too readily are those of unraveling and unhitching. When I was an infant and a strange new word sent my mind in search of yours, I imagine these encounters were imbued with a purity that I can no longer find in our later ways of relating. If such a purity existed, it was surely bought and paid for by my own ignorance. I knew almost nothing; you appeared to know everything. I was the Moses on your mountain, and my pilgrimage was rewarded with fresh knowledge again and again, and so I continued my ascents. But there came a time when, carrying my tablets downhill, I had an uneasy sense of their fragility. Your words didn't always make sense to me. They sometimes required that I revise my theory of your mind, and this unsettled me.

As I grew older, I wandered off in search of other mountains. I began to question the meanings of some of the words you taught me. After some time, it seemed we spoke different languages from each other.

The poet Czesław Miłosz writes, "Everything would be fine if language did not deceive us by finding different names for the same thing in different times and places. . . . A word should be contained in every single thing / But it is not."

It is not, and we learn that language is no guarantee of rapturous union. We learn that words do not bind us together inside a sacred truth; they are mere attempts to fumble our way toward each other. Meanings are fallible. They can become corrupted and unrecognizable to us. And where language once drew us into another mind, it can also reveal the canyons that have opened between us.

As children, we sense that there are risks to merging minds with others. Deceptions may lurk within language, and we learn to distrust those who propagate them. In the psychologist's laboratory, a young child eagerly sops up a new word uttered by a stranger, deploying all the usual strategies of mind joining. But learning is preempted if the child has earlier witnessed that stranger trying to pass off a false name for a familiar thing—calling something a dog when it is plainly an apple. That person may offer an enticing new word ("Here is a blick!") on the heels of this linguistic betrayal, but the child holds back. This stranger may display the new word's meaning with all kinds of vocal and bodily demonstrations, but a fissure has opened up and the child does not cross over. A suspicion blooms in the child's mind: This person speaks, but is not to be trusted. He has violated the practices of our language guild. There is no telling what he might be capable of.

From the very beginning, as we gain mastery over language by opening our minds to others, we simultaneously learn to select, to exclude, to close our minds to certain influences. When we were tiny infants, the calls of lemurs might have triggered a search for meaning as we scoured the world with our eyes. A few months later, we have learned to disregard such sounds; they no longer have anything to tell us about the world. They do not come from our kind. A few months later still, we learn to disregard the sounds of other languages, sounds that make a different music from the one spoken by those we have come to love. We have learned that those sounds do not come from our kind. They no longer have anything to tell us.

Alongside their many observations of children's eagerness to join minds with others, scientists have also witnessed the walls that children erect as protection. After all, if language can reshape mental landscapes, one must guard against those who would terraform it to suit their own purposes or whose own knowledge is defective. A child's willingness to accept a new word from a speaker is tempered by vigilant evaluation of that person's competence. A person who has made obvious errors, who displays uncertainty ("I'm not sure, but I think this is a blick"), who appears too young to have reliable knowledge—all may be regarded by the child with suspicion; even when invited, the child does not saunter freely into the open gates of these minds.

The endless questions of a preschooler ("But why?") may

be more than idle curiosity or an annoying way to prolong a conversation with an adult; they may be the child's way of probing the depth of the adult's knowledge, gauging whether their words can be taken at face value. My own niece, at the age of three, took a direct approach. When confronted with a new assertion, whether it was that carrots are good for you or that the stars you see at night might already have died by the time their light reaches your eye, she would demand, "How do you know?"

Moreover, the child is on the alert for signs that the speaker's interests clash with her own, that the speaker may have a hidden, uncooperative agenda. Trust is not handed over automatically, with the purity of trust that Helen granted her teacher or that I imagine I granted you in my earliest years. Even as toddlers, children seem to be aware of the power wielded by someone using language—that to accept something as true based solely on someone's words is to accept a reality that one has not seen or heard for oneself—and are wary of ceding too much of this power to a person who may prove to be untrustworthy. Even the simple act of accepting the meaning of a new word involves a leap of faith. The child must believe that whoever uttered the word belongs to the particular guild of language users that she herself is eager to join, that the word is uttered with good intentions, as an invitation into that guild, without trickery.

An assortment of studies reveals the reluctance children have to learn new words from certain speakers, people from whom they withhold trust. Not surprisingly, their confidence in strangers is fragile: when children were shown unfamiliar objects whose names were unknown to them (a cocktail pourer, a rubber squeegee) and heard different names assigned to them by a teacher they knew from their own preschool ("That's a snegg") and a teacher they had never seen before ("Actually, that's a yiff"), they more readily accepted the name from the teacher they knew.

In their attempts to judge the knowledge and intentions of each speaker, children erect barriers between others' minds and their own in ways that resemble the barriers that exist among adults. Children are more willing to learn new words from a speaker who is deemed attractive than one who is rated less attractive; from someone who is formally dressed rather than a speaker in casual clothing; from a speaker who belongs to their own racial group over someone of a different race; or from one who sounds like a native speaker of English over someone with a foreign accent. Like adults, their loyalties may be startlingly arbitrary: children who were assigned to a blue-aproned "team" learned more eagerly from a speaker of their own team than from a red-aproned speaker.

And so, a child's openness is conditional. Before deciding how deeply to plunge into the thicket of another person's mind, she is constantly testing: Is this person to be trusted? Does he speak, act, or dress like others that I presume to be trustworthy? Will others follow him? Has he shown himself to be fallible? A liar? Delusional? What are his motives? Where are the limits to his knowledge? *How do they know?*

Eventually, these questions can be turned against the ones closest to us, the very same people who have initiated us into the rites of language.

When we know nothing, a word is an opening, an invitation gratefully accepted from someone we trust. The more we come to know, the more our words become private islands from which we scan the horizon for approaching ships.

As I grew, I encountered the same words I had used with you, but now they appeared in different times and places, and so my words began to change shape. They accumulated the detritus of my own experiences, apart from you. "Bread," in our home, meant a soft white substance that could be pinched off the loaf and rolled between the fingers into a dense, sweet clay. The word referred only to the loaves I shared with you. When I began to eat meals in other homes, the same word acquired other traits: coarseness, a deep color of caramel, the resistance of seeds between the teeth, an unexpected flatness. Today, after thousands of meals away from each other, we no longer conjure the same thought when we say the word "bread." I've noticed, too, that we no longer conjure the same thought when we say other words: "God," "sex," "duty," "success"—even the word "love."

All of this, I suppose, was to be expected, language's way of ensuring that I would not be hemmed in by the scope of a single mind, no matter how blissful the union. As I ventured further from you, I used words as levers to pry open minds other than yours. At times, other people exerted pressure on my lexicon, pulling at the meanings I'd collected, pressing them into certain molds. I experimented with opening and closing my mind, learning how to dole out my trust. Like

Helen, I conflated language with love. I chose my teachers and loved them for the epiphanies they sparked.

But these excursions strained the invisible lines stretched between your spirit and mine. They took me into landscapes that were wholly foreign to you. And the more I became aware of the limits of your knowledge—the more I sensed you capable of betrayals of language—the more I closed my mind to yours. I watched as our future intimacies shrank and darkened.

How many years passed like this? Twenty? Thirty? The words I had once shared with you split and drifted like continents moving away from each other, words upon whose meanings we could no longer agree.

The loneliness of private meanings is intolerable, and because of this we search for enclaves of agreement. As adults, we constantly hunger for the lost intimacies of childhood, when we felt a purer alignment with other minds. Perhaps it's the pain of separation from those we first loved that drives us to try to recapture those lost moments of communion. We try to assuage this pain by driving out of our consciousness anything that threatens a sense of shared meaning, by turning away those whose meanings are discordant with ours.

And thus, separate vocabularies arise between coast and heartland, boomers and millennials, urban dwellers and country people. I have read studies suggesting that entirely different thoughts are summoned when people of liberal and conservative political leanings say the words "right" and "wrong." What words could be more elemental? We cannot live without saying these words; they are like the essential words "Daddy," "milk," and "shoe" for a toddler learning to make sense of her world. But the meanings of even these most fundamental of words diverge: A conservative, apparently, would utter the word "wrong" when confronted with a person cleaning their toilet with a national flag they have just taken down, or by a person taking a chicken home from the supermarket and fucking it. A liberal, though dismayed or disgusted, might say: Where's the harm? I'll tell you where the harm is. The harm is in the disenfranchisement of the poor and the racialized.

Linguistic betrayals of this magnitude send us scrambling for comfort among those whose words are recognizable to us. We cannot bear to be alone in our meanings. Like Helen making her hand signs, frantic for some shared understanding, we send signals into the world, where they collide with countless other frantic signals. We scrutinize our social networks, deciding whom to trust and whom to disbelieve, which websites and TV channels and newspapers and acquaintances speak the language of our kind. Cloistered within our selected clans, our languages begin to diverge ever more, much as the accent of Detroit has slowly but surely edged away from the accent of Louisiana, each wanting less and less to do with the other's version of English. The words we once shared with certain others dissolve like the pages of a dictionary left out in the rain.

When I hear the words uttered by the citizens of present-day America, it is all too easy for me to draw up a partial list of the words upon whose meanings we cannot, as a nation, seem to agree:

> Citizen. Threat. Greatness. Person. Oppression. Hope. Family. Privilege. Purity. Science. Wilderness. Corruption. Mother. Woman. Selfishness. Freedom. Fairness. Evidence. Work. Leader. Goodness. Father. Sanctity. Nation. Degradation. Deformity. Knowledge. Responsibility. Power. Seduction. Baby. Genius. Delusion. Heritage. Manliness. Animal. Loyalty. Wealth. Community. Evil. Order. Profanity. Injustice. Strength. Progress. Treason. Dignity. Markets. Elite. Culture. Authority. Savagery. Marriage. Pride. Origins. Faith. Homeland.

We may live in an illusion of agreement, believing ourselves to speak the same language, but these words reveal the canyons that have opened up between us.

III. Joining attention

Language would not exist if the members of our species did not have the capacity to merge attention with each other. The ancestor to all the words that exist in all languages is the impulse to point at something and say, "Look!" The desire to sit and jointly contemplate a thing and, in that contemplation, to share with the other what has drawn our notice about that thing, what emotions rise up as we look at it, what we've learned about it. This impulse precedes words. When I used to walk with my toddler son in our neighborhood, he would point—to a truck, a flower in bloom, a dog—with his gaze locked on the object of his fascination while his free hand tugged at my coat to emphasize the urgency of drawing my gaze to it, too. "Dat!" This was his general-purpose word for fastening my attention to his. In return, I would hand him a finer-wrought word, as I'm sure you did when I was at that age. "Truck." "Flower." "Doggie."

My son's simple act set him apart from other mammals. Chimpanzees, whether mothers or babies, do not point to draw the attention of other chimpanzees to an object of interest. And while one chimpanzee can learn from another by imitating it, it does not seem to have the sense, unlike very young humans, that it has been born into a fellowship of beings who are eager to share their knowledge and experiences. The desire for such exchanges is our birthright, but to fulfill this desire, we require words to be forged as tools of meaning. Necessity is the mother of invention. And our desire for joining attention requires so much more than a tug on the sleeve and an exclamation of "Dat!"

When Helen Keller lacked words but was full of the impulse to merge attention, she attempted to forge her own tools, through gestures. But words cannot be manufactured in solitude. To become the instruments through which thoughts are transmitted, others must agree to weld *this* set of gestures of hands or mouth with *this* meaning, and none other. Helen was not able to secure such agreements from those around her; they were already equipped with their own set of precision tools forged out of speech. As a result, her overtures to merge attention remained crude and unrefined, having the quality of vague private meanings rather than that of finely calibrated instruments.

$$\wp$$

As it turns out, dictionaries—perhaps like all sacred texts— are not legal prescriptions but approximate records of the agreements struck by people who decide to inhabit the same language. Lexicographers know they do not legislate. They compile a history of our attempts to fumble our ways toward each other; they document our moments of linguistic convergence; they monitor the adjustments we make to our truces of meaning. They know that language exists only because humans are capable of crafting such agreements; no deity breathed it into us or inscribed it in stone for us. Language was created word by word, each word conceived in a moment of yoked attention, one person proposing and another acquiescing to a particular union of sound and meaning. Language is the totality of such moments, multiplied within the kaleidoscope of an entire community.

Dictionaries tell only a partial truth, however. They do not log our moments of painful separation. They describe the containers of shared meanings, but not the idiosyncratic memories, experiences, and visceral sensations that spill over their edges. They omit the tensions that pull meanings in different directions, threatening to snap a word in two. As such, they can give a false impression of convergence.

I suspect that many people prefer it this way. Turning a blind eye to the slippages and cleavages between their words and those of others offers the soothing illusion of a more perfect union than can ever be achieved. All the better if one clings to the fiction of a sacred text, to the idea that meanings are dictated by a higher authority. Best not to acknowledge that every linguistic exchange contains within itself the seeds of a discordant Babel. Believe hard enough in the uniformity of meanings, and one may forget the sting of being expelled from the childhood garden.

But I have been expelled. I understand how it is that I first received words from you, back when you and I sat together in that garden long ago and I trusted you to be my provider of meanings. What I don't know—what no clever scientists of language have been able to tell me—is how to negotiate the meanings of words with you now. Perhaps the only way to start is by accepting that I can never return to that infantile state of innocence. It is over for us, the time when I sought to merge my mind with yours at every opportunity. I am now burdened with knowledge that separates me from you. My meanings are not arbitrary. They bear the inscription of all the moments of my life and all my chosen loves. So it is for you as well.

Perhaps we can find a way to join our attention nonetheless. Perhaps we can lay our words side by side, see where they resemble each other, relate the stories of how they came to diverge. If I can stop grieving for those mystical moments when you ignited language for me, moments that I can neither remember nor re-create, we may be able to fumble our way toward each other, even now.

Let me begin: Come sit with me. Mother. Teacher. Beloved other mind. There is something I would like to contemplate, together with you.

Feral polyglot

Parenthood has succumbed to technocracy. The arrival of a new child provokes a sudden, intense focus on order and policy: There is a list of objects that must be stockpiled, even before the child makes her howling entrance. Perhaps a room is freshly painted in sleep-conducive tones; regulation-compliant furniture is arranged into an assembly governed by principles of feng shui. New standards of cleanliness rule the household. Schedules are optimized, in consultation with an app that predicts sleep patterns and cluster feeding.

Parents become apprentices in developmental psychology, committing to memory a litany of milestones, the ages at which their child is expected to sit, roll over, stand unaided, search for objects that have vanished, enunciate first words, compose first sentences, name the letters of the alphabet. Daily life is structured around activities that will ensure these milestones are met, as with the production quotas of a nation governed by a regime hell-bent on meeting its Five-Year Plan.

Above all, anything the child takes in must be monitored. Foods are introduced neither too soon nor too late, lest allergies be provoked or aversions take root, and they are delivered in textures and quantities that avoid courting catastrophes of swallowing. Visitors are screened for possible contaminants of all biological and nonbiological varieties. Books, films, songs, stories, programs—these are censored and sorted so they do not instill anxieties in the child, or taint the child with problematic norms and stereotypes, or induce complacency with content that is too simple or a feeling of defeat by material that is too difficult. Influences that risk sending the child's moral compass into a spin are kept at bay. Consistency is the antibiotic for confusion, which must not be permitted to overtake the child's undeveloped spiritual immunity.

And languages. Languages, too, are regimented, their dosages carefully supervised. Lesser languages are not to compete with the indispensable one, lest they stunt its development. If more than one language is spoken in the home, these should be quarantined from each other: one parent is the designated speaker of one language and the other parent speaks the other. Once the child enters school, slowly, slowly, one can introduce foreign languages into the academic diet. These outsider languages are kept sequestered, in separate rooms and within separate time intervals, apart from the essential language.

Every obsession with order reflects, to some extent, an underlying terror. The language policies that have afflicted childhood in America (and elsewhere) have a long history, and they reveal a dread of certain dangers that might lurk within the borders of a mind that has admitted more than one language. Though often phrased in bland and soothing terminology—in terms of "best outcomes for the child"—they well up from anxieties endemic to a nation formed by a ragtag collection of rebels and conquerors and stressed by a succession of wars fought within and outside its own borders.

Within such a nation, the hygienic quality of monolingualism has long appealed. Until the latter part of the twentieth century, even language experts were warning parents about the dangers of bilingualism, which, some claimed, could lead not only to linguistic confusion but also to schizophrenia or intellectual disability. One has the feeling that linguistic confusion was considered as grim a condition as the other two.

Other languages were viewed as parasitic upon English, such that learning one risked draining the lifeblood of the unifying language. So essential was English to the alleged health of America's citizens that for many years profoundly deaf children were sent to schools whose primary purpose was to silence the language that flowed most naturally from the hands of those who could not hear. Parents were told that a signed language would cripple their child's potential to learn English. In reality, few of these children could penetrate a spoken language of any kind. Still, a pretense of an education in English was deemed preferable to a real education in a language that was not even its distant cousin.

Similar anxieties persist to this day. Parents worry that a mind occupied by two languages will always be divided against itself. That the languages will squabble, in constant friction with each other. That the breadwinning language will be held back by compromises made with the other, that it will sacrifice too much of itself and fail to achieve its glorious destiny. They worry that the child's languages will not know their places in the world and that they will be distorted beyond recognition by each other.

Beneath the fear of linguistic confusion is, perhaps, an existential terror that we do not really know who we are.

Not all children live such regulated lives, of course, whether due to their parents' unruly temperaments or the unruly circumstances in which they find themselves. My own childhood was linguistic bedlam. After my family's abrupt departure from Czechoslovakia as refugees, we ping-ponged back and forth between Austria and Italy in search of a livelihood and a permanent home, eventually flinging ourselves across the ocean to the linguistically divided city of Montreal, in which speakers of one language were planting bombs in the mailboxes of people who spoke another language.

Languages entered and left my life and my mind, heedless of timetables or planning. My parents were too consumed with the daily labors of keeping us fed and sheltered to make any attempt to regulate our intake of languages, or much of anything else. My memories of that time are a blur of movement: trains shuttling us from one place to the next—here to a frenetic city where traffic sounds went on long into the night, there to a farm where crickets closed down the evening—and people entering and leaving our lives, lugging their various languages with them. We were left in the care of whoever was willing to supervise us, a shared language often being a luxury too exorbitant to consider. We moved in and out of households, wearing the languages of others like hand-me-down clothing.

My mother tongue, which was just beginning to come into focus, yielded to a fog of German in my Viennese preschool,

which in turn was usurped by an Italian streaked with the
Czech of relatives and expatriates who lived near us. Later, as
I sought admission into the packs of neighborhood kids that
roamed the Montreal streets, it was mostly Québécois French
that bounced off the walls, a language I still associate with
the sweet liberty of long summer twilights outside the range
of adult eyes and ears. But also vying for attention were many
strains of English. These were spoken in a hodgepodge of
accents and proficiencies by the immigrants with whom we
found ourselves in social circulation.

I encountered a uniform, tidy version of English for the
first time in kindergarten, when I walked into the classroom
as the incarnation of a teacher's nightmare of linguistic confusion. Back then, there were no special classes for children
who had arrived at school clinging to the life rafts of other
languages. When I entered school, language was an ocean
whose floor plunged straight down from the coastline, no gently sloping beach serving as a ramp. My fingers were pried
from the other languages I had dragged with me; I bobbed
around on an English that stretched out as a rippling expanse
in all directions, indistinguishable from the sky.

As children do when confronted with the authority of
school, I soon yielded to the linguistic order imposed upon
my verbal life. I accepted the implicit laws that elevated one
language above the others. School English was the language in
which to mold myself; all exertion and aspiration were infused
with its sounds. French had a place in a corner of the curriculum, and also in a corner of the schoolyard, as a temporary
lingua franca that patched up certain linguistic deficiencies.

But I knew better than to attempt to speak in any of the other languages that had accompanied me throughout my childhood; school was the wrong place for any of these languages. I understood that in my classroom, and in much of the world beyond it, I was meant to speak English and to imitate the habits and tastes of those who spoke it.

The elevated status of the English language made clear who I was supposed to be, and I got to work being it. Until then, when in school, I kept my mouth shut.

A language that raises itself above other languages lives in constant fear of being deposed. And so, to conscript an army of defenders, legends are circulated about the dangers from outside, about those marauding languages that threaten the order of things. Among these legends is the notion that children who hear multiple languages willy-nilly are unable to distinguish between them, that their linguistic development will be compromised by a mental ensnarling of tongues. As the legend goes, structure must be imposed at the outset; each language must be kept in its proper place.

But claiming that children muddle languages unless they are laid out separately in straight lines is like claiming that it is impossible to learn to distinguish between plants unless they are geometrically arranged within a Parisian-style garden. Language, like the rest of the natural world, has its own inherent order. And children, like other animals, are instinctive detectors of the structures and regularities they encounter in nature.

Even at birth, babies can distinguish certain languages from others. They may not have a sense of what a language is, or that it can be bolstered by schools and armies, but they can tell that some stretches of speech sound different from other stretches of speech. First, they register the rhythmic properties that are audible before birth through skin, blood, muscle, membranes, and fluid, noting how each language has a distinct heartbeat that is made from its own particular ways of grouping the openings of vowels with the closures of consonants, its own ways of combining strong and weak beats. These coarse properties are like ones that can be spotted in a plant from a distance, through blurry eyes—its general size and shape, the color of its blooms.

A few months later, infants can separate even languages like Italian and Spanish, whose rhythms are very similar. By then, they have learned to attend to subtler cues, much as neophyte botanists begin to note the number of leaves of a plant, their textures, and whether they are arranged in opposite or alternate patterns. Babies observe that languages differ in the details of their consonants and the contours of their vowels, in the clusters of sounds that fraternize with each other, how certain sounds never or always appear next to certain others. An early typology takes shape in the infant's mind.

None of this learning is impeded by exposure to more than one language at a time. Infants born into a two-language family know that these languages are distinct from each other—even when they are not anchored separately to each of their parents. They can even distinguish between languages they hear in the laboratory over loudspeakers, produced by a faceless stranger. If one language is played until the child becomes bored, her gaze begins to wander, but a switch to the other language renews her interest; she pivots her gaze toward the loudspeaker once more, having registered this stretch of speech as different in kind from the one that came before.

Clues of languages' identities are everywhere. By four months, children can tell which language a person is speaking simply by looking at the speaker's face, without hearing any of the speech at all. This ability is strengthened among children who live in two or more languages; knowing that a windfall of information can be harvested from the movements of lips and tongue, these children develop the habit of looking intently at the mouth of a speaker.

As their expertise grows, children notice that the rules for arranging words vary. One language may allow verbs and their accompanying nouns—subjects and objects—to change their positions from one sentence to another like reeling square dancers, while another may require them to line up in a rigid processional order. One language may dress verbs in an elaborate regalia of prefixes and suffixes, a formal dress code that signals when an action was committed, by whom and to whom and for whom, whether the action came to completion, whether it was part of a repetitive habit or a singular occurrence, and so on; other languages prefer their verbs nude. The appearance, habits, and habitats of each language make themselves clear, without any need for them to be artificially segregated. Children know not to press the sounds of Italian into the syntax of German, even when both languages grow wild in their vicinity.

It is true that children raised in two languages do sometimes mix them together, and anxious adults may read this as
confusion, an inability to learn each language in its pure state.
But such mixing is negotiation, not confusion. Within multilingual communities, nothing is more natural than to draw
on the resources of all one's languages, sometimes within the
same sentence, to achieve one's purpose. I'm sure I did this as a
child, when confronted with another person who spoke mostly
in a language I was just beginning to learn. Lacking a certain
word, I would proffer the most plausible one I had and hope
for the best. You never know. The worst that can happen is in-
comprehension, but this is far better than no engagement at all.

At times, the mixing is expressive rather than pragmatic,
a sign of linguistic virtuosity. Among bilingual adults, those
who blend their languages tend to have deep mastery of both.
They pluck words and phrases from each language and arrange them artfully, just as a florist surveys her buckets of
flowers to make the most vivid and arresting bouquet. They
choose a word from one language for its edgy connotations, a
phrase from another for its hint of tenderness, yet another for
its comedic sounds, irreproducible in the other language; they
may shift mid-sentence from the mainstream language into a
scrappier one, to sound a note at once rebellious and intimate;
they may beckon the hearer to lean in closer, using an abrupt
change of language to signal that what comes next is worthy
of heightened attention.

But the legend of language confusion persists nonetheless, perhaps because when these speakers defy the rules
of linguistic segregation, what they are really saying is pro-

foundly subversive: that languages are not interchangeable, that their value goes beyond what is needed for serviceable communication. Intimately familiar with the gifts each has to offer, these speakers harvest them for meaning, sound, cadence, insinuation, and lush undertones.

In doing so, they assert that languages have little to fear from each other, that they can occupy the same spaces without provoking a fight to the death or an existential terror.

When I left the wild linguistic landscapes of my early childhood and stepped into the regimented realm of school, what was it I learned about language?

Being taught to abandon my languages at the door of the classroom almost certainly did not accelerate my learning of English, despite the pedagogical wisdom of the day. Keeping languages apart did not help me to distinguish the rules of grammar of Czech, French, or English—lessons for which I had no need anyway. It did, however, help me to distinguish their speakers and to learn the rules according to which they occupied their slots in social hierarchies.

I learned that one must declare allegiance to a language; in Montreal at the time, one could be a Francophone or an Anglophone, and if you were an Allophone (that is, a speaker of another language), you had to become naturalized in one of the official languages. It was best to hide any knowledge of unofficial languages; simply speaking these in earshot of others, I discovered, could incite probing, suspicious glances.

I learned that while some languages were displayed in the

front gardens as showpieces, others were best grown by the kitchen door, where they could be used to flavor the soup but had little value otherwise. Still others were to be considered weeds.

And I learned how useful it could be to pass as a person who had declared allegiance to a single language.

These lessons fell onto fertile soil, as they do for all children. Some psychologists believe that an eagerness to bind language to identity has evolved in us over time and that children are tuned like radios to pick up linguistic signals that set one social group apart from another. To children, language—even more than race—is the bedrock of the self; they are more willing to believe, for example, that a Black child can grow up to be White than that a child who speaks English can become an adult who speaks French. As preschoolers, they choose friends more readily on the basis of accent than on the basis of race. And if asked which language will be spoken by a child who was born to Portuguese parents but adopted at birth into an English-speaking family, preschoolers believe the child to be destined to speak Portuguese.

It is as if children think that the language one speaks is immutable, the very stuff of which one is made. And perhaps with some reason. Unless a person learns a language from a young age, they are marked as an outsider by their accent and grammatical foibles; the ease with which small children master the intricacies of sound and syntax begins to fade around puberty. Language, then, is one of the most reliable ways for humans to know where someone is from, who mothered them, who taught them their way in the world.

Even among adults, something of the child's magical thinking about language persists. Many people believe that simply learning a new language will imbue them with new properties or a fresh way of perceiving the world, when in reality it is the new experiences one has in the language that are the source of any transformation. And mountains of evidence show that adults project certain traits onto others—intelligence, friendliness, attractiveness, physical height, even the degree to which one can believe factual statements they make—solely on the basis of hearing a snippet of their speech. A bilingual person may be judged to have quite different qualities depending on the language they are speaking at the time.

Just as children are able to disentangle languages and perceive the order intrinsic to them, so too can they discern the order that structures the world of people and assigns them value. The talent for the linguistic task is pressed into service for the social one. At first, infants are preoccupied with sorting the familiar from the strange, the "we" that promises safety and belonging from the mysterious, unpredictable "they." At six months of age, babies prefer to look at people who speak their own language with a native accent rather than an unfamiliar foreign accent. As they grow older, they are more likely to accept toys or food from a person who speaks the language of their family and community, or to imitate the actions of such an adult.

But by the end of preschool, they have sensed another way of sorting people, aside from "we" and "they"; they begin to notice that certain speakers are held in higher regard by others. They notice that certain languages are not heard in schools, shopping malls, or places of worship and that certain accents are met with curt replies or cool suspicion. As this awareness seeps in, they begin to prefer to associate with children and adults who speak the favored language, even if it is not the language of their own family.

And so, a fissure opens within families who have the misfortune of speaking a lower-status language. More and more, the child begins to emulate those who speak the more valued language and edges away from the language of her own parents. If they speak English with a foreign accent, theirs is not the English she will adopt as her own. Instead, she will grow up to sound like the native English speakers she hears. She may even stop speaking, as do scores of second-generation immigrant children all around the world, the first language that flared like love in her infant mind.

For such children, it's no longer possible to tell from their speech who mothered them, who first taught them their way in the world.

When I was young, it was a matter of pride to be mistaken for someone who was born into English, as someone who was made of no other languages. Now I wonder: What was there to be proud of? What does a monolingual mind have that mine does not?

It is true that knowing only one language comes with a certain efficiency in using it. Among people who know two or more, a slight vacillation between languages can be recorded in the lab: there is a tiny lag between thought and speech; a fraction of a second longer is needed to remember and recognize words compared with people who speak a single tongue. Like wearing the same shirt every day, there is a streamlined simplicity to never having to choose between one's languages.

It is also true that the presence of a second language very subtly alters the shape of the first one that took up residence in the same mind. The vowels of the two languages may drift slightly in each other's direction; the borders of categories encircled by words may soften. For example, a person who grows up speaking Greek—a language that enlists separate words to refer to light and dark shades of blue—may find, after acquiring English, that the distinction between the two has blurred somewhat, even in the native tongue. To invite another language in is to risk being influenced by it.

Knowing a single language, then, is a bit like being unencumbered by family. It comes with certain freedoms. One can move lightly and swiftly, without the burden of consulting others or the exertion of ignoring their unwanted advice. The habits of others do not encroach. But these freedoms come with a narrowing of perception.

A brain's allegiance to a single language is a form of selective hearing. Neurons learn not to respond to the sounds or patterns of other languages. As infants, we were able to distinguish between subtle contrasts of sound in many different languages, but over time we learned to ignore those not relevant to our own. The longer one spends hearing only the sounds of one language, the deafer one becomes to the subtleties of others. A child raised in an English-speaking family gradually becomes insensitive to the difference between *t* and its slightly breathier counterpart t^h, a difference that a Thai child knows to be essential for distinguishing between words of different meanings. A life lived in contact with a single version of a single language leaves other tongues less intelligible. On the other hand, familiarity with the sounds of multiple languages is a wedge that keeps the door of perception open. Even hearing one's own language spoken in a variety of foreign accents makes it easier to understand an accent never heard before.

I suppose that the advantage of a monolingual mind, a mind that has dug a moat to protect one language from all others, comes down to this: it becomes highly efficient at understanding a diminished range of human speech.

For me, growing up meant converging on a single language. My family settled and left behind our nomadic polyglot ways; my schooling fixed my gaze upon English; in adulthood, I moved away from the language-addled city of Montreal and came to live in American neighborhoods where other languages were rarely heard in the streets; I steeped myself in higher learning, soaking up texts written in the one language to reign over them all; I married an English-speaking man and raised our Anglophone children. In theory, confusion over who I was should have subsided.

In reality, convergence *was* the source of confusion. If the foundations of our souls are laid down in childhood, then the monolingualism that later spread over my life had the effect of obscuring the true substances of which I was made. I may look and sound as if I have declared my sole allegiance to the English language, but in truth I am a cacophony of voices, influencing each other, at times assisting each other, at times getting in each other's way, always vying for turf. I do not always agree with myself. Each of my languages comes not only with its own patterns of sound and methods for arranging words but also with its social habits and its judgments about what to forgive, what to condemn, and what to revere. They do squabble.

This cacophony may seem like confusion, but what if it is really the natural state of being human? Who among us, regardless of the number of languages they speak, is subject to a single set of influences? Who can say they are of one mind about what they forgive, condemn, and revere, that they are never blown about in multiple directions? Does a person of uncomplicated allegiances exist, anywhere, in any language? Perhaps when our societies converge upon a single language, it is also a way of obscuring who we really are.

In her memoir of immigration from Poland to North America, Eva Hoffman writes of the battles between the Polish- and English-speaking halves of her self. These halves would argue, in their respective languages, over how she should live her life, each vociferous about staking its claim to core values and aesthetics. Once in college, however, she saw that her internal conflicts were not much different from those of her monolingual, American-born friends: "marriage, divorce, career indecisions, moving from city to city, ambivalences about love and work and every fundamental fact of human activity." Her peers were no more protected than she was, she realized, from the strains of dislocation or the need to cobble together an identity from multiple influences, outside the protective folds of a single, enduring tradition. "In a splintered society," she wondered, "what does one assimilate to? Perhaps the very splintering itself."

These splinterings, with the clouds of dust they have kicked up over all lives everywhere, have sent us scurrying to the false promises of order, to the clean enclosures of our fengshui'ed living rooms and approved procedures of child-rearing, designed to achieve the best outcomes for the child, to keep confusion from encroaching. It's a natural human instinct, I suppose, to fear chaos and contamination, whether they come from another language, a set of morals we can't comprehend, or invisible organisms that threaten to overwhelm our bodies. We order our lives and obey stringent routines of physical, social, and mental hygiene to tame these terrors. We believe we can erect borders between ourselves and all kinds of foreign elements, biological and nonbiological.

But our habits of believing our selves to be entities that can be kept separate from the muck and muddle of the world are catching up to us. New generations of experts are now warning of the perils of too much hygiene imposed on a human life. We are told that the strict regimens prescribed in the past have led to an epidemic of new allergies and immune disorders. We were wrong, it turns out, to have been overly scrupulous about cleaning, to have kept all pathogens and allergens away from our children. In truth, our bodies do not belong to ourselves alone; each of us contains multitudes. We are now taught that it is healthy to host a flourishing population of microbes; rather than trying to eradicate all alien organisms that live inside us, we are better off letting our bodies learn how to accommodate them.

Perhaps it is the same with our minds and with our languages. A zealous hygiene may soothe us with the illusion that we are not hosts to a multitude of influences. It may feel as if we have managed to keep the dangers at bay, that we have prevented an inflammation of conflict by imposing strict rules and hierarchies. Nonetheless, we do host multitudes, even when we require all of them to speak the same language. The multitudes inside us must learn to reach a truce. Sometimes the negotiations need to take place in numerous tongues.

When I see the sterile routines upheld by friends and relatives who have little ones, I become fiercely nostalgic for my own childhood, ripe as it was with chaos and unfiltered influences. Lacking the resources to keep me separate from the complicated, sometimes grubby, often tumultuous world outside, my parents had no choice but to send me out to live in it. In the end, what better preparation could I have had for living in a confused and chaotic world than to be left to play in the dirt and run wild with all the languages I liked, all of which became—gloriously and unhygienically—a part of me.

Prosthesis

No one knows how I learned to read. At some point, people noticed that I was handling books in ways that were surprising for a child not yet taught to decipher print. On one such occasion, my mother entered the room when I was supposed to be napping, but was in fact reading. With what must have been a guilty conscience, I jammed a book of fairy tales back under the pillow where I had been hiding it. My mother demanded to know what I was concealing from her. I showed her the book. It was one that did not have many pictures, which seemed to puzzle her. "What are you doing with it?" she asked. When I told her I was reading it, she asked me to show her. Not convinced by my reading—perhaps she believed I had committed the story to memory—she left the room to retrieve another book, opened it somewhere in the middle, and asked me to read from it. I did, haltingly. Many of the words were unfamiliar to me, and I thought she would be disappointed by my fumbling attempts to decrypt the lines on the page, but this, more than my earlier fluent reading of the fairy tale, seemed to satisfy her. "Hm," she sniffed, with interest. "So you can read." This is my earliest memory of being aware that reading was something you had to learn to do.

Other memories of my early reading days have a similar quality: of surreptitiously fixing my attention on a book when I was supposed to be doing something else and then losing myself in its vortex, of my engrossed state catching the eye of an adult, and then—astonishingly—of there being no punishment or disapproval upon the discovery that I was wallowing in text. In the corner of my kindergarten classroom, I sat absorbed in a book I had taken off a shelf when I noticed my teacher standing next to me, watching me intently. Rather than scold me for having failed to join the activity taking place on the rug in the middle of the room, she led me to the classroom next door and pulled the first-grade teacher out into the hallway to serve as witness to my reading ability. "Who taught you to do that?" the teachers asked; in my school, reading was not officially taught until the first grade. I shrugged, a little baffled.

In retrospect, I must have had some teaching. It is telling that no one ever asks a child who has just uttered her first full sentence who taught her to do that. Children do not need speaking lessons. No curriculum is designed to teach children how to converse in their mother tongue; they learn their language's intricate laws for bundling and ordering nouns, verbs, adjectives, adverbs, and articles, all without learning how to describe these laws. I have met perfectly articulate college students who cannot reliably tell me if certain words are nouns or verbs. To raise a fluent child, it is enough to simply include her in the back-and-forth reciprocity of daily language. Parents instinctively speak in a way the child can learn to understand; the child instinctively discerns the patterns that make up her language.

Reading is different. Left to their own devices, children rarely (if ever) spontaneously burst into reading, even if they are surrounded by text, even if they are lovingly swaddled in rituals of bedtime reading. Upon reflection, this is odd. Objectively, learning to read should be much easier than learning to speak a language; it is far less impressive an achievement. To break into the written word, all one has to do is discover the trick of matching a handful of visual marks on the page with certain sounds. The rest is parasitic on spoken language. But to learn the spoken language in the first place is to extract from rivers of sound enough bricks of meaning to fill a warehouse, and then to discern all the secret, untaught rules that organize these bricks and combine them in limit-less ways—a set of rules so complicated that it takes the life-long labors of many linguists merely to describe them. Why does reading require pedagogical intervention at all, when the miracle of speaking does not?

Reading, unlike speaking, is not intrinsic to our species. In the history of our articulate existence, claimed by some to stretch back as far as two million years, writing is an af-terthought, existing for a mere sliver of time of possibly less than six thousand years. Up to the present moment, many human societies have run their affairs perfectly well without a written code; their lack of literacy is no impediment to com-posing epic poems, crafting contracts and treaties, or pass-ing many generations' worth of knowledge down through many more. But no wordless human group has ever been found.

Children who grow up without knowledge of text do not

invent their own writing system out of some essential need to store their thoughts for safekeeping. But children wholly deprived of language do create their own. When groups of Deaf children converge in one place, for example, never having learned language, they make an entirely new language with their hands, one that may be as different in its grammar from the language spoken by their parents as Urdu is from French. A number of distinct signed languages around the world have birthed themselves in exactly this manner.

The botanist and writer Robin Wall Kimmerer writes of her delight at discovering the Potawatomi word *Puhpowee*, whose translation into English, she learned, could be approximated as "the force which causes mushrooms to push up from the earth overnight." *Puhpowee* is the unseen, animating force that inhabits the natural world, the hot breath of life. Spoken language—along with its manual sibling, signed language—is surely imbued with *Puhpowee*. Language springs from children's minds like mushrooms after a rain, mysteriously, seemingly overnight, with little evidence of the forces that pushed it up from the damp soil of the unconscious mind. Language scientists have formed various theories of what these forces are and how they took hold of human minds, but there is little doubt about their vital, thrusting power.

Written codes are not animated by their own life force. They do not push themselves into existence wherever there are humans who strive, as they inevitably will, to connect minds with each other. Alphabets are fabrications—objects designed and manufactured by clever, enterprising people after long consideration of an engineering problem and its possible solutions. In humans, literacy does not unfurl naturally, as limbs do, growing from buds as a fetus takes shape. To become part of a person, text must be attached from outside, like a prosthetic leg.

When I entered first grade, reading instruction commenced, slowly and systematically. Thick workbooks were filled with drawings of everyday objects and with words pinned like butterflies to the page, split apart into their components. My classmates and I devoted many hours to circling pictures for words that began with certain consonants, then moved on to underlining vowels, matching clusters of consonants, mastering the subtleties of diphthongs. The work was repetitive, circling back over the same ground again and again, like a person searching for a lost set of keys in the grass.

Among scientists who study reading, there is agreement that such laborious, explicit teaching is necessary. The number of children who learn to read without much help from adults is exceedingly small, and why a small number do remains something of a mystery; such children do not necessarily display extraordinary intelligence, and being gifted is no guarantee of being able to bypass the many hours of work in which attention is shuttled between symbol and sound, symbol and sound, symbol and sound.

There is much about reading that is unnatural, that pushes against our senses. In learning to recognize letters, children have to train their minds to believe that an object is strictly bound to a certain orientation; learning that *p* and *b* and *d* are different things is like asking the mind to believe that a cup becomes a different object if it is laid upside down or with its handle facing left instead of right. Such a way of seeing runs counter to the ways of the world.

Even more unnatural is the slicing of speech into segments that can be paired off with letters of the alphabet. To a literate mind, it may seem self-evident that speech is made of letter-sized bits, the obvious atoms of language, but this belief is an alien one, absorbed only after a long indoctrination. It is not an insight that eagerly leaps into the mind. It is just as unnatural to separate speech into such pieces as it is to cut a ballet into fractions of gestures or leaps. Children as well as adults who have not learned to read find it difficult to identify, for example, that "pen" and "pot" begin with the same sound, or to predict that removing the first sound from "pink" will result in "ink," or to count the number of individual sounds in the word "pan." Asking children to perceive speech this way is much like asking them to revise their way of perceiving the world; instead of seeing the world as populated by entities such as rabbits, cars, and cups, they are instructed to see such entities as bundles of fur, paws, and hindquarters, as compositions of hubcaps and handles.

When learning to speak, a child rides with the current, carried along on ways of seeing and thinking that are native to being human; to learn to read, she must swim upstream, against her nature.

It's unlikely that such strange habits of mind would have occurred to me without prompting. It is entirely possible that a parent or an aunt or an older sibling at various times pointed out the marks in books, drawing my attention to the forced marriage of symbol and sound; in the chaotic eddy of my childhood, the steady accumulation of such moments might have escaped my mother's notice. Certainly I do remember being an avid watcher of *Sesame Street*, a children's program that blatantly propagandizes the dissection of speech into segments that can be crammed into the alphabet. And no doubt, I was helped along by the fact that the earliest books I read were in Czech, a language in which the pairings between sound and symbol are more monogamous than they are in English.

I would have been an eager student, though, convinced that the efforts channeled into learning to read would be well worth it. What *was* obvious to me from an early age, far more than the shifts of mind I would need to break into the written code, was that a book could give you something that the physical world, gorgeous as it was, could not give you, that even the people you loved best could not give you, that there were longings that could be satisfied only by the quiet turning of pages. My mother voiced daily her resentment at the lack of time to sit by herself and read. My older siblings could not be lured or bullied or pouted into play when engrossed in a book. And when my father opened a book to read out loud to us, it was a ceremony.

Like all prosthetic devices, text becomes useful only once it is incorporated as though it were a natural bodily part. The external object must be embraced by the brain as one of its own. A hearing aid is mere annoyance until the brain submits to the new signals coming in, reconfigures its auditory circuits, and reclaims neural regions for sound that have been given over to other uses. Only then does speech emerge, clean and clear against the noise of the world.

A prosthetic hand begins as a thing, as foreign as a stick tied to the body, but with time the brain adjusts its sense of the body's boundaries. Just as my own mind has intimate knowledge of the edges of my hand so that I can grasp a coffee cup without knocking it over, or scratch my nose without smacking myself in the face, the mind of a person with an artificial hand comes to know exactly where the device ends and the rest of the world begins. The more a prosthetic limb is used, the less distinguishable it is from flesh and blood; with increased use, certain visual areas of the brain respond to a photo of the device just as they would to a picture of the body's own hand, with a leap of recognition.

Other objects, too, through many hours of use, can come to be treated as (detachable) parts of one's body: skis, violin, surgical implements. Being alive for us means having the capacity to transcend and extend our bodies, to incorporate the products of others' ingenuity into our very selves.

So it is with reading. With time and much repetition, the brain accepts this new technology and changes itself in response. Unnatural ways of seeing and hearing come to feel natural. Distinctions between sounds that are represented by different symbols sharpen; the sounds wedded to *p* and *b* come to seem as starkly different as the symbols themselves. Areas of the visual brain that were previously devoted to recognizing faces are squeezed into a smaller space as tracts of neural real estate are appropriated for the speedy recognition of letters. As artificial as it is, deciphering text can eventually come to feel as organic—as *inevitable*—as inhaling the meaning of a parent's words.

Perhaps this is why the pedagogy of reading is prone to such dissent. Once text has infiltrated the body, it is hard to remember it was once an outsider. Some educators over the years have resisted the painstaking methods I encountered in my first-grade classroom, those repetitive exercises designed to fuse sound to symbol in young minds. To a teacher for whom literacy feels as agile and sinewy as her own hand, or perhaps even like a vital, beating organ, these exercises in phonics must seem drained of all life. They did so to Horace Mann more than two hundred years ago, when, as secretary of the Massachusetts Board of Education, he railed against the tedious exercises for teaching children to recognize letters, objects he described as "skeleton-shaped, bloodless, ghostly apparitions." When books pulse with life, when they are the hot liquid of thought passed from human mind to human mind, how can it be right to introduce them to children through such dreary methods? "It is no wonder," Mann concluded, "that the children look and feel so death-like, when compelled to face them."

And yet the implantation of the foreign object must occur. What to say to the teacher in the throes of language love who balks at the distance between worksheets and poetry, who finds it difficult to see how one could lead to the other? I would say that there is a long way indeed to travel between worksheets and poetry, and that traveling this ground is at the very heart of what it is to be a teacher of the language arts. But to neglect the slow grafting of text onto child is like expecting a person who is hard of hearing to thrill to a recitation of Rilke with their hearing aid turned off.

&

As a child, I used to watch a television show called *The Bionic Woman*, in which a tennis player who survives a near-fatal skydiving accident is surgically rebuilt with artificial limbs and implants. The reconstruction leaves her better than before, endowed with superhuman strength and the ability to hear the slightest of sounds over extraordinary distances. I was fascinated with this show, which flaunted an idea that would soon drench our culture: that technology could not only restore us to ourselves but leave us enhanced. Its techno-optimism was an inversion of the tragedy of Mary Shelley's Dr. Frankenstein and his botched creation, written a century and a half earlier.

Shelley's Dr. Frankenstein dares to blow his own hot breath of life into an inanimate thing, but tragedy ensues because he can't bring himself to embrace his creation as his flesh and blood; the gulf between human and artifact cannot be bridged. And yet the novel itself would never have come to life had it not been for the implantation of literacy into human minds. Those ancient precursors of Frankenstein, the creators of alphabetic scripts, dreamed of animating the bloodless, ghostly apparitions of letters. And it turns out that even these skeletal things can become the objects of human love, though they lack the *Puhpowee* that runs through speech.

By the time she wrote her novel, Mary Shelley's brain had no doubt embraced text as if it were indeed her own flesh and blood, as if reading had budded and grown within her. She had been enhanced.

When I learned to read—to *really* read so that the marks on the page ignited thoughts the instant my eyes passed over them—I felt myself transformed into someone with new powers.

Like the bionic woman, who could overhear conversations from miles away, I suddenly found myself privy to the thoughts of people who were not in the room—people who could *never* be in the same room as me because they lived oceans away, or were far more important than I was, or were dead. I enjoyed intimacies that were impossible within the limits of my physical world, even had I been blessed with poise and charm rather than being the shy, poorly dressed immigrant kid that I was. Next to my literary companions, my conversational partners were pitifully few in number, and those I had were all more or less alike. They were unlikely to reroute the path of science, or to rouse a freshly founded nation, or to murder anyone.

The fact that all this took place under the cover of solitude is what transformed me from one kind of child to another. Reading allowed me to vault beyond the grasp of parents and teachers and their ideas of who I should be and how I should think. In retrospect, I find it slightly odd that the adults in my life, who professed to be concerned with my formation, smiled so benignly when they caught me reading and then left me alone. There were certain girls, not to mention boys, whom I would not have been allowed to bring home. But as long as they could be hidden between the covers of a book, I could smuggle any dubious companion into my room and shut the door. In solitude, I could revel in their influence, egged on by their scandalous lives and outlaw philosophies, free to think or feel whatever I thought or felt about them without the burden of commentary or moral guidance from the official authorities in my life.

There was no price to pay for the enhancements I gained, unlike the bionic woman, who was powerful but enslaved. Her implants, financed by a federal agency, were a debt she had to repay with years of docile servitude as their undercover agent. I did not repay my benefactors in any way, least of all with obedience. In fact, I wonder: Would the adults in my life have been so willing to take up the labors of instruction if they had known how my eventual mastery of reading would dim their power over me and strengthen my own? How it would foment my rebellion against them?

Reading was sheer liberation, from the limits of my here and now, from parents and teachers—in the end, even from the authors whose words I consumed. I was a pliable child, easily molded by the approval of others. When people spoke, I monitored my own responses, as if through their eyes—did I display on my face the right shadings of assent or outrage? A conversation left little room for my own thoughts; I was too busy rearranging myself. But inside my fortress of solitude, invisible to the author, all my doubts and quarrels could run free. There was no hardness of a bodily presence against my mind's soft clay, and if the author's words failed to have their desired effect, I paid no penalty for it. It was in those hours of reading, particularly of books that appeared in no curriculum, that I quietly incubated my own power.

Maybe I had a sense, from the day I scrambled to hide that book of fairy tales under my pillow, that this was a power best concealed. Much of my reading took place under a haze of guilt at what I was reading or its effects on me. I rarely talked with adults about books, even—or perhaps especially—when I felt myself altered by them. I thought my reading should unsettle them. But it never did. With my nose in a book, I was granted an extraordinary exemption, permitted to have any thoughts that came to me, even when they sprang me loose from everything I had ever been taught. Under the placid gaze of my parents and teachers, who no doubt felt that by encouraging my bookishness they were molding me in their image, I plotted my escape.

It amazes me still that I got away with it.

Crevasses

When I was twelve, I asked my mother if I was pretty. She looked at me and considered. "It's more important to be smart than to be pretty."

This exchange is an apt summary of our relationship at the time.

I spent my adolescence convinced that I was ugly. Not for me was the shelter of a mother's admiring gaze. No reassuring words to make me over and conceal my blemishes. I faced the world raw skin out. It was a world that appeared to teem with girls skilled in the arts of lip gloss and contouring, girls who knew how to compose themselves inside their clothing, how to angle a shoulder or a hip, how to liquefy their movements, who steered the gaze of boys in their direction and were happy about it, girls who appraised and ranked other girls. Girls, I was convinced, who knew their mothers thought they were beautiful.

Many years later, my husband, who did think me beautiful, prepared me for a day of walking on a glacier. Though it was summer, snow covered much of the ice, and one had to be aware of the treachery underfoot. It was possible, while walking, to punch right through the thin snow and drop down into a crevasse, a deep crack that had opened up some time ago as the glacier moved over uneven terrain. Once inside, it would be futile to try to scale its vertical walls, as uncompromising as glass.

Mountaineering magazines offer dire accounts of climbers or skiers who have fallen to their deaths in these great fissures, their bodies at times washed away by the torrents of ice water that run through a glacier's arteries.

Crevasse dangers are quantifiable, though numbers do not tame the hazards. An article published in the journal *Injury* reports that between the years 2000 and 2010 a total of 415 individuals were reported as falling into crevasses in the Swiss Alps, ranging in age from six to seventy-five (mean age: forty), 84 percent of whom were male, 67 percent foreigners, with the majority of accidents (73 percent) occurring between the months of March and August. The average depth of the fall was sixteen and a half meters. The spectrum of injuries ranged from benign to fatal; the likelihood of death "seemed to be determined primarily by the depth of the fall."

᷿

These are the words that I heard that my mother did not say:

I can't lie to you and say you are pretty, because you are not. But really, you should stop obsessing about this foolish question, because it's more important to be smart than to be pretty.

Language, too, has many crevasses. Its surface appears trust-worthy, as if one can rely on solid meaning underfoot. But between the words, there are unseen gaps. As I grew older, it became clear to me that people often did not say what they meant, nor meant what they said.

My mother, leaning into the bowels of the grimy stove she was scrubbing, muttered through gritted teeth to an unseen someone, "Thank you very much, I'm so eternally grateful for this work."

In fourth grade, I had a young teacher who wore pantsuits and tall red shoes, who feathered her frost-tipped hair and ap-plied makeup as if it were tempera paint. At the end of each day, she had all the girls line up at the door to kiss her cheek before releasing us into the clean, outdoor air. I demurred. The only kissing I had ever done had been of skin that was not lacquered over, of faces that had not been doctored for public presentation because I was not the public. The fake intimacy of the whole thing made me squirm. After tolerating several days of my resistance, during which I would take my place in line but slink past the teacher with eyes downcast, she sighed heavily and announced with loud, simulated sorrow, "Julie doesn't like me." Which was a true statement, actually. But what I heard was an imperative sentence. I lifted my face to kiss the cheek.

One day, I brought home my report card, proudly showing my father the 97 percent I'd been awarded in seventh-grade English. His eyes wrinkled at the corners, but then he said (uttering a question that I thought only he could ask, but that I have since learned is the universal question of immigrant parents everywhere), "Where did the other three points go?"

How could I answer? What did he mean by this? Was I meant to reflect on what I had done to squander those percentage points, which were rightfully mine? Was I being warned of the dangers of a bloated sense of self? Was it a reminder that academic perfection was the only fair trade in exchange for my parents' sacrifices?

What I think now is that he was attempting to say (but did not), *Daughter, you fill me with pride.*

Philosophers tell us that much of the meaning that appears to come from language is in fact imagined. Language is less substantial than we think. We hear someone report, *Sofia had an affair with her ski instructor. Her husband flew into a rage, and the poor woman ended up dead.* We absorb the news of the affair and the outburst and the woman's demise, taking the first to be the kindling for the second and third events, believing them to have occurred in sequence, as strung together by syntax. But we ourselves have conjured the causal links, we ourselves have ordered these events in time; there is nothing in the language to make it so. The language has not even committed itself to the claim that the husband belongs to Sofia—it is we who have equated Sofia with the pronoun "her," which merely points to some female entity—or that she is the same poor woman who is no longer alive. These identities have never been asserted, merely gestured at, with a limp vagueness of reference that we are only too eager to augment.

We believe we have been told a tale of murderous revenge by a cuckolded husband. But the tale is in fact a mosaic we ourselves have assembled from pieces of language. Upon hearing a recording of the statement in court, we might be forced to acknowledge that the speaker was being truthful, though badly jumbled, if using this language to relate a series of disconnected events, involving people of unclear identities, with indeterminate relationships to one another.

A proposed test to separate imagined meanings from those that are baked into language: language is responsible only for what *must* be true if it is to avoid perjuring itself. That is, if I say, "There is a bird in the tree outside my window," when in fact the only thing in the tree is a squirrel running to and fro, I have lied, violating the laws of language. But if you have imagined a robin perched in the tree when in reality there is an emu reclining in its lower branches, no perjury has occurred. The meaning of "bird" has been adhered to. It is you who have imagined a different kind of bird from the one I had in mind when making my truthful statement.

If I provide further clarification to rein in your imagination, but am not forced to retract my statement outright, then the laws of language have also been preserved throughout. I can say, "My mother was an austere woman who rarely praised me, and I have grown up seeking affection in dangerous places." If I then add, "But I doubt that the two are connected in any way. I'm just saying we all have our stuff," I may be canceling the meaning you have imagined, but not the meaning of my original statement, which continues to be true.

When my mother said that it was more important to be smart than to be pretty, that was not a lie.

She had committed no violation of language.

So who or what was responsible for the injury that ensued?

It is in our nature to imagine meanings, filling in the crevassed fields of language with a light snow of inference that leaves the surface appearing unbroken. What we think has been said is merely our theory of what the speaker surely must have meant by using the words she did, a theory that is grounded in our own beliefs about what a reasonable person would have meant by those words and in our beliefs about the words a reasonable person would have used instead had she meant something different.

A reasonable person, we presume, would relate events in an orderly manner, mindful of the linear logic of time and the calculus of cause and effect; she would avoid strewing them about when speaking, with no thought to their arrangement. Is it not safe to believe, then, that the order of her language reflects her sense of the order in the world?

A reasonable person would not withhold information without cause; if she's asked how many children she has, we do not expect her to answer that she has two when she also has a third, unless there is reason to be secretive about one of her offspring.

A reasonable person would not casually mention that there is a bird in a tree, inviting us to think of robins or sparrows when there is a fucking *emu* in the tree.

A reasonable person would address the question at hand; she would not respond to a query about her marital status with a discourse on asparagus—and if she does, surely what she *means* by it is to rebuke her interlocutor for asking the question. Moreover, if the question at hand is whether her twelve-year-old daughter is pretty, her answer would illuminate the question, would it not?

So eager are we to provide the meanings that words do not that we become enablers: we give language the license to tolerate among its ranks a contingent of spindly, anemic creatures.

Take a weakling like the word "some," which offers the scrawniest of meanings; on its own, the best it can commit to is that it means "more than one." (Its vagueness is apparent from the fact that it is possible to say, without being nonsensical or acknowledging a lie, "I've read some of your books; in fact, I've read many of them, and perhaps all.")

But a person who asserts that she trusts some men will likely be taken to mean that she does not trust many, let alone most or all of them. Otherwise, the reasonable listener infers, surely the speaker would have used a different word; she would have said that she trusted "many," or "most," or "all." In the absence of any added clarification, the listener takes it upon himself to enrich the speaker's meaning.

What we understand as meaning, then, is really a calculation of what has been said against other possible ways of saying.

I once heard a friend refer to her mother as "the woman who ejected me from her uterus." I understood this to be a renunciation of her female parent, a declaration that the woman had no right to claim all the imagined meanings that are spring-loaded inside the word "mother," the word that my friend could not, it seemed, bring herself to say.

Between reasonable people, a sumptuous conversation can unfold despite an austerity of language. An intelligent hearer enlarges meanings against an appraisal of what might have been said but was not; a cooperative speaker foresees the hearer's construal and avoids leading her into a crevasse.

Still, there are many opportunities for falls, ranging from benign to deadly. Our imagined meanings are only as solid as our theories of reasonable speakers. We build these up over time, depositing layers of knowledge into the gaps left by language—knowledge of other humans, what they know, what they desire, how they wield language to achieve their desires; knowledge of the customs that dictate which words may or may not be used; knowledge of the intimate details of the present situation; of how all of these forces have come bearing down on the speaker at this very moment.

Only once many layers have been packed down into a firm mass is it safe to take a step.

The Japanese are known for their penchant for obliqueness. They do not flash meanings out in the open. They understate their own achievements, hint at their desires rather than declare them nakedly, and divert language from the path of confrontation. Conversations require depths of calculation, and their results are rarely determinate. Beneath drifts of ambiguity, one must probe for the meaning intended by another, much as one would insert a probe stick into snow to locate the body of a person buried under an avalanche.

The Japanese term for such careful conversational probing is *kuuki o yomu*: "reading the air."

I have a friend who grew up in Kyoto, whose residents are famous even within Japan for their indirectness. Local lore has it that if a person is vexed by guests who have overstayed their welcome, she should offer them *bubuzuke*, a humble dish made of hot green tea poured over steamed rice. This invitation, my friend tells me, is meant to convey something like this: *Naturally I am honored and delighted by your visit and I'm eager to invite you to share a meal with me. I wish I could offer you food that is worthy of guests, but all I can prepare is the simple meal of* bubuzuke. Reasonable listeners will hastily exclaim that they must be going, are expected elsewhere, are already late for their appointment.

To an American accustomed to down-to-earth bluntness, such communication feels not only hazardous but inefficient.

To burden the hearer with such an excavation of meaning is an affront to the American sensibility. A reasonable listener would not feel guilty for abandoning the attempt to understand a speaker so disinclined to say what he means.

In Japan, a person who drops the burden of careful listening risks being ridiculed. He may be called a KY—a slang term short for *kuuki ga yomenai* (unable to read the air). On a recent Japanese reality TV show named *Love Village*, a participant repeatedly misread signals from female members of the cast, believing them to be romantically interested in him when they were not. Throughout the show, he was mockingly labeled a "misunderstanding monster."

Such a person might wish to hone his social skills by playing the video game *Kuukiyomi* (Consider It), which is all about reading the air. In the game, the player is confronted with delicate social situations and must decide how to respond. An example: You are a man who has asked his female bowling companion, "If I knock down the last pin, will you go out with me?" She says, "Yeah . . . okay." Your dilemma: Should you knock down the pin or deliberately miss?

I admit I can find the Japanese style a bit aloof. I suppose I have been trained to link directness with intimacy. When speaking with a Japanese person, I sometimes feel myself held at arm's length from the other, as if, deemed untrustworthy, I have been denied entry into her true thoughts and feelings.

My Japanese friend tells me that I am mistaken in this. Her culture's obliqueness, she says, is an invitation to intimacy. To decipher a person's meaning, you have to read her face and body as you would read the snow over a glacier, alert for patches of sagging snow that hint at the abyss beneath. You have to take the time to probe for the meaning under the surface, and you must plant your steps with care. A person who conceals meaning beneath layers of language is saying, *I trust that you will find me worthy of making the effort to uncover what it is that I mean but do not say.* She is beckoning you to lean in close.

I remember often having the feeling that speaking with my parents was like speaking with people from a foreign culture, inscrutable in their otherness. Which I suppose it was. If someone was beckoning me to lean in close, I missed it.

My husband told me of an accident report he'd once read, describing how a nine-year-old boy accompanying his father on an ice-field walk had fallen into a crevasse. His father and others attempted to pull him out, but the boy's body was firmly wedged in the crack. As he struggled, his movements only succeeded in wedging him ever more tightly into the cold, hard grip of the glacier. Eventually, the boy died, whether from asphyxiating in the snow, from hypothermia, or from having his lungs compressed by the icy walls of the crevasse, my husband did not recall.

I listened to this tale with horror, thinking of all the invisible dangers into which a child might fall.

Children are chaotic imaginers of meaning, because their theories of reasonable speakers and possible ways of saying are still poorly formed. For them, the breach between language and intended meaning may be too wide to leap over. They know too little about how other minds operate, too little about how *this particular other mind* operates, what experiences it has accumulated, what its agenda is, what the world looks like from behind its eyes.

At times, children take refuge in the literalness of language, not daring to venture further. It is not until they are eight or nine, for example, that most children can fully recognize sarcasm for what it is, accepting that a person of sound mind can intend to mean exactly the opposite of what they are saying, let alone understanding what that person may be trying to accomplish by twisting language in such a manner. (My own daughter was eventually taught by an English teacher that the purpose of sarcasm was "to tear flesh, using wit.")

Children may accept weak words at face value, without fattening them in the ways adults do. Most adults, when asked whether it is true that *some giraffes have long necks*, deem the statement false, hearing the unspoken claim *not all giraffes have long necks*. Most small children, however, accept it as true, perhaps not yet having a firm grasp of what a reasonable speaker would be expected to say under the circumstances.

A toddler may ask, "Can I have a cookie?"

The mother answers, "It's almost dinnertime."

The child persists. The mother snaps, impatient with the child's attempt to bulldoze through a refusal, and a power struggle ensues. But has the child understood the refusal? No "no" has been uttered in response to the question. To comprehend her mother, the child must understand that the timing of dinner is a principle that governs the distribution of sweets, and that drawing attention to this fact is a reasonable way in which to turn down the request for a cookie. Without this knowledge, the parent's response is as informative as if she had responded, "Your shirt is blue." The parent, who has taken pains to soften the bluntness of a hard refusal with a loving explanation of why denying her child's desires was in fact in the child's interest, bristles at evidence of her daughter's stubbornness. In the gap between minds, conflict brews between parent and child.

A child is also at risk of over-imagining meanings, as I undoubtedly did from time to time when I was small. From my self-important viewpoint, I absorbed every glowing statement my parents uttered about another child as an indictment of me; surely, there could have been no other reason for them to comment on a child's virtues in my presence other than as commentary on my own self. I had never been a parent; how could I possibly throw myself into the space behind their eyes as they looked at their child, and imagine what meanings they might mistakenly predict I would calculate? How could I possibly imagine that my own emotions—my roaring fears and blazing jealousies—were not, for them, the loudest, most visible things in the room?

I keep thinking of children stumbling and pitching

headfirst into the cracks of language. The trouble is that met-
aphors, too, are mystifying to children. To warn a child that
language is filled with crevasses is not a warning that can
keep her safe.

⸙

I recently asked my mother what she'd had in mind, that day
she told me, her twelve-year-old daughter, in response to the
question at hand—a question I had asked with my heart in
my mouth—that it was more important to be smart than to
be pretty.

"Exactly that," she said.

I should have taken refuge in the literalness of her words.
I should not have stepped out onto the snow.

But I did, and the fall I took, where the solidity of language left an opening, was deep, very deep.

When I review the accident report with others, they now
tell me that a reasonable speaker should have foreseen and
forestalled the danger. My mother should have known that the
question at hand was indeed not foolish but predictably salient
for a girl standing at the precipice of adolescence, a girl made
aware in several multitudes of ways that the question of her
beauty was a crucial, urgent question. My mother should have
known that a reasonable listener, under the circumstances,
would infuse any answer to the question "Am I pretty?" with
the substance of assent or denial, that in fact the question at
hand was not really a question about her daughter's beauty
but a question about how to survive in a world that demanded
beauty as proof of worth, and that a reasonable twelve-year-old

listener would take her mother's unspoken denial of her beauty as an indictment of her worth. How do you face the world with a face that not even a mother thinks is beautiful?

Was my mother, the woman who ejected me from her womb, being reckless in her disregard for the mortal dangers at my feet?

I'm not sure. There is more than meets the eye to this question of reasonable speakers and reasonable listeners. My mother tells me that when she was twelve, the question of a young girl's beauty was an abstraction, not an insistent, thrumming beat. Growing up under the privations of communism, she was not tormented by catalogs of beauty products circulating at school, stuffed with glossy photos of full-lipped, high-cheeked standard-bearers of female worth. At my mother's school, everyone—girls and boys—wore overalls and hand-stitched pants passed through a long chain of siblings. A young woman's stock rose or fell with her skill at turning monotonous food staples into flavorful meals (an uncle-in-law was fond of saying that it was worth marrying into my mother's family for the soups alone), or with her ability to thrive under dictatorial constraint. Sturdy calves and ankles were a female asset, not a reason for self-recrimination.

The ground my mother stood upon as a child bore little resemblance to the surface on which I planted my feet—how could she assess the terrain and foresee its hazards? It is hard for me to hold her responsible.

But there is no doubt that the terrain we walked over as mother and daughter in those years was riven with cracks and that we were poorly equipped to deal with its perils.

My husband taught me that when traveling over a glacier, all members of the group must be tethered together by means of rope and harnesses. They must also carry ice axes, snow pickets, pulleys, carabiners, and various cords and slings.

If the snow collapses under a person, the others try to arrest the fall with the weight of their bodies. In order to avoid sliding into the crevasse as well, they may need to plant their ice axes into the snow to use as a brake while kicking their feet into the snow for additional stability.

If the person has fallen too deep to climb out of the crevasse, the others must haul him out. To do so, one companion will build an anchor in the snow while the others keep their bodies in place to prevent him from falling farther. Once the anchor is in place, the weight of the fallen climber is transferred from his companions to the anchor, freeing them up to assist in the hauling. Prior to hauling, they must place an ice ax or a backpack under the rope at the lip of the crevasse to prevent the rope from cutting deeper into the crack.

My husband made me repeat each step multiple times, until he felt sure I could correctly build the anchor, tie the knots, set up the pulleys.

I found all of these preparations somewhat unsettling. Imagining the yank of my husband's heft that I would feel on my body in the event he took a fall, I looked for reassurance. "But you'll be careful. You won't fall into a crevasse, right?"

His eyes locked into mine. "You have to assume I'll fall," he said. "And be prepared to save me."

Perhaps this is what my Japanese friend was trying to tell me: if you are going to travel over language filled with cracks, you'd better be roped to your companions.

When I think back to my fourth-grade teacher with the lacquered face, it occurs to me that neither one of us said what we meant.

What I meant was, *Please don't make me kiss you.*

But I said nothing. I averted my gaze and tried to evade her dolled-up body, which was, unfortunately, occupying most of the doorway.

What my teacher said was, *Julie doesn't like me.* (A statement that, incidentally, I meant, but could not say.)

What she meant was, *Kissing me is obligatory.* (A statement she probably could not say.)

As I saw it, only one of us was permitted the luxury of misunderstanding the other.

Some time ago, I read an essay in which the author described the experiences she and other women had with unwanted sex involving men. These episodes were described as failures of language. In some cases, the women, frozen into verbal paralysis, said nothing at all. In her own case, writes the author, she did say "no," but "could not rise to the challenge of confrontation, much less frank talk, which required an intimacy that he and I did not share." What she needed that night, she suggests, was a "linguistic rip cord"—perhaps the phrase "red zone" would do—that would serve as "a quick, unemotional way to telegraph how deeply uncomfortable I was, without having to explain to someone I barely knew just how deeply uncomfortable I was." Finding herself unable to utter words that would have required a deeper intimacy than she'd achieved with the man she was with that evening, the author suffered an unwanted physical intimacy that left her profoundly disturbed.

In courts of law, some judges have attributed events like these to misunderstandings between reasonable people. It is hard to fathom, they suggest, what it was that kept these women from simply sitting up and saying, "Look, I just don't want to have sex with you right now. You need to leave." One can only assume that if a woman fails to clearly assert her unwillingness to have sex, she must not be that unwilling to have it. Surely, the prospect of sexual violation would jolt even the most diffident woman into communicative clarity.

The prescription appears obvious: instruct women to speak their minds directly and clearly, and impress upon men that they must pay heed.

Perhaps my Japanese friend would understand why such a prescription would not guarantee a woman's safety. There are unwritten laws that we all come to learn, beginning as children, about the things we cannot say, and when and where we cannot say them, and to whom.

These laws are so powerful that at times, a penalty as dire as the prospect of death is not enough to jolt a person into communicative clarity, even if one is not Japanese. The deadliness of linguistic crevasses is not only figurative. In 2001, it was determined that a British patient by the name of Wayne Jowett died as a result of receiving an injection of vincristine into his spinal fluid. A junior doctor who took part in the procedure suspected the drug should not be administered in this manner, but failed to challenge his senior colleague. An external report concluded that a contributing factor in Mr. Jowett's death was a work culture in which senior medical staff were not to be questioned.

Later, a German study found similar lapses of communicative clarity among physicians and nurses who participated in a surgical simulation in which the attending doctor committed seven violations of standard procedure, including ordering two potentially fatal drug administrations. If the junior medical staff intervened at all, they resorted most often to oblique, even nonverbal communication; feigning ignorance, they might ask why a particular dosage was ordered, hoping the attending doctor would correct the error, or they might reach for their own surgical mask to hint to the doctor that he should be wearing his. When the medical staff became aware of an error that required verbal intervention of some sort, 72 percent of them chose to remain entirely silent. When asked why they had remained silent, 37 percent had no answer.

Researchers who study communication styles find that obliqueness can be predicted in specific situations. You are especially likely to be oblique if your social status is lower than that of your interlocutor. You are especially prone to indirectness when delivering unpleasant news, whether you are declining a social invitation, divulging a grim diagnosis, or criticizing someone's surgical skills. And in the seven-veiled dance of seduction, a dance that thrives on mystery and concealment, social norms provide little room, with someone you have just met, for frank talk about the degree to which each of you does or does not wish to have sex with the other.

Women who try to fend off unwanted advances often find themselves in all three situations at once. And they find that only one person in the room seems to be permitted the luxury of misunderstanding the other.

A much-cited article introduces Western readers to sixteen ways in which a Japanese person might refuse a request without saying "no." These include saying "yes" and then launching into a lengthy explanation that in the end amounts to a detailed account of why fulfilling the request is difficult or impossible; being vague and evasive so that the other side loses track of the issue; abruptly changing the subject; suddenly assuming a deeply apologetic tone; silence.

Psychologists have documented the various ways in which Western college students might refuse a sexual overture without saying "no." These include listing the other person's admirable qualities followed by the word "but"; sidling away from the other party; abruptly changing the subject; turning on the television; suggesting sex at some later, unspecified time; silence.

One study found that when rejecting a sexual advance, both Japanese and American college students said they preferred to deliver a soft and oblique refusal rather than flat out saying "no." But while Japanese students on the receiving end of these gentle demurrals understood them to be as clear in their meaning as stark refusals, American students—whether male or female—did not.

One might conclude that this state of affairs—a predilection for subtle signals by the pursued coupled with their lack of clarity to the one pursuing—sets Americans up for catastrophes of communication.

Some researchers have claimed that there are rifts of communication between women and men, offering evidence that some signals—dressing sexily or talking about sexual topics—are taken by men as willingness to have sex when women may not intend them as such. "These behaviors," suggests one paper, "are some of the most likely to result in honest disagreements about consent."

But other authors object, citing evidence that men are perfectly aware of the subtle means by which seduction is advanced and rebuffed, and at times simply choose to disregard them.

Tacit in much of the debate is the presumption of innocence of a man who sincerely believed that a woman meant something other than she did, who is afterward surprised and horrified to learn that she experienced a violation. It does not consider that misunderstanding itself can be monstrous—a moral failure, not merely a sad but blameless accident.

What I have learned about traveling over a glacier, thanks to my husband:

1. Choose your companions carefully. Do not travel with those who are not trained in the techniques of crevasse rescue.

2. The ropes can stay in the backpacks while you are traveling on solid ground. But as soon as you step onto the glacier, especially if you are traveling in summer when the snow is thin, the safety gear must come out.

3. It does not matter if your companions are heavier or lighter than you are; in the event that one of them falls into a crack, it is your responsibility to haul them out, regardless of the weight differential between you. In the event that you fall in, it is their responsibility to haul you out.

4. Take care in deciding how much space to leave between companions who are tethered together. Leave too much space, and it will be difficult to stop a companion's fall, allowing them to smash onto ice below rather than dangle harmlessly mid-crevasse. Leave too little space, and you risk being swept into the crevasse with them.

5. The person who is most experienced at reading the terrain should walk in front. This person is the most likely to notice telltale dips in the snow and to be able to navigate around them.

&

Somehow, my mother and I managed to navigate our relationship without any deadly falls. It has taken us decades to refine our theories of each other.

Today, she is the woman who ejected me from her womb, the woman who taught me things, some of them indispensable and some of them erroneous, the woman who loved me, at times with gritted teeth, throughout her bewilderment with me, the woman I still crave to be near, the woman who became a greater woman than the woman she was when she gave birth to me, the woman who is the deserving claimant of all the imagined meanings spring-loaded into the word "mother."

These days, when my mother and I travel together over treacherous terrain, we know to bring ropes and ice axes. We are prepared for rescue in the event of a fall through flimsy snow. And I have become well-versed in the art of reading the surface, alert for signs of ravenous air underneath.

But when I was twelve, all of this was still in the future. First, I would have to meet the man who taught me the ropes. And before that, I would have to cross over vast ice fields unprotected, encountering traveling partners of the sort who would leave you behind in the crevasse if you slipped, who would cut the ropes, even, given half a chance. Who would not grieve for you if your body was washed away in the glacier's ice-cold blood.

PART II

&

Maturity

The rectilinear movement of time

A few months short of my eighteenth birthday and well into my first year of university, I had the sense that my future was assembling itself into semisolid form and all I had to do was point myself in its direction as it continued to harden into reality. That future dissolved on the day I stepped into an introductory linguistics course.

Before that day, it had seemed inevitable to me that I would be a writer. This meant writing novels or possibly poetry; I had not yet read other kinds of books that smoldered with aesthetic intensity or set my synapses alight. I chose a class in linguistics not because it sounded interesting (it did not: its course description made reference to notions such as syntax and grammar, which I had encountered only in desiccated and prescriptive forms) but because it seemed that knowing about such things might be useful for a writer.

I thought I knew a great deal about language already. I had by then wandered in and out of five languages and was adept at comparing and contrasting them. My teachers had routinely praised my ability to manipulate language. But more than that, I felt I was *made* of language—that my soul was the product of all the language fragments that had blown my way and accumulated into a semblance of a whole, all of them held together by my ardor for their alchemies of sound and meaning. Nothing else in the world drew the same bodily response from me (I was just beginning to have an inkling that sex might have similar possibilities). I could imagine no version of my self that was not about language. I thought I knew language intimately, in a way that made me possessive of it.

What happened in that linguistics classroom was a shock to me. After the first session or two, I was certain that my life had changed, though I couldn't have said exactly how. I did know that I was about to abandon my plans of majoring in English and becoming a novelist.

A few years later, I came across a painting by Rembrandt that explained what had come over me. The painting is titled *The Anatomy Lesson of Dr. Nicolaes Tulp*, and it depicts the sort of public dissection anyone (who was male, presumably) could attend at the time for a fee. At the center of the image is a cadaver, awash in cold, pale light. The presiding Dr. Tulp, with immense composure and dignity, has peeled back the skin on the arm of the corpse, revealing its muscle, tendons, and bone. A ring of men, all in black coats and white starched collars, stand on the periphery and dissolve into shadow; several of them lean far into the light, their faces transfixed by the body displayed before them.

All their lives, these men had seen bodies much like the one lying on the slab in front of them, everyday bodies walking, sitting, limping, swaggering, swinging an ax, hoisting a child, dipping bread into soup, glugging a mug of beer, kneeling in prayer, dying. Bodies they knew intimately, some perhaps even possessively. But here, under an unflinching light, they were offered a completely new way of seeing a body. And they could see that until this moment they had known nothing.

Here, underneath the skin, they found revelations they hadn't realized they needed. They could see that blood did not slosh around in the body or soak deep into sponge-like tissues, but traveled in its own intricate channels radiating from the heart, gathering to fortify itself within the balloons of lungs. They could see for themselves the secretive machinery that animated all movements, the circuitous journeys that were traced by food and drink. Their faces reflect the religious feeling that had not yet begun to bleed out from science; to understand the container of man's soul, with the help of scalpel and cold, pale light, was to move closer to God.

In that first linguistics class, I had been like one of those men in black, leaning hard into the light. I had not imagined it possible to look under the surface of language in the way we were being taught to look. I had not dreamed of the structures—the systems of cooperating organs—that lay there for anyone to see, once language's skin was sliced open and peeled back.

It came as a revelation, for example, to learn that all vibrating consonants in my mother tongue of Czech became whispered versions of themselves at the ends of words, so that *d* became *t* and *z* became *s*, and that they could be restored to their true selves by the presence of an adjacent vowel within a suffix that sheltered them from the cliff edge of the word. For example, the word *hrad* (castle) was pronounced as "hrat," its spelling notwithstanding, but the *d* sound ventured out in the plural form *hrady*. I realized that this pattern ingrained in Czech was likely behind my parents' charming pronunciation of the English word "bald" as "balt," though they had no trouble with "balding."

When I pointed out to my mother the facts of her pronunciations, in both Czech and English, she was astonished—it's not the sort of thing anyone ever notices spontaneously, especially about their own mother tongue—and then entranced. (She, too, was a leaner into the light.) I was able to inform her that English sounds also had unstable identities, as with the plural tag on "beds" versus "bets"; although both are written as the letter *s*, the former is pronounced as a vibrating *z*, relinquishing a part of its identity to the preceding *d* sound. Our conversations at that time often veered into my new discoveries of language and her exclamations of wonder and delight when I shared them.

Countless patterns like these lay hidden under the membrane of conscious awareness. Even accidental slips of the tongue submitted to a concealed order. I learned why it is common to exchange the first sounds of words in errors of speech—saying "queer dean" when one meant "dear queen"—but less common to exchange the last sounds, as in "dean queer" instead of "dear queen"; why it is even less likely that one would exchange the first sound of one word for the last sound of another ("near queed"); why nouns are readily exchanged with nouns in error and verbs with other verbs, but rarely one with the other; and so on. There are good reasons for all of this. An exquisite logic runs through language even at its most disheveled.

How can one not be transfixed by this view into language? To encounter the science of language for the first time is like lying in the dark with a lover of many years, believing that you have already learned most of what is knowable about him, when he turns his face to yours with a certain look. You sense that he is about to crack open the door to hidden rooms inside himself, ones that have long been sealed off from you, that you hadn't even known were there. He invites you in. There is more sweet discovery ahead, much more than you had ever learned to expect.

Who would not thrill at such an invitation? What kind of lover would not whisper a tremulous "yes"?

More than a decade after my first encounter with linguistics, after I did not become a novelist but did complete a PhD in linguistics, I took on the mantle of a Dr. Nicolaes Tulp and found myself in classrooms where students were having their own first encounters with the science of language. One day, after I had given the first lecture of the semester, a woman came to the front of the room. She was older than most of the students and had the self-assured air of someone whose identity had stabilized. She thanked me for the lecture, but wanted to let me know she wouldn't be continuing with the class. It was not at all what she had expected, she explained. This analytical approach, this "dissection of language" (her exact words), was just not for her. "You see, I'm a poet," she said, by way of explanation.

As if loving language required cultivating a degree of ignorance of it. As if this love would burn up under the cool light of knowing too much. As if to learn more about language risked snuffing out its spark of the divine.

When I started to be serious about linguistics—not just devouring the knowledge produced by others but adding to it as well—the questions that captivated me were ones that dealt with the miracles and mishaps that took place in people's minds as language passed between them. A sentence was not given whole by one person to another, like an apple or a hunk of bread. It unfurled and revealed itself moment by moment, owing its very existence to the flow of time.

Time struck me as a cruel master, lording itself over language at every opportunity. Here was a speaker rushing to transmute her thoughts into language, preparing to enter the conversation's relentless stream: mentally laying the foundation of her sentence; choosing *this* structure from among the many ways she might have expressed the same thought; selecting her words; snapping them into the sentence's frame; converting it all into the liquidity of speech; all while releasing sounds, drop by drop, into a shared acoustic space. Here was her listener, gathering up those drops one at a time—but quickly, quickly, before they melted into nothingness—and assembling them into a shape capable of yielding meaning, fixing structure and meaning in memory while scrambling to pick up new drops of sound the moment they were released.

All of it, always, came down to a matter of time. The instruments of my trade allowed me to slice time into the thinnest of increments: I used computer programs to measure, down to the millisecond, how long it took my subjects to read certain words, begin to utter a sentence, respond to a question. I tracked their eye movements to discern where in a sentence their eyes landed and how long they lingered there, or how much time it took them to fix their gaze upon an object while obeying a verbal command. Tracing the path of their eyes over a picture as a narrative unfolded, overlaying eye gaze with speech, I could see how their interpretations were often tightly yoked to the stream of speech, but sometimes lagged behind or stumbled, and sometimes leaped ahead.

Not all of my fellow linguists were as preoccupied as I was with the relationship of language to time. These temporal questions belonged to a subdiscipline known as "psycholinguistics," a term that always struck me as odd—as if language could ever be disconnected from the psyche, from which it emitted and in which it resided. But many linguists treated language as if it could be, at least for the purpose of examining it. It was useful, they claimed, to view language as a thing unto itself, an abstraction that could be pried away from individual speakers and their circumstances, the limits of their minds, their cultural contexts, even from the strictures imposed by time. Sentences, splayed out in their entirety and frozen in time, were the primary objects of study.

Following the lead of Noam Chomsky of MIT, who had helped to drag the study of language out from the plush lounges of philology departments and under the fluorescent lighting of the information age, linguists were drawn (and really, who could resist?) by his ambition to discover and describe not just one language, or several, but the very essence of Language. His core insight was that a relatively small collection of mathematical rules for combining words (referred to as a grammar) could expand, universe-like, into a limitless number of sentences, each as unique as a constellation. Moreover, he claimed, these grammars were constrained by a genetic endowment common to all humans. Small variations in this set of rules could yield the abundance of patterns seen across all the world's languages; the genetic constraints could explain why certain patterns never appeared among the world's languages while others were found among many. All of this was knowable. Many linguists at the time were electrified by the possibility of capturing the sum total of these rules, of squeezing infinitude into a compressed informational space.

In this grand intellectual project, the mere *implementation* of language, that is, what happened in the back-and-forth between speakers and listeners—in *real time*, as we called it—was often seen as mere drag, the equivalent of friction rubbing annoyingly against the purity of the physical forces that held the universe together.

But I could not fathom separating the essence of language from its subservience to time. To think of language as outside time seemed like trying to understand the anatomy of a bird without taking into account the force of gravity that was so determined to pull the creature back to the earth's surface. It was like failing to consider that the structure of the bird was the very expression of its struggle against gravity's unrelenting, unalterable demands. Perhaps you could describe a bird's structure from this vantage point. But could you ever truly understand why it was the way it was?

Besides, it was not the elegance of mathematics that stirred me. It was my love for language—not as an abstraction, but as an embodied thing, in motion, implemented in, yes, *real time*. I loved language the way you adore a person, in their details, in the way they have taken control of your senses. I loved how language could shape the vagueness of a human voice into something precise, how easy it was to recognize a familiar voice not just from its timbre but also from its habits of speech—the crisp tap of her *t*, a slight looseness of the *s*, the slant of her vowels. I loved how language constantly jolted me—how a sentence could proceed smoothly and unremarkably and then upend all rational expectations, whether through its own genius or its own clumsiness. I loved the sweaty effort of forming a sentence and the satisfaction when it flew straight and landed clean.

Would Nicolaes Tulp's anatomy students have been so moved by their first dissection if they had never loved any particular human body, if they had not thrilled at its grace and prowess, been stricken with anxiety at signs of its frailty? If they had not experienced the strains and pleasures of their own bodies?

I wanted my study of language to stay close to my own experience of it, sweetly imprisoned as it was by time.

☙

Saint Augustine ruminated about time and language more than a millennium and a half before I ever did, and long before technology made it possible to split time into thousandths of a second, allowing me and my colleagues to observe its demands on language. More accurately, what Augustine ruminated about was the mystery of the present moment—the only location in time in which we truly exist—and he used language to pry the mystery open.

He began by noting that we have the sense that some syllables are short and some syllables are long. (Indeed, the distinction lies at the heart of classical Latin and Greek poetry, and in many languages, such as Czech, the length of time spanned by a syllable is an indispensable clue to its meaning: *byt*, "residence," and *být*, "to be," are pronounced identically except that the vowel in the second word is longer than in the first.) But how can we know that syllables differ in this way? wondered Augustine. How can we measure the time spanned by syllables? In the fourth century of the common era, there were no devices capable of doing so. But it was not a problem of technology that preoccupied Augustine. It was a problem of philosophy.

While I'm uttering a syllable, I cannot measure it, because it has not yet ended; one can't measure the time of something that is still ongoing. But as soon as I have finished uttering it, it is in the past and no longer exists. How can I measure something that doesn't exist? And yet we are convinced, wrote Augustine, that some syllables are short and some long—a conviction that is firmly borne out by poetry and by languages such as Czech, which assign different meanings to syllables of different length.

What we are measuring is not the syllable itself, concluded

Augustine, but our memory of the syllable, the mere imprint of it in our mind after it has stopped existing. That syllable is no more real than the dream we have of a future that has not yet come into being.

All of this points to a vertiginous conclusion: what we experience as our life is mostly contained within periods of nonexistence, the past or the future. Only the present moment exists, but this moment is so small as to be virtually nonexistent. As Augustine points out, "Time flies so quickly from future into past that it is an interval with no duration. If it has duration, it is divisible into past and future. But the present occupies no space."

What would it be like to occupy a present that could be fixed and held still, a reality that had substance and existence, that was not merely the vanishing point where the lines of past and future meet? That, asserted Augustine, is something that only God can describe. To fix the present and hold it still would be to experience eternity—"the sublimity of an eternity that is always present."

Augustine was no psycholinguist, being preoccupied with mysteries far greater than the ones that concerned me as a young language scientist, but he put his finger on an inescapable truth: we experience language, as we do everything else, through the pinhole of the present. The future is out of view, visible only in our imaginations, but it comes rushing toward us, flickering before our eyes for an unmeasurable instant before it flies out of view once more, recoverable only as a fallible, grainy image reconstructed by memory.

It's no wonder that the nothingness of the present became

apparent to Augustine when his contemplations turned to language. Almost nothing in the human experience has as little stability in time as speech; it is by its very nature evanescent. In every divisible moment of time, its qualities are different. As such, it brings into painful relief the paradoxical impossibility of living in the present moment.

As my chosen field of psycholinguistics grew more sophisticated at studying language in "real time," it became all the more apparent that language, in its everyday use, involves a frantic negotiation between future and past, though we ourselves are trapped in those pinhole moments between what has been uttered and what has yet to be spoken. How do you create something coherent from these minuscule fragments of ever-changing sound? Your grasp of syllables, let alone entire words or sentences, depends on your ability to imagine the future and remember the past, to knit together the two nonexistent tenses in order to hold still a meaning that is hurtling itself through time.

Every sentence you utter illustrates the problem. Before you speak, you must have a sense of what you are going to say. To convert ideas into language takes time. Like a sculptor, you carve your sentence from a block of thought, first hacking out the coarse outline of its shape, then chiseling in the details of specific words, then refining its surface of sound.

Unlike the product of a sculptor's labors, though, your creation is not made of material that can persist through time. You must form an utterance before you can speak it, but even as it forms in your mind, it rushes from future to past; its shape is already a memory even before you have opened your mouth. As best you can, you try to fix its image in memory as you prepare to speak it. But a full sentence in all its detail contains more information than your memory can easily hold, and if you wait until your sentence is completely formed in your imagination before you begin to utter its first syllable, it will have already begun to dissolve.

To outrun its decay, you begin to utter the first portion of the sentence while hurrying to put the finishing touches on the portions that will come later. Indifferent to your struggles, the future bears down on you. At times, your planning lags behind your speech: you reach the point in a sentence where you are to utter a certain word, only to find that you have not yet decided on what it will be, and all you can do is vocalize an empty sound (*uhhh* . . .) to mark its place until you complete your work. At other times, you have rushed and your tongue slips; in your haste to ready your material for speech, you have lined up the wrong word or sound or syllable.

You are constantly ferrying between past and future; to choose the word or phrase you are going to say, you have to leap back into memory and conduct a frantic search. You can't spend too much time there, because the future will be here any instant. You reach for the first word that comes to mind, the most common phrase, a word you have just heard, whatever lies at the top of the memory heap. You speak, hoping for the best.

Time is no kinder when it is your turn to listen. As your interlocutor's sentence streams into the nonexistent past, you strain to hold its image in memory. To forestall the sentence's inevitable decay, you rush to squeeze meaning out of it as soon as words begin to spill from the speaker's mouth. Sometimes this task is complex, and it takes some time to translate language into thought; then you risk being buried under a new avalanche of incoming speech. Sometimes, this task is simple; then your mind is freed from the burden of holding on to the past and so you leap into the future. Before the sentence has revealed its shape, you predict the form it might yet take. This too requires shuttling between tenses, because predictions themselves rely on memories—how else do we know what to expect in the future, other than by remembering what we have encountered before? If your prediction turns out to be correct, all is well. If it is not, you stumble, take time to recover. In the meantime, more speech has piled up on top of you.

In this back-and-forth, pressed between the walls of past and future as they close in on each other, language seems a fragile thing, in constant danger of being crushed.

❦

My work as a psycholinguist was to explain how language manages to survive nonetheless, despite being trapped in such a perilous space, wholly dependent on the human ability to anticipate and shape the future while keeping the past from melting into oblivion. My colleagues and I built and tested theories to understand what the mind is doing as it scrambles between tenses.

To an outsider, the daily work of these investigations would likely seem pedestrian: much of my time was spent designing sentences, making minute adjustments to this or that crucial feature, poring over reams of numerical data from willing subjects who had volunteered to produce or decipher language. But to me, the work felt profound, revelatory. I was toiling at the heart of a gorgeous mystery: how it is that we humans create meaning while occupying the pinhole of the present, in which the thinnest shaving of language exists.

The greatest revelations came from the lapses and failures of our subjects. From these emerged a vision of language truly pressed against its limits. Language as we know it would not exist if we were equipped with slightly lesser minds, if we had a somewhat diminished capacity to prevent scraps of information from sliding into an irretrievable past, if we were less able to synchronize all of the many time-jumping mental activities that fall under the label of language.

If you knew how to look, disfluencies and slips of the tongue revealed many details of how past and future were stitched together in the act of speaking. Certain patterns of speech errors revealed that speakers chose words well in advance of uttering them, but waited until the last moment before speech to attend to their pronunciation. That is, when a word is plucked from the past's storehouse and lined up for future utterance, it is a naked concept, not yet clothed in sound, presumably to avoid the burden of holding in active memory all the details of its pronunciation. One can imagine memory as a harried stage manager, able to keep track of which performers are to exit the wings in what order, but not the details of their costumes; these are left to a wardrobe specialist who hastily dresses each performer before they step onto the stage.

Thus, a speaker might easily say, "We ordered a new library for the third floor of the desk," having exchanged the words "library" and "desk" in error. The error reveals that the word-concept "library" was pulled from memory well before its appearance in the sentence, and as a result it was milling about backstage, where it was mistakenly tagged by the manager for premature entry; the wardrobe assistant, not questioning its place in line, compliantly clothed it in its designated sounds. But psycholinguists noticed that speakers never seem to say, "We ordered a new lesk for the third floor of the dibrary," having exchanged the first sounds of "desk" and the still-distant "library." When speakers exchange sounds, they almost always do so between words that are adjacent to each other, saying, for example, "sam handwich" when they meant "ham sandwich." At this close distance, while the speaker is preparing to utter "ham," the word "sandwich" has already been dressed in sound, waiting for its imminent appearance, when one piece of its outfit is hastily snatched by the word lined up ahead of it, in exchange for a sound the inadvertent thief has carelessly dropped.

Under these and many other investigations, the act of speaking reveals itself as an acrobatic, time-defying performance that is somehow pulled off—but just barely—by a troupe of artists pushed to the very edges of their energies and abilities. The whole show rests upon a precise choreography in which the utterance of a sentence is the result of many coordinated steps, each involving behind-the-scenes preparations conducted by various specialists. The performance is rarely perfect; as fellow speakers, we are forgiving of the inevitable slips and stumbles. After a few glasses of wine, the troupe's control over timing turns precarious, and it is best to pack up the show and head for home.

As with the planning and implementation of speech, psycholinguists have looked to the places where comprehension strains as the mind attempts to construct meaning while pinned between remembering and anticipating. Even in reading, certain structures court failure. A reader's eye moves smoothly and easily over a sentence such as "The senator who poisoned the president was a traitor," but it might lurch and stumble—or at least linger slightly longer—over "The senator who the president poisoned was a traitor."

At first sight, the difficulty is puzzling: the sentences seem equal in complexity of structure, each containing a relative clause nestled inside the main clause. They could be diagrammed as follows:

[The senator [who poisoned the president] was a traitor].
[The senator [who the president poisoned] was a traitor].

Some suggest that the difficulty with the second sentence lies with too many unresolved relationships that must be held aloft in memory. The senator appears as the subject of the sentence, but upon encountering the relative pronoun "who," readers know they must wait for its role in the main clause to be revealed, and they also know that the senator will play an additional, yet-to-be-revealed role in the embedded clause. Then the president is introduced, and now there are two elements floating untethered in memory, their roles and relationships in the sentence still mysterious. It is not until the verb "poisoned" appears that any of the elements in the sentence can begin to be connected to each other. In the first sentence, by comparison, the early appearance of the verb "poisoned" allows at least one of the senator's roles to be resolved without placing unreasonable demands on memory.

Adding another clause to the difficult sentence, like adding another ball to the juggle, risks collapsing all sense of coherence. Most readers can make no sense whatsoever of the following theoretically grammatical sentence:

> [The senator [who the president [who the journalist exposed] poisoned] was a traitor].

Once again, it is deferred resolution and not the sheer number of stacked clauses that appears to be the trouble; too many nouns are released while the reader must wait for the verbs that reveal how they are connected. It is much easier to squeeze sense out of the following sentence, which is equally complex but links the nouns together as the sentence unfolds:

> [The journalist [who exposed the senator [who poisoned the president]] was a traitor].

By examining sentences and observing how people decipher them, psycholinguists have discovered how we struggle to hold on to bits of disconnected information, how easily we are overwhelmed by ideas begun but not completed. Our minds can't afford to gather up all the elements of thought and hold them in one place before piecing them together. We are compelled to assemble meaning as quickly as speech pours out, and if we are unable to do so, the various parts of a sentence are swept away in the current of time. Language, in its ephemeral nature, turns us into creatures who leap at the opportunity for coherence before it is lost forever.

So eager are we to leap that at times we leap too soon and in the wrong direction. Below the taut surface of language, different structures—each with a different meaning—might be concealed beneath the same words. Impatient, we guess at the structures underlying incoming fragments of sentences, drawing on our past experiences with language to predict the sentence's trajectory. When our predictions lead us too far astray, comprehension runs aground, as it often does with the following sentence:

> *The patient told the psychiatrist that he occasionally*
> *dreamed of about his distressing murderous thoughts.*

The first half of the sentence lures the reader into an interpretation too tempting to resist—that of the patient recounting his dreams to a psychiatrist. But then, beginning with the word "about," most readers run aground. There is no way to make the rest of the sentence fit with what has come before. Recovery hinges on recognizing another meaning for the first half of the sentence, one in which it is the psychiatrist who occasionally enters the patient's dreams.

How and why do we make certain predictions and not others? By fiddling with sentence variants and foisting them on my volunteer subjects in the lab, I was able to catch glimpses of a nimble human intelligence that awed me. In our scramble for coherence, it turns out, very little of past experience goes to waste. It seems that we carry with us a personal history of language and are so practiced at running through its statistics—computed over past occurrences of certain words, syntactic structures, events—that we are able, for the most part, to game the probabilities of meaning. We lean hard toward meanings that our past leads us to believe will occur again in this particular future. When the evidence is conflicting, we hold back, reluctant to commit.

Thus, we pitch ourselves into the future of a sentence, relying on memory's access to an ever-growing mountain of moments that exist no more, keeping a delicate truce between what has already happened and what is yet to come, between an imagined future and the possibility of error. The shape of all human language is the outcome of such negotiations.

If language's shape is an expression of its imprisonment in time, then so is a human life. At some point—in those years while I was completing my studies, building a new lab and reputation as a young professor, waking at four in the morning to prepare my lectures, birthing and raising children, being whiplashed by the joys and torments of an increasingly untenable marriage—it occurred to me that my intellectual preoccupations with language's struggles against time were contained within the same pinholes as my own struggles to create a sense of coherence from the fragments of my present. Is there ever a moment for a young professional mother when she isn't frenetically scanning the future to assess her obligations, or scouring the past to weigh her failures? Understanding my life was not much different from understanding a sentence: plunder your past experience for material you can use to anticipate the future so that you are not caught, shocked into incomprehension, when that future comes crashing into your present, as it inevitably did, relentlessly and without reprieve, at the breakneck speed of speech.

I'd had the sense, from that first day in my linguistics class, that language was the true container of the human soul—and therefore worthy not only of reverence but also of dissection and examination under all available light. The more I studied it, the more lessons it offered about what it is to live a human life. Language was proving to be an archaeological site of the human condition. By patiently sifting through its layers, one could discover not just our urge to enter other minds, or the inevitable gulfs that remain between us, but also what it means to live within the substance of time. Like language itself, we cannot escape time; thanks to language, we are painfully aware of our own captivity.

In her book *The Human Condition*, Hannah Arendt remarks that humans are the only beings on earth that are mortal—not because humans alone die, but because we alone have the awareness of our individual lives as distinct from the rest of our species and the rest of nature. An individual life is bounded by birth at one end and death at the other. Unlike the life of a species, which continues through repeated cycles of death and renewal, an individual human life cannot loop back on itself; once we have lived a present moment, it is forever in our past, never to return. "This individual life," she writes, "is distinguished from all other things by the rectilinear course of its movement, which, so to speak, cuts through the circular movement of biological life. This is mortality: to move along a rectilinear line in a universe where everything, if it moves at all, moves in a cyclical order."

We rarely know how long the line of our individual life will be, but we do know that the further we travel from our nonexistence before birth, the nearer we are to our nonexistence after death. As with a sentence, there is silence at either end. Or, in the words of Vladimir Nabokov, "Our existence is but a brief crack of light between two eternities of darkness." The lyricism of these words does nothing to soften their devastation. On the contrary: it sharpens the blade of awareness.

Is it the knowledge of these dark and silent eternities that compels us to stuff as much as we can into the length of our lives? If the importance of an individual life is separated from the larger whole of which it is part—and more so in the contemporary West than at any other time or place—it becomes unbearable to forgo any of the blessings of life: motherhood, work, ecstatic love, family, travel, friendships. Perhaps in our era, the significance of an individual life is so great that our compulsion to fill it is always running up against the limits of how much it can contain.

Time itself does not proceed any more quickly than it did decades or centuries ago (and the lines of our individual lives have generally lengthened, postponing the silence of death), but many of us are trying to ram a great deal more complexity into them. Our lives become like the sentences that flummoxed my subjects in the lab. We nest more structures inside each other than can be managed, stacking unresolved tasks and goals, one on top of another, until we risk a collapse of coherence. The moments stream by, but we are unable to gather them up into a meaningful whole. We feel ourselves to be constantly starved of time—more than anything, of the time needed to make sense of all the things with which we have filled our lives.

As a young scholar, I had made some progress in understanding how humans make sense of language, trapped as they are in the fleeting present, but I had little idea of how humans make sense of a life, trapped between birth and death. I knew even less how to make sense of my own.

Our modern age does not offer much in the way of useful theories. Everyone longs for Augustine's eternal present, but it seems to me that prescriptions for "mindfully" living in the present are little more than tricks of attention that blunt our senses to the rectilinear movement of time. I often try these exercises. In one of them, I contemplate an apple for ten minutes, paying attention to the sheen of its skin and how shadows drape themselves over its near-spherical shape. This is possible to do because the apple changes almost not at all in these ten minutes; by narrowing the beam of my attention, my mind is freed from everything else in the world that is undeniably different than it was a moment ago. In another exercise, I close my eyes and direct all the resources of my attention to my breath, following it as it swells and recedes within my chest. My breathing is a changing thing, different in this instant than it is in the next. But it does not move in a line. As each breath recedes, I know another will follow, followed by another. I have been reabsorbed into the circular movements of the universe.

Either way, the line of my own life fades from view. I relinquish the struggle for coherence. I give up on shuttling between past and future and forgo the effort of creating meaning that links them together, into an idea I can grasp.

Yet it seems to me that this cure for time starvation is only ever a temporary respite. Just as human beings can't seem to live without shaping slices of speech into sentences—those miracles of syntax that connect separate nouns and verbs, themselves made of streams of sound, and reveal the relationships that bind them—we also need some way to create meanings that bind together the slivers of time that make up our existence. I do not think that people can easily endure a life that is composed only of present moments that come and do not return. To be indifferent to the meaning contained within one's individual life is to be not entirely human—to be like a swallow that has given up resisting gravity and has decided that it will be forever earthbound.

We mortals rebel against the linear shape of our lives, bounded by silence at either end. Is it any wonder, then, that we do the same with language? And miraculously, we succeed. Tucked inside language itself is a means for escaping the tyranny of unstoppable time without forsaking meaning: the transfiguration of language into literature.

Many linguists have felt compelled to explain why no human society exists without language. Its universality is the bedrock upon which prominent theories are built. These theories, argue their proponents, hold the key to understanding the human mind, that which makes us different from other animals; many careful dissections of sentences and their internal organs have been conducted as a result. But much less has been said by scientists about the fact that human societies rarely, if ever, exist without a literature—without a body of stories, mythologies, epics, poems, dialogues, essays, or histories—whether preserved in writing or through oral tradition. What does this tell us about the essence of the human mind?

I believe that literature is the way we endure lives trapped in the rectilinear movement of time. Both oral and written forms of literature make language more elastic, invite an escalation of complexity, free us from the chains of real time. Through literature, we create meanings that transcend the limits of an individual mind held inside the pinhole of the present.

The problem of speech is that "there is no way to stop sound and have sound," as noted by Walter Ong, who studied the historical shifts from oral to written cultures. Oral cultures find ways to have sound over and over again. In oral literature, the line of a sentence is bent so that it arcs back deep into the past and spirals far into the future. Repetition keeps language from being swept away into nonexistence: its recurrence stabilizes the line of a sentence in collective memory and—provided that oral traditions are left undisturbed—guarantees that it will resurface in the future. Language cheats human time by becoming circular.

Oral traditions ease the strains on memory through cycles of return and by imposing patterns, formulas of rhythm and sound that anchor language in the mind and keep it from blowing away. When a sentence or poetic structure is revisited again and again rather than built anew in each present moment, the demands of creation are spread out over many moments so that complexity survives the journey from mind to speech. There is space for innovation made in increments, for variations, alterations, additions to meaning that do not risk its collapse. Listeners too can reach into communal memories of language; they are not left to decipher an epic tale or poem all at once before it vanishes forever. Instead, meaning accrues over time, with something new added with each repetition, and is distributed among many minds and over many moments in time.

In written cultures, the problem of speech is solved by the radical technology of text. Text emulates Augustine's eternal present, by converting speech—that fluttering, ethereal presence—into a form that persists. My meditation apple has long decayed since I first contemplated it on my kitchen table, but sixteen centuries after he wrote them down, I am still able to read Augustine's ruminations on the transient present, as if I were God himself, surveying all of time held motionless before me.

Even the act of creating or reading a written sentence occurs within a present that is stretched far beyond its pinhole shape. When composing a sentence, the writer can forestall the future. Words need not be selected and pronounced at the rate of speech; the writer can pause mid-sentence to wander through her lexicon. In speech, words must be chosen while still sonically nude, but the writer can take the time to mentally dress each word, examining it in its full apparel, rejecting this one for containing too many syllables, selecting that one for having consonants that strike a harmony with those of its neighbors.

Syntax, too, becomes more layered in writing than in conversation; clauses stack upon clauses in a way that would not be possible in running speech. In the lab, as I watch the movement of eyes over text, it becomes clear why certain sentences can be read but not easily understood as speech: the reader's eye does not sweep smoothly from left to right. Instead, it jumps from one word to another, in uneven fashion, spending a brief moment here but stopping to pause or linger there, occasionally skipping over short or predictable words without a single glance, often stopping in its tracks and then backtracking to an earlier part of the sentence. Words that have slid out of memory's grasp are revisited. Errors of prediction are detected, diagnosed, and corrected. The mind does not encounter language a sliver at a time as it does with speech. When language is fixed to the page or the screen, held still across time, we see how it makes room for itself, how language expands to fill an enlarged present moment. It can hold complexities that would oversaturate speech. Certain forms that are found in text almost never occur in speech, being too unwieldy to assemble from memory; when spoken, language reverts to the direct, well-trodden paths.

Some scholars have argued that writing has reshaped the syntax of its host languages. Embedded clauses, especially those that allow several unresolved relationships to pile up on top of each other, are rare in transcripts of oral literature or in a culture's earliest written code. An old Hittite text from the fourteenth century BCE, for instance, still reflects mainly oral patterns of language, stringing clauses like beads added to a necklace, one after the other:

> I drove in a chariot to Kunnu, and a thunderstorm came, then the Storm-God kept thundering terribly, and I feared, and the speech in my mouth became small, and the speech came up a little bit, and I forgot this matter completely, but afterwards the years came and went, and this matter came to appear repeatedly in my dreams, and God's hand seized me in my dreams, and then, my mouth went sideways, and . . .

Similar patterns were found in the earliest known clay tablets preserving the ancient Akkadian language, dating to 2500 BCE. But seven hundred years of writing later, an Akkadian sentence from Hammurabi's Code of Law displays the convolutions of a line pulled from a contemporary legal brief or from a Henry James novel or from a psycholinguist's experiment that pushes the human capacity for language to its limits:

> If, after the sheep and goats come up from the common irrigated area when the pennants announcing the termination of pasturing are wound around the main city gate, the shepherd releases the sheep and goats into a field, the shepherd shall guard the field.

Written language offered more than the space to unfurl a sentence. It shifted language away from communal practices into private ones. Text released writers from the chains of inheritance that hold an oral culture together, allowing them to cultivate a voice distinct from others. It allowed readers to interpret these writings through the lens of their own personal histories. Written literature pulled an individual life ever more forcefully apart from other human lives, and to the extent that it made salient the boundedness of a single human life, it cast a pitiless light onto mortality. (Witness the sense of loss we feel upon hearing that a beloved author has died.) At the same time, it made mortality bearable by joining the minds of reader and writer. It offered a means by which the thread of an individual life could be entwined with other lives into a sturdy rope; the separate, unrepeatable mind of a writer could now reach into the dark eternity ahead, and the lonely mind of the reader could cast itself into the dark eternity before.

The arrival of text in a culture changed it slowly rather than all at once. Though Augustine had the tools of reading and writing, language for him still occurred mostly through sound. During this period and for a long time after, writing was a method of flash freezing sound until it could be thawed out again; texts were often dictated to a scribe from memory, then set aside to be stored until a time at which they could be read aloud to an audience. It was not until the advent of print, which packaged text inside cheap and compact objects one could carry home, that a habit of reading silently and alone spread throughout the population. Only then were ordinary people able to experience a form of language that was cut loose from voice, speech, and the harshest restrictions of time.

I am aware how much of my self I owe to being born at a specific point in human history; by the time I became a literate child, the habit of private reading was so taken for granted that the adults in my life rarely objected (and often praised) my long retreats into bookish solitude. While reading, I experienced an agency that was not possible in other spheres of language. I was no longer bound to the plodding pace of a spoken sentence. My eyes could leap over text, dismissing what was easy or dull, lingering on what was lush or unexpected. If a sentence perplexed me, I was not left to desperately chase its acoustic shadow; I could reread, mull over, and reread again. It was only when I began to read, and then to write, that I became aware of language as a thing that could be paused, moved back and forth in time, studied from all angles. And became aware of just how much meaning quivered inside its skin.

Incredibly, there are some who agitate for an acceleration of language. Instead of seeing freedom in the stilling of the present, they seize upon the eye's ability to read faster than the speed of speech. It is now possible to run text through an app that will accelerate reading by presenting each word on your screen for the briefest of moments, allowing you to read at a rate of 300, 500, even 1,000 words per minute. (The rate of speech is sluggish by comparison, at roughly 150 words a minute.) This, assert the developers, rids you of the wasteful habit of moving your eye over text at uneven speeds, and of backtracking to linger on portions of the sentence that you have already passed through. In other words, it undoes exactly that which the invention of text has made possible. It wrests away from the reader any power over time. Unable to allocate time in accordance with the complexity of the text or the richness of the thoughts the text might arouse, the reader sets upon a high-speed forced march through language.

At a thousand words per minute, it would be theoretically possible to read the average novel in a little over an hour, or Tolstoy's *War and Peace* in less than ten. Maybe this is enough time to recognize the individual words as they are thrown up on the screen, one after the other, and even enough time to join most of the words into the frames of their sentences, parsing the links between subjects, verbs, and direct objects. (And if some sentences are too complicated, well, you get the gist.) It is emphatically not enough time to translate sentences into sensual experiences, to read between the lines for the unwritten essence of the text, to allow anticipation to rise or pleasure to collect in the cistern of consciousness. It is not enough time to reflect on what this novel reveals about us in our present day or how it helps us to predict the inscrutable future. It is not enough time to entwine the mind of the reader with the mind of the writer.

I suspect the app holds little interest for anyone who has ever read a book in such a way as to merge with it. But new technologies everywhere are rearranging the relationship of language to time. We are more awash than ever in text, but the lines between written and oral language are blurring. On television, we watch actors exchange dialogue that has been crafted in a writers' room. We read transcripts of interviews.

We listen to novels over headphones, perhaps while cooking or jogging. Instead of speaking over the phone, we send each other texts—written snippets that are as informal and interactive as conversational speech. We type messages on social media, often as impulsively as we would blurt out a comment in "real time."

Decades ago, Walter Ong proposed that we were on the cusp of an era of "secondary orality," in which the elements of speech were encroaching onto territory previously held by the printed word. More recently, the literary scholar Tom Pettitt has embraced the term "Gutenberg parenthesis," arguing that the centuries between the printing press and the internet were a departure from the normal state of human societies and that we are returning to modes of language that have much in common with the lives of medieval peasants—and that this is no bad thing. More and more, our uses of text are coming to absorb some of the properties of oral cultures. We are using text communally and cyclically; we sample, remix, transform, send it back into the pool of text that we've dipped into.

An optimist might speculate that we will come to harvest the best of both written and oral cultures, or that this blurring will rein in some of the excesses of printed text—its imprisonment as a fixed and unchanging object, its separation of the author from the river of humanity. Perhaps we will become less rigid and more liquid in our uses of language, adept at the full range of expression between oral and written poles.

A pessimist might worry that we will discard the best of both, thereby forfeiting our mastery over time. The literature of an oral culture knits a community together in rituals of language so that the bonds between its members rescue it from the ephemerality of speech. What happens when language is created within amorphous communities, as is the case with the language of the internet, detached from physical life, forever shifting and dissolving? How long can such language endure? And at the same time, will we have lost the skills of slowing language down through the deliberate practice of writing that which can't be spontaneously uttered and the habit of reading in a way that manipulates time?

There is much anxiety about the latter, and rightly so. Our world is more complex than ever, but we've invented technologies that risk undermining the best means we have for absorbing complexity, for making coherence out of the endless flow of information that streams by. (It is ironic that these technologies are the gifts of a society at what may be its apex of literacy.) There is evidence that people read less deeply on digital devices than on paper, conditioned by a reading environment of repeated distraction and interruption. Eye movements on screens hint at readers who do not dwell inside the meanings of individual sentences or consider how one builds upon another; instead, they graze, flit, zigzag over the text, landing on key words at the beginning of the text, darting to the end, and occasionally sampling from the middle.

Reading in fragments may be suitable for much of the text that meets our eyes, but the neuroscientist Maryanne Wolf invites readers to consider whether it is becoming the default manner of reading, "whether you have moved, unaware, from the home that reading once was for you. . . . Perhaps you have felt a pang of something subtle that is missing when you seek to immerse yourself in a once favorite book. Like a phantom limb, you remember who you were as a reader, but cannot summon that 'attentive ghost.'" She reserves the greatest worry for children who might never have learned to read deeply, deprived of the thousands of hours of sheltered reading that are needed to learn to read with a still and quiet eye.

I think of the hours I spent cloistered in my room, and I try to imagine what my childhood would have been like if, during every attempt to lose myself in a book, I'd been harassed by my brother, had my parents breathlessly announcing the train derailment the next town over, my friends chiming in with a deconstruction of the outfit I wore to school that day, and worst of all, other readers clamoring to tell me what I should think about the book I'm doing my best to read. I might have never entered a book so fully that it altered me. I might have grown up to believe that ingesting a book at a thousand words per minute sounded like a good idea.

I, too, worry about such children and the adults they may grow to be. Maryanne Wolf suggests that the tools of science—the scanners, the trackers, and the theories to which they speak—are the best hope we have for understanding and forestalling what we are at risk of losing. This is undoubtedly true, but only if the scientists themselves do not abdicate all temporal control. Universities were once places for contemplation, places that stilled time much as text does; now they have edged closer to the model of the factory. The assembly-line belt is in relentless motion. We churn out scientific discoveries at the steady rate required. But these discoveries can be like piles of nouns whose place in the sentence we don't have time to work out. We may have little idea what these discoveries mean or how to predict their effects on the future. And so we risk being unable to imagine the existential dangers waiting for us, in a life lived only in present-moment slices.

Many years after I first set eyes on Rembrandt's *Anatomy Lesson*, I came across a piece of writing by the philosopher Sarah Kofman about the same painting. Her essay—still unfinished when she plunged into her second dark eternity—describes a very different experience from the one I'd had. In Kofman's reading of the painting, the "scientific gaze" of the men attending the dissection obscures as much as it exposes. Even as the cadaver is opened to reveal new insights, its viewers are blinded to something they had previously known: Kofman writes that the body's "fragility, its mortality, comes to be forgotten, even though it is exhibited in full light." The dead person on the table becomes "not a subject but an object, a purely technical instrument that one of them manipulates in order to get a hold on the truth of life." The men "seem to be unmoved by any feelings for him, for someone who, just a short time ago, was still full of life. . . . They do not see in [the body] the image of what they themselves will be, of what, unbeknownst to themselves, they are in the process of becoming."

Moreover, claims Kofman, the eyes of the men are fixed not on the corpse itself but on the anatomy text that is propped up by the cadaver's feet. The men gaze at this text "with the same attentive fervor as that found in other paintings in which the evangelists are poring over the sacred books from which they draw the confirmation of their message." One authority and its way of seeing has been entirely supplanted by another. The scientific text has overwritten the mythologies of meaning.

When I read this essay, my thoughts strayed to the poet who had attended exactly one of my linguistics lectures and then turned away. It occurred to me that, like Kofman, she was alert to a danger that had not resonated for me in the presence of the scientific gaze: the danger that science might obliterate other texts of importance.

At the time, I was baffled by this student's response; my own experience of science was only that of opening, of uncovering. I felt as if I had grown a new organ of perception. Far from leaving me unmoved by any feeling, science attuned me to beauties in language I'd been unable to discern. I had no fears then of erasure or replacement. I did not worry then that one way of perceiving language might be supplanted by another, only that it added to it.

I have to admit that, several decades later, the poet's fears seem less irrational to me. The thrill of new discovery has never left me, nor has the sense of a widening of vision. But it is true that, after years of keeping pace with the daily demands of a scientific life, I allowed my attention to literature to slip. I rarely opened a text that was not scientific. My neglect of other texts of importance was, quite simply, a matter of time. As my vision grew sharper in details related to science, entire regions of thought and feeling went unattended, much like a neurological patient who suffers from hemispatial neglect, in which one half of the visual field is completely ignored. Such a patient might fail to eat the food on the left side of their plate or shave the left side of their face. In extreme cases, they may fail to acknowledge the left side of their body as their own.

If I, an individual scientist, find myself with too few hours to read widely and to think deeply, this is merely a private loss, albeit a profound one that leaves me frustrated, sensing that there is something out there that I am just not seeing. But if I am just one fish in a shoal, all of us schooling together in the same direction, this is a crisis, a collective partial blindness. Kofman's interpretation of the *Anatomy Lesson* has, I fear, become a dominant one. It is telling that the terms "science" and "humanities" refer to segregated, nonoverlapping disciplines, as if the practice of science had nothing to do with being human, and as if the habits of mind that are needed to practice it were severed from—even incompatible with—all other methods we've ever had of leaning into the light.

If I were to meet that poet today, I would still insist that the scientific gaze need not leave one blind to other ways of seeing. (I am guessing that after Nicolaes Tulp's anatomy lesson, all the men went home and read from the Scriptures.) I would promise the poet that immersion in the science of language would open her to unexpected pleasures when reading literature. I would let her know that this immersion was like a baptism to me, that reverence has never left me. Not even after decades of poring over lab data did language ever become a slab of cold meat or a purely technical instrument.

But I would also say: We are mortals, traumatized by the

inexorable flow of linear time. From the pinhole of the present, there is only so much sense making we can do. If that pinhole is stuffed to its limits with the pursuit of science, it is true that we are left with no way of creating coherence from discovery. We have no way to entwine our minds with other minds. We risk living out our brief lives as a mere procession of still-life frames, unmoored from the swells and cycles of narrative. If we do this, our own mortality will become unendurable.

So stay. We need you to stay. Bring your beloved texts with you, the ones that arrange the long and short syllables of your life into poetry. Bring your friends, the storytellers, those alchemists who turn language into time-cheating meaning. Bring the painters, who understand how light works and how vision receives it, who can render religious feeling in pigment, who know how to alert us to the dangers of looking at a body under the floodlight of science and seeing nothing but a corpse.

Resolving ambiguities

scene (seen)

Two viewings of the same film serve as brackets around a period of my life; one viewing marks a time before my first marriage began to end, and the other occurs at a time after it was over. They face each other, these moments, but at their backs are stretches of time as different as two parts of a life can possibly be; they are like gateways through which you enter separate territories, each with its own requirements for citizenship. On these separate occasions, my own responses to a particular scene in the film were in such opposition to each other it was as if the same scene had been viewed not by one person at different times but by two friends who were no longer speaking to each other.

In the scene in question (which appears in the film *When Night Is Falling*, directed by Patricia Rozema), a couple is at a moment of crisis. A man has just discovered that his fiancée is having a secret affair with another woman, a circus performer. He tries to salvage his relationship by forestalling his beloved's confession. He tells her that there are things they do not ever need to speak about, things that may churn below the surface but that will eventually pass and that can be kept hidden from each other without destroying their partnership.

When I first watched this scene, I was filled with sympathy for the man, who, in my eyes, was behaving with admirable restraint. Although a religious man, he did not unleash a torrent of judgment or rage upon his partner. Instead, he was prepared to overlook the signs of his partner's erotic and emotional turmoil, willing to patiently wait for the seas to calm once more. I felt that only a very strong person could make such a proposal; by this time in my marriage, I suppose, I had a sense of the exertions that such a suppression would require.

The second time I watched this scene, I was horrified by what the man was asking of his partner. It was as if he were pleading with her that their union could still be perfectly viable, if only she would agree to relinquish her two legs. No, he was not condemning her, or even requiring her to give up her lover. But he was suggesting that she enter the marriage as a portion of herself; she could not bring with her whatever it was that roiled her with such urgency. Inside the territory of their marriage, this part of her would never assert itself or present itself for inspection, or even be acknowledged as real. This struck me as more sinister than if he had made a scene, erupting in rage and insults and ultimatums, which, after all, would have involved admitting that he had *seen* who she was. All of my hair follicles were warning the woman to run the hell away.

Throughout my second viewing of this scene, I was aware of the reaction I'd had the first time I had seen it, but this was a disembodied memory, as if I were remembering how a

friend had described her own response to it. It was an interpretation I perceived as ludicrous and wildly off the mark, the
sort that makes you wonder if you and your friend have even
seen the same movie. Somehow, in the time between viewings, I had shifted from being a person who constructed one
meaning into a different kind of person who was incapable of
seeing how anyone could ever arrive at that meaning.

right

Which meaning did the filmmaker intend? The movie's ending, thick with symbolism, is not enigmatic. The protagonist
does wind up fleeing her relationship, rejecting the terms set
by her fiancé. She entrusts herself to her new lover. She literally hands over her body, consenting, with great trepidation,
to a hang-gliding expedition; as she ascends, harnessed to her
partner, her face reflects an inner journey from terror to joy.
While the credits roll, we see the protagonist's dog, which had
been presumed dead and buried in a snowbank, bound to life,
having burst its way out of its frozen grave. Not dead after all.

Still, the director could very well have resisted steering
her film toward a single meaning. In art, we accept that the
artist may withhold evidence of her intentions and leave it to
the audience to construct their own meanings, even to vacil-
late between them or to allow multiple meanings to occupy
their minds at the same time. Perhaps the artist herself does
not know what she means, has decided she does not need
to or cannot know regardless of how much she might wish
to. We concede that in art there is space for ambiguity, for
an indefinite postponement of certainty, for the sublime and

agonizing tension of being hung on a wire between possible realities.

But this permissive space often feels cordoned off, like a protected park that one can visit from time to time, as a respite from the rigidities and demands of the modern world. It is a space that is set apart from the daily efficiencies of language. Art has a special status; it is seen as subverting the normal rules of human communication in which clarity is the desired state. After all, if language has any use, it must be governed by laws of functionality. Surely, it has evolved precisely to serve this purpose, to transport useful information between minds as expeditiously as possible, with slippage of meaning kept to a minimum.

Even among writers and editors, who ought to know better, I often encounter the view that language is *by its nature* exact; it is the purpose of *literature*, they might say, to deform language in interesting and provocative ways. Artists of language are allowed to play with their medium the way a child might play with objects, repurposing them, using a banana as a weapon or a teacup as a ship for a doll to sail away in. In the real world, a banana is a banana, and not a gun.

But the illusion of single meanings is just another example of language hiding its true nature from plain view. In fact, it is the nature of language—not just literature—to repurpose itself. It no more avoids ambiguity than the human body avoids containing water. Oddly enough, it is often scientists of language, and not its artisans, who recognize this, even though the former are singularly committed to using language with exactitude and with a minimum of semantic slippage, herding in any stray interpretations with formally defined terms, scientific jargon, mathematics, and explicit, defensible conclusions.

Writing for *Language Log*, a blog for technical discussions about language, the linguist Geoff Pullum laid out evidence for its inherently ambiguous nature. He began by pointing out that there are about 200 trillion possible words that combine no more than ten letters from *a* to *z*. In contrast, the total number of words used by English speakers is somewhere between 25,000 and 250,000. "What I'm saying," he wrote, in case the math didn't speak for itself, "is that English could *easily* have a distinct letter sequence for every different meaning, using letter sequences *much shorter* than the present ones. It doesn't because the language in general shows *no signs* of being the slightest bit interested in that."

And in case this wasn't clear, he offered specimens: a single three-letter word that is used for meanings that convey "understanding, judging, experiencing, finding out, dating, visiting, ensuring, escorting, and saying farewell." (The word is "see.") And a single two-word phrase used to talk about denigrating, ceasing to hold, making notes, and euthanasia. (The phrase is "put down.") And in case any doubt remained about his intended meaning: "Nobody who thinks about English for a few seconds could possibly believe it shuns ambiguity. It doesn't give a monkey's fart about avoiding ambiguity."

train

The more seconds one spends thinking about language, the more it becomes apparent that much of our verbal lives must be lived between meanings. Our minds are tossed about in ambiguity's constant flux—and yet we rarely feel it. Awareness seizes on the moment when we finally grab hold of a single meaning and cling to it. To our conscious selves, understanding a word is like the moment of pulling in to a train station; even though most of the journey was spent in the in-between blur of not yet having arrived anywhere, what remains in our consciousness is the standstill of destination and not the hours of landscape hurtling by.

Because a single set of sounds or letters can multiply into many different meanings, those stretches of time before we arrive at the station are spent not just between destinations but across parallel universes, the tracks within each universe leading to a different station. Before the arrival, many destinations are still possible. There are stretches of time, almost entirely unperceived and unremembered, during which we sit at a window and pass by a multitude of possible meanings.

As a scientist, I found myself fascinated by these stretches of semantic possibility and by our obliviousness toward them. When language is spoken rather than written, its ambiguous nature is especially evident. In speech, words can't be gathered up in a single glance. Instead, they form a procession, the last sound straggling in sometime after the first. Not just words but fragments of words—syllables, or even smaller slivers of sound—open up to many possible meanings. We hear the sound "can," and we have no way of knowing whether the word has reached its end, or whether it is about to continue as "Canada," "cancer," or "cantaloupe."

I have spent an inordinate number of seconds of my life

trying to study ambiguity with as much precision as possible. The trick, as with all psychological studies, is to avoid being taken in by the fictions that the mind eagerly narrates about itself and its activities. Several years into my graduate studies, some of my colleagues hit upon the idea that we could follow the flickering movements of eyes as a way to observe a person's transit through semantic possibility. Eye gaze reveals the ways in which attention alights here and there, outside the jurisdiction of the conscious, narrating mind, and this being the case, we might see a physical reflex of the various meanings being considered and abandoned, before the mind has a chance to pull in to the station and announce its arrival at a single destination.

Our first willing subject allowed an eye-tracking device to be placed on his head (in those days, a heavy contraption mounted onto a bulky helmet) as he followed simple spoken commands to handle everyday objects laid out in front of him. On a screen to the side, we watched as a cursor representing his gaze flitted over the array of objects. *Pick up the candy.* And there it was, the vacillation: after the speaker's release of the syllable "can," our subject's gaze danced over to a candle that also stood on the table, and hovered there briefly—for just two-tenths of a second or so—before the speaker released the sounds of the second syllable, sending the eyes scuttling over to the candy, obviously the intended meaning. And then came the disavowal: when asked, our subject denied considering, even for a fleeting instant, any destination other than the candy. When confronted with his ambivalence—evidence on videotape of his eye movements played back to him—he shook his head in wonder. As if he had no memory of ever being a person who had traveled toward another meaning.

Time after time, person after person, the procedure revealed the same events: an unstable stretch of time, during which the person's eyes would flit to one or the other or both objects at chance, followed by a clamping down of the gaze on a single object and a stated certainty that the person had never wavered in the path toward the intended meaning, the lure of any alternatives already submerged from attention. And upon being pressed, a disavowal of the seductiveness of other meanings, a denial of where the eyes had clearly been.

But submerged as they were, these meanings had been there—it was all on videotape!—and trailing along with them, an entourage of companions. Partway through hearing the word "log," a person's eyes might alight on an image of a key, by virtue of its friendly association with the briefly considered but soon-to-be-disavowed meaning "lock."

What fascinated me, as much as the evidence of various meanings and associations popping like fireworks, was the ruthless efficiency with which the mind settled on a single meaning; in one instant, it was nimble and responsive, open to all considerations, and in the next it was dogmatic in its suppression of all but one. We were seeing among our lab participants the result of years lived in language's ambiguous landscape. By the time they put on our eye-tracking machine, they were exquisitely trained in the art of stifling unwanted meanings.

We never did have Virginia Woolf in the room wearing an eye-tracking helmet, but if we had, she might not have been as quick as the others to disavow the stifled meanings. In her essay titled "Craftsmanship"—which she opens by calling attention to the duplicitous nature of the word "craft," a single word that describes both "the making of useful objects of solid matter" and "cajolery, cunning, deceit"—she makes the same point as the linguist Geoff Pullum did. She uses not mathematics, though, but language that itself streaks by in a blur. Words, she writes, "have so often proved that they hate being useful, that it is their nature not to express one simple statement but a thousand possibilities."

Imagine standing at a tube station, she suggests, waiting on the platform for the train, and seeing on a signboard the phrase "Passing Russell Square." These words are useless at conveying one meaning, because along with their surface meanings they carry with them many "sunken meanings." The word "passing" might evoke "the transiency of things, the passing of time, and the changes of human life." Upon hearing the word "Russell," one might hear "the rustling of leaves and the skirt on a polished floor also the ducal house of Bedford and half the history of England." Hear the word "square," and you might see "the shape of an actual square combined with some stark angularity of stucco." Words cannot help being full of multiple meanings, echoes, associations—after all, as Woolf notes, "they have been out and about, on people's lips, in their houses, on the streets, in the fields." Even the simplest of phrases brings with it all the meanings and memories and various uses its words have traveled through.

The trouble is, writes Woolf, we deny words their liberty: "We pin them down to one meaning, their useful meaning, the meaning which makes us catch the train, the meaning which makes us pass the examination. And when words are pinned down they fold their wings and die."

direction

The trouble with my marriage was that, like Virginia Woolf, I longed for the blur between train stations, where more than one meaning is still possible. Or at the very least, I could not bear to live confined inside the single meaning my husband had clamped down upon and insisted we share. It was getting harder and harder to avert my gaze and stifle the evidence of alternative meanings.

But I came to learn that there's agony and peril too—and not just freedom—in ambiguity. One can get lost in its endless folds. And I did get lost. For half a year, I vacillated, tossed about between destinations as I considered whether to snap my life into two segments, the *before* and the *after*. My memories from that period of my life have a dreamlike quality, but not a pleasant one—not the languid reverie of sitting at a train window with an untethered, wandering mind, but more like a feverish nightmare in which scenes abruptly shift and nothing holds its shape or its sense across time. Nothing has settled, everything can be terrifying. The future can warp into anything at all. Love can grow fangs and be willing to use them. Children can melt, like Dalí's clocks, forgetting their form. When I should have been sleeping, my mind kept jumping tracks between possible ways of interpreting my marriage and the continuations (or discontinuations) they implied.

Getting lost between meanings was a pervasive symptom.

When my husband and I visited a marriage counselor, we were asked to fill in a questionnaire to measure, on a scale of one to five, our respective views of the health of our relationship. My husband, who wished the marriage to continue on precisely the same track it was currently running, mostly circled fives. My questionnaire could not be scored, the counselor informed me; on a number of the items, I had circled both one and five for the same question.

There are good reasons why our minds have evolved to stifle useless meanings. Scientists point to certain frontal regions in the brain as responsible for subduing signals that do not serve the purpose of the moment. Some part of our mind must be willing to step forward and chair the meeting, draw up an agenda, form a strategic plan, set priorities, and direct energies and resources where they can be most effective. Without this director, language would be, admittedly, useless as a means of communication. Each mind would be trapped in a loop of its own reverberating meanings, memories, and desires.

In the lab videotapes, when we saw the vacillations come to an end and the gaze settle with steady purpose upon a single object, we were seeing evidence of the director taking the reins, steering straight toward the meaning best borne out by the current evidence. People who have damage to certain frontal regions of the brain, or who show a pattern of difficulty in squelching unwanted information from their attention—that is, who have deficits in *cognitive control*—can have trouble settling on the most appropriate meaning of an ambiguous word.

Or they can become stuck within meanings, mired in one

interpretation of a sentence that began with great promise but is no longer tenable. Language scientists call these trajectories "garden path sentences," to highlight their deceptive nature. A sentence might begin, "My husband accepted the letter," and one might feel tempted to interpret "the letter" as the direct object of "accept," as in the sentence "My husband accepted the letter of apology I wrote." But the same words can splinter off into a very different future in which relationships, grammatical and otherwise, must be dramatically recalibrated: "My husband accepted the letter he wrote only served to bring our marriage to its end." It is natural to feel disoriented.

In making one's way through a garden path sentence, the reader has to know when to abandon a meaning that has reached its dead end. In extreme cases, the first meaning that one alights upon is so inviting and appears to have so much evidence in favor of it that a person can find himself unable to consider any other. Many who read the phrase "The wife passed the test" can find no way to reconcile it with the continuation "refused to fill it out." They have been lured into certain commitments—that the word "passed" refers to a verb whose meaning signals the clearing of a hurdle, that "the wife" is its subject and "the test" is the hurdle in question—none of which make any sense upon encountering the verb "refused." Some readers will not be able to make the shift between being a person who has embraced one meaning and being a person who has rejected that meaning and is able to make the leap to a new one, in this case, a meaning in which the wife who has been handed a questionnaire declines to complete it. "The wife (who was) passed the test refused to fill it out."

A measure of cognitive control is indeed useful if one is to avoid getting stuck in these sand traps of ambiguity. People with less of it are more likely to get stuck—including children, whose frontal brain regions are underdeveloped, the brain's managerial abilities being among the latest functions to fully mature. A lack of cognitive control leaves a person prone to getting lost between meanings, wandering about aimlessly when the garden path leads to a brick wall.

But children are said to be creative in ways that adults are not, and to some extent inventive thinking has indeed been found to be linked with a looser control of attention, whether in the brains of adults or children. It does not surprise us that Virginia Woolf's literary genius might in some way derive from her ability to freely roam among the many possibilities that words allow, from the fact that she does not make a beeline for their single, useful meanings. We have long accepted that artistic genius is the product of minds less restrained than ours; perhaps we have even romanticized the tinge of madness that we believe to be the blessing and curse of the great artists. Some of us may seek out art as a temporary excursion into the unfamiliar wilderness of madness, a wilderness that is nonetheless comfortingly contained within the covers of a book or the walls of a museum.

Ultimately, though, the romantic vision of the mad artist is deceptive. It fails to acknowledge that art requires control as well as freedom. Virginia Woolf's essay on craftsmanship is no untamed wilderness. It is, among other things, a beautifully wrought cage that contains within itself the opposing meanings of the word "craft," letting them quiver and warble at each other so that the melody of each grows more complex and resonant as a result of their facing off against each other. It is a garden path that meanders its way back home, through mud puddles and brambles that leave their residue on the person who travels there. It's a device for jumping between universes of meaning without getting lost. It invites a multiplicity of meanings, but the center holds; it never falls apart into incoherence.

Woolf's essay, with its masterful tension between freedom and control, has its scientific correlates: brain imaging studies have shown that creative thinking does not require the utter silence of the managerial functions of the prefrontal cortex; a deep dysregulation of these brain regions is of no help to the artist, it turns out. Rather, creativity thrives when the mind's director knows when to step in and lead and when to let the associative fireworks of the brain do their work. At various stages in the creative process, the prefrontal cortex is engaged, then disengaged, then reengaged. Too much micromanagement, and thinking becomes rigid and constricted. Too little direction, and ideas battle each other, irreconcilable and chaotic, having nothing to say to each other.

In fact, artists know full well that total freedom leads to aesthetic disaster. They praise the virtues of constraints—the regimentation of line and meter, the shape of a villanelle, the arc of the epic narrative—much as certain lovers extol the pleasures of bondage. Such constraints are a way of supplying, from outside the artist's brain, a measure of cognitive control.

An absolute absence of constraint can feel like hell. My half year of vacillation in my marriage felt to me like the primordial chaos of madness. I was becoming unmoored from a single, useful meaning, but unlike Woolf's artful essay, nothing held my life or my thoughts together. I felt on the verge of disintegration, as if the molecules that composed me could no longer agree to coexist.

Perhaps Woolf also had stretches of her life that were like this. I have no way of knowing, but I can imagine her near the end of her life: having thrashed for months chasing sleep, up to her ears in a roaring freedom but no way out of it, desperate to stop the endless travel from one meaning to another. In her exhaustion, she dreams of the swirling river and of sinking into the stillness of having—at last—arrived somewhere.

sentence

When judgment finally arrived, it felt inevitable. My marriage had become like a garden path sentence that had reached its dead end. Try as I might, I could not see a way of wringing sense of the version my husband clung to, and we could not jointly agree on abandoning it for a new one.

Just as with the subjects in the eye-tracking lab, my shift from ambivalence to resolute certainty seemed almost instantaneous. I was on an airplane, in transit between cities, engrossed in Carol Shields's novel *The Stone Diaries* when I came upon these sentences: "How does a woman know when a marriage is over? Because of the way her life suddenly shears off in just two directions: past and future." In the time it took to read these lines, I felt myself clamping down on one meaning and shucking off the other, and I knew my marriage was over.

The court document cited irreconcilable differences. When

people asked me, I struggled to explain what these differences were. I could point to the usual cataclysmic events, or an accumulation of grievances, or diverging desires for the future, but while all of these were part of the story, they were not responsible for the end of the marriage. What was fatal was that we now lived in separate interpretations: I did not believe I was the woman he believed me to be. He did not believe he was the man I believed him to be. As a result, our actions and motives had become utterly incomprehensible to each other and pregnant with hostilities.

In fact, this was not what was fatal. What *was* fatal was that our relationship did not allow both interpretations to coexist; one would have to subdue the other, and then this becomes a fight for existential survival.

He fought for his in spectacular fashion. My leaving triggered a three-year court battle, ostensibly over the partitioning of house, money, hours with the children. But as with movie plots and domestic squabbles, court battles are rarely about what they claim to be about. At regular intervals, I turned up in the courtroom for the face-off. He hired, then discarded, then newly recruited one lawyer after another, doggedly fighting his way through a prolonged divorce trial that was patently not in his best interests. Nonetheless, it offered him a theater into which he could bring witness after witness to testify: that we had seemed happy, that our division of roles was harmonious, if not tilted in my favor, that he had played the part of the faithful satellite to my ambitious planet, that our marriage as he had defined it had been perfectly viable and—were it not for my abrupt, inexplicable departure—could still be smoothly cruising along in the same direction.

I understood what he was fighting for—but it was the one thing I could not agree to regardless of the skills of any mediator we were ordered to work with. With a collapse of coherence behind him, and an ambiguous, terrifying freedom in front of him, he was in a death match to preserve the only narrative of our lives that he could make any sense of.

resolution

It dazzles me still that we humans ever manage to understand each other at all. It is a daily miracle, the way we can live amid the buzz of a thousand possible meanings and still manage, well enough, to settle on meanings that are mutually agreeable. It reveals an astonishing agility. With minor variations, we are all equipped with a mind whose aperture can widen to semantic possibility and then quickly contract to admit but one meaning. Unknowingly, we perform these acts of opening, selecting, suppressing countless times a day, like the rhythmic openings and closings of gills on fish, unbothered by the ambiguities in which we swim.

How is it, then, that we can be so undone by certain ambiguities, precisely those that perturb our sense of who we are in relation to others? We are undone by them whether our temperament is to wander about in open semantic fields, like Virginia Woolf, or take cover in confined spaces, like my former husband. With these dangerously personal meanings, we struggle to find our rhythm. We dilate too wide and drown in unresolvable contradictions, or we shut down too soon, deluding ourselves with certainty.

My crisis of ambiguity did appear, at last, to be resolved. My life sheared off in two directions. Having extricated myself from the narrative to which I had once committed, I found myself becoming a different person, in exactly the ways one might resolve to remake the self upon reaching the boundary of a significant birthday or the turn of a new year. I fell in love with and married a different man, more Woolf-like this time. For the most part, our opposing meanings agree to share the same space.

But the old meanings lurk; a rupture of sense is rarely that clean. In the language lab, when people read garden path sentences, there is some evidence that remnants of the discarded interpretation latch on to the new one, even when the new meaning appears to have successfully subdued the old. Like barbed seeds from a dying plant, they are carried forward, finding a way to persist. Consider that difficult, duplicitous sentence: "The wife passed the test refused to fill it out." A reader might be able to understand that someone handed the wife a test that she did not fill out, the only meaning that remains grammatically viable by the sentence's end. But if asked, "Did the wife pass the test?" that same reader might also answer yes.

Music, that shadow sibling of language, acknowledges the impossibility of resolution. Many different musical genres make use of the device of the coda—a restatement of the thematic melody, a return to the main musical preoccupation—as if to remind us that despite all of the numerous ways in which the theme has been turned this way and that, inside and out, tensions variously prolonged and finally settled, we are once again back where we started. We may believe we have traveled from one landscape to another, that we have remade ourselves. But here we are, facing the same music all over again, re-solving the ambiguities we thought we had solved.

I have certain recurring dreams, and their repetitive patterns now serve as the codas to my waking life. In them, marriage is the musical line being endlessly worked over. In some of these dreams, I am remarrying, once again, my current husband; though it's never clear why, there is apparently a pressing need for a new wedding to take place between us. In other dreams, I find myself reunited with my former husband. In these dreams, I can't for the life of me remember why I am back together with this man whose memory now fills me with pain. I can't work out how I reneged on my resolution to remake my life, or how to get out of the whole mess. I know only that I am, once again, in the blur between train stations. I wake up realizing that the meanings I thought I had shucked off are not done with me yet.

How to be a success!

---

1. It's all about the signal

I am surrounded by people wearing crisp business attire. Even I am wearing a blazer. We are at an event sponsored by the local chamber of commerce, as part of a program meant to incubate new businesses. The room is not particularly warm, though; I imagine this would stultify the ambition that is required to nudge a new start-up out of its metaphorical egg. Cooled air pours from the vents, and there are only tables, chairs, and a coffee urn in this rented room, which, like a minimalist stage that must accommodate many different performances, avoids the risk of containing props that are at odds with the purpose of the moment.

The session is designed to allow aspiring entrepreneurs to seek the advice of so-called experts about their plans for new companies. I'm attending in the guise of a so-called expert, here at the invitation of a marketing firm in the city. I've been invited because I have co-written a book about the language of advertising and have some knowledge of the psychological mechanisms of persuasion.

A small cluster forms around me, and a young man begins outlining his ideas for the new consulting firm he hopes to launch. Midway through, another so-called expert—the host of the event, in fact—strides over to our group. He is stocky but not flabby. He moves his body in a way that suggests he knows it can be perceived to have the qualities of a concrete wall, should that perception be useful. As the young man continues talking, the expert nods his head energetically, indicating that he's heard every sentence before, or ones very much like it. He wants to know what the young man is planning to charge for the new company's services. He interrupts as the young man begins to tell him. "You should charge eight hundred or even a thousand dollars per hour," asserts the expert. "This sends the signal that you're in demand and offer a service that is unique." He deploys a thousand-dollar grin, designed to appear intimate and conspiratorial, an expensive accoutrement to information shared only among the elite: "Don't think of pricing as economics. Think of it as communication. It's all about the signal."

2. Strive for perfect fluency

Many aspiring entrepreneurs have, I suspect, found themselves at one time or another in a similar minimalist room, in the company of fellow members of Toastmasters International. The stated purpose of this club is to impart skills of public speaking and leadership. Salutary effects, as advertised on the club's website, include "maximizing your potential" and "enjoying unlimited personal growth."

I don't doubt that many have found their participation in Toastmasters to be useful, even empowering. But I've always been struck by a particular fixation the club seems to have with speech hygiene. Members are urged to cleanse their speech of any filler words—interjections such as "um," "ah," and "you know." Even the connectors "and" and "but" are undesirable when the speaker has recruited them not purely for their logical function but as a way of pausing the sentence while rummaging for their next words.

The club's philosophy is stern on this point; such "empty" fillers are allegedly distracting and irritating to listeners, adding noise to the smooth transmission of meaning between speaker and listener. Their total eradication is the ultimate goal. When someone gives a presentation at club meetings, one of the members is designated as the "ah-counter," reporting on the number of offending fillers that have marred the speech, draining it of its effectiveness.

The club's rationale is patently false. Filled pauses, as they are known to language scientists, are signals. They warn the audience of obstacles ahead as speech struggles to form itself while caught in the raging current of forward-moving time.

The problem of speech is this: it takes time to transform thought into language, but language survives in memory for only the briefest instant. Unless it has been rehearsed many times so that it is fixed, as if in amber, a sentence forming in the speaker's mind begins to wash away even before its first sounds can be uttered; it is like a sand mandala that is brushed into oblivion before it can be completed, a tower of blocks being hastily stacked in the presence of a destruction-hungry younger sibling.

The way out of this paradox is to speak and prepare to speak at the same time; one makes a leap of faith and utters the first part of a sentence while continuing to work out the rest of it. The sentence never exists as a whole object, but is in continual transit between the mind of the speaker and the mind of the listener, who for his part must rush to extract meaning from the sounds of speech before these are lost to time.

On occasion, speech outruns preparation, creating a backlog of half-formed language. The speaker comes to an abrupt stop until the logjam is resolved. This tends to happen when the idea to be expressed is complex, its linguistic form uncommon or convoluted, or the speaker has a vast body of knowledge or vocabulary to riffle through as she plans her sentence; highly knowledgeable speakers, it turns out, speak less fluently than others about their subject of expertise. To reassure the listener that thought is ongoing and will soon be making its appearance in the form of speech, the speaker emits a sound that is familiar to them both: "ah," "um," "er," "sooo," "you know," "aaand," and so on.

These vocalizations are not acknowledged as meaningful in any dictionary, but they are far from empty. They are a way for the speaker to alert the listener: *Hold on. I'm doing something difficult. I'll be with you momentarily.* The equivalent of a spinning circle on a computer screen, if you will. The listener takes note. Anticipating a reason for the delay, his mind snaps to attention; after all, something that is difficult to say is likely to be difficult to understand. Thus alerted, the listener recognizes the subsequent word more quickly. At times, he may even be able to anticipate the speaker's meaning from the disfluency, inferring, for example, that she is trying to describe an unusual object rather than a common one—a melon baller rather than a spoon, for example. Even small children, it turns out, are attuned to the useful function of disfluencies, using them to narrow the beam of their attention. When narrative speech is stripped of all disfluencies in the lab, listeners find it more difficult to understand or remember than when it is naturally seasoned with "ahs" or "ums."

Scorned by Toastmasters as "verbal crutches"—signs of weakness, in other words—these filler sounds allow speakers and listeners to sync up their minds with each other. Both interlocutors face the tyrannical demands of time upon language; each must decide how to ration their mental resources in proportion to the complexities of the moment. By revealing the slippage between speech and thought, a moment of stress in the production of speech, the speaker invites the listener to align his mental resources with hers. Precisely because of the vulnerability it reveals, an "um" has the capacity to yoke two minds in their joint labor of making and recovering meaning, united against time's efforts to erase it.

In banning all filled pauses, the Toastmasters club is perhaps less preoccupied with the alignment of minds or the clear expression of ideas than it is with a certain kind of signal: the point is not so much to communicate well as to perform well. The speaker is a character, her speaking self an avatar. Her primary goal is not necessarily to be understood but rather to be understood as a person for whom complexity appears trivial.

The ah-counter at these meetings reminds me of a firm governess, entrusted with instilling the proper habits and behavior of her young charges so they might take their rightful place in society. The proper habits of speech are like posh table manners, which serve no useful function in delivering food to mouth in the most efficient way. But they are prized as a signal that a person has invested time and energy in mastering a difficult maneuver to the point of seeming effortlessness. They are a signal that one has undertaken the preparations necessary to enter the club where such maneuvers are required and can be counted on to perform accordingly. Not surprisingly, it is those trained in the same arts of performance who are most readily distracted by filled pauses, upon whose ears they grate the most, who perceive them as lapses to be corrected at all costs.

3. Don't. Ever. Cry.

A colleague once related a story about her time as a young graduate student. Her advisor was a woman of formidable intellect, also known for her thoughtful and generous treatment of others. One day, my friend found herself in the advisor's office with some difficulty or other—perhaps it was a failed experiment, or some harsh criticism of her paper by a reviewer—and tears of frustration sprang to her eyes. Her usually gentle advisor gripped her by the shoulders, stationed her face inches away from my friend's, and commanded, "Stop crying. Don't. *Ever.* Cry."

My colleague chose to tell me this story because earlier that week a young student had burst into tears in her own office, and she found herself, without meaning to, reenacting her advisor's response. She handed the student a tissue, but said sternly, "You can't cry. You can't ever cry." As we shook our heads over this involuntary outburst of terrible advice, we began listing the many concealments we had conspired in over the years.

How I had submitted, four weeks after the birth of my first child, and without a waver in my voice, when my department chair proposed that I take over the teaching of a large class after its original instructor reneged on his commitment at the last moment. This was shortly after I'd overheard a conversation in the faculty lounge about how a pregnancy at this critical juncture in my career signaled my lack of seriousness as a scholar.

How my friend rarely brought her husband to work-related social events, despite their devotion to each other; with his blue-collar job and lack of education, he was not well suited to playing the part of spouse to an ambitious young academic.

How I denied ever missing my children while away on conference trips, how I made no mention of missed sleep due to serial ear infections, blocked milk ducts, or the viscous grief of miscarriage. How my friend and I, separately and privately, monitored and edited ourselves, always on the alert for the threat of tears, shudderings of rage, shrugs of impatience with colleagues (usually male) who signaled that they knew more than we did. The effort we spent to hide what it was costing us to succeed at our work and to make the hiding seem like no effort at all.

And here we were now, the ah-counters for the next generation.

4. Be the voice of authority

A great deal has been written about how women speak in "powerless" language. Allegedly, we are prone to hedging, hesitating, qualifying, or tempering an assertion with a question tagged onto its tail or by an uplift in intonation, and all of this is purported to be evidence of our being unable or unwilling to speak with the voice of authority.

As with filled pauses, the folklore around such language—labeled "tentative" by some scholars—is alluring in its simplicity, but it misses the quiet work accomplished by these conversational elements. They do more than leak insecurity. A question tagged onto an assertion ("This meeting's running late, isn't it?") might well flag a person's uncertainty about the truth of the statement, or it might be a solicitous attempt to draw the listener into the conversation, an expression of solidarity, or an effort to spare the listener's feelings by softening the sting of criticism. After analyzing the context in which tag questions were uttered, one researcher concluded that men were more likely than women to use them as markers of uncertainty whereas women more often used them to lubricate interactions with a conversational partner.

A similar richness of function has been documented for uptalk, the much-maligned practice of raising the pitch of one's voice at the end of a statement to give it the intonational contour of a question. (In New Zealand, uptalk is especially prevalent in Māori English, possibly linked with that culture's emphasis on social sensitivity and cooperative conversation.) If a speaker says, "I walked into the meeting and there was this admin guy?" she is probably not asking the listener to fact-check her, but she might be alerting him to take note of this detail; the admin guy's presence will be important in the story. If she says, "I'd like to give you some advice?" she may be testing the listener's reaction before barging into a room where she is not welcome.

Uptalk, like filled pauses, can direct the beam of a listener's attention if they are alert to how it is interwoven with other cues: often it serves to hold attention on the statement that ends with the rise, perhaps to elicit some response from the listener, but if the lifted syllable is stretched out in time, it may instead shift attention to what will come next. If you say to someone, "I'd like to give you some adviiiiice?" you may be signaling that what is about to come is delicate—delicate enough that you are weighing your words carefully and delicate enough that the listener may wish to steel herself.

One study found that uptalk, in combination with the degree of stretch on syllables, shifted listeners' attention either backward to what was just uttered or forward to what came next, in such a way as to influence how quickly they recognized words at certain points in the speech stream. It also found that listeners would ignore these cues if they were told that the speaker was an expert who was confident in his or her assertions; the presumption of the speaker's competence rendered listeners less attuned to the signals present in the speech.

This last result offers a hint as to why the same kind of talk can elicit different reactions depending on whether the speaker is male or female. Listeners filter the signals of speech through their prior expectations about the speaker and through their own mythologies of language and power. Several studies found that when female speakers delivered a message with the markers of "tentative" language, they were found to be less persuasive than their assertive counterparts; the influence of male speakers, on the other hand, remained undiluted by the presence of hesitations, hedges, or qualifiers. Perhaps a presumption of competence dulled the listeners' perception of signals present in the speech.

Women are often counseled to speak in the style of a (male) leader, to don the verbal equivalent of the power suit. But to follow this advice blindly, without exquisite attention to social context, is to trip over hidden land mines. As with the sartorial dilemmas that women face, it is no easy matter to calibrate the appropriate force of authority in one's voice for the particular occasion; one could spend hours paralyzed in front of the linguistic closet, obsessing about the correct mixture of power and femininity.

Evidence from research hints at the difficulty of the task. In one study, tentative language rendered a woman less influential in the eyes of other women but more influential in the eyes of men. In another, women who negotiated for a higher salary were more successful if they spoke less assertively. (Men's negotiations were unaffected by their choice of language.) The latter finding is echoed by another, which found that uptalk, a stereotypical marker of powerlessness, patterned differently for male and female contestants on the *Jeopardy!* game show. The lower a man's winnings, the more uptalk was evident in his speech; for a woman, the *more* money she'd amassed, the more likely she was to lift her statements into questions, perhaps out of instinct to avoid the appearance of gloating. And yet another study found that while lower pitch of the voice signals authority, women should be careful not to dip into the basement of their vocal range, into what is known as "vocal fry" or "creaky voice," because this could affect how they are perceived in a job interview. (Men were penalized much less for allowing their voices to creak.)

Easy enough to advise women to speak for success; more difficult to know exactly what that is. More difficult yet, apparently, is listening to what a woman is saying rather than how she is saying it.

5. Project authenticity

On one of my first dates with the man who is now my husband, we went to see a film about the tragic life of the Mexican artist Frida Kahlo. As the movie ended, I turned to him and saw that his face was slick with tears. I felt my internal organs shifting and rearranging themselves, as if in silent willingness opening up a space for love.

At such moments, a current surges between humans. You sense that someone has taken you—and perhaps only you—into the back room, where the costume is dropped to the floor and the performance is over. A promise hangs in the air: in this space, perhaps you too can be liberated from the strains of performing. Perhaps here, the true costs of meaning making can finally be revealed. Behind the stage, the two of you can stammer, pause, revise, and retract your way toward knowing each other. No one is counting anything.

This is the space in which seductions can occur.

Those who are in the business of seduction know all this. They know that we long for such intimacies and the freedoms they signal, even with strangers. They know that we bristle at sensing we are the audience to a performance we have not asked to see. A salesperson whose speech is flawless is felt to be less trustworthy, some researchers have found. The listener discerns that speech without the ripple of disfluency is a hint that it has been rehearsed or scripted; there are no moments in which she feels she has been drawn into the back room where language is being assembled, no moments where minds sync up together against the onslaught of time.

Ever mindful of simulating human connection, designers of robots have taken note: they are busy studying the patterns of disfluencies in human speech and testing whether deliberately planting them into artificial speech—as a signal of spontaneous, effortful, unscripted language—makes people feel a warm current sparking between self and machine.

The secret to success, then, is far more subtle than what one might learn at the Toastmasters club. It consists in knowing what to conceal and what to reveal. Signals that the performance has been suspended can be worked into the performance, to one's advantage. But the rules are complicated.

What is perceived as unguarded openness in one person may be seen as contemptible weakness in another. Witnessing the signs of internal struggle sometimes leads to an alignment of minds and a deeper understanding; at other times, it provokes scorn and dismissal. Much depends upon who is speaking, and when, and where, and upon who is watching. Much depends upon what we expect a person to bear without visible effort, upon preconceptions of a particular speaker's strength or competence, upon a sense of whether the performance is ongoing or has been suspended.

I watch a hearing at which a woman accuses a man of past sexual crimes. Her face and voice do not leak, and there is no crying or shuddering of rage or other emotional eruptions to add noise to the smooth transmission of her message. Her voice is steady and her words are evenly spaced even though she is describing horrifying actions of which she claims to be the victim. The man's voice and face are not steady. He releases torrents of outrage as he defends himself against accusations he insists are false. He pauses at length as he describes how the accusations have affected him and his family, filling the pause with the visible effort of suppressing tears, a signal that he is in the midst of something unspeakably difficult.

No performance would be complete without critics to weigh in on it, and as I listen to other watchers, I'm struck by how little they agree with each other. Some comment on the woman's self-control, seeing a person who has succumbed to legions of ah-counters to the point of hiding deep wounds; others see a calculating strategizer intent on destroying a successful man. Some view the man as an actor blustering in front of an undiscerning audience, inserting false pain between his words to simulate vulnerability; others see in his outburst a genuine outpouring of the anguish of a man wronged by the mob; still others view it as an alarming symptom of an unstable temperament.

The watchers can't agree, it seems, on who is strong and who is weak, who is human and who is robot.

6. Always be at the cutting edge

The host of the chamber of commerce event is perfectly fluent. He is fluent even when he is addressing a question, directed at me, by representatives of a local marketing firm who are wondering how best to incorporate some of the latest scientific research on language into their work for clients. He is fluent despite—or perhaps because of—his utter lack of expertise in this area, which has quickly become apparent to me regardless of the signals he confidently emits. He finishes dispensing his knowledge, such as it is, and then indicates that he is in demand by rushing off to help another group across the room.

The women from the marketing firm watch his solid, retreating back. Then they turn expectantly to me, waiting for me to answer their question. Something passes between us—in the pause while waiting for him to be out of earshot, in the way their eyes hold mine for an extra beat—that signals that a shift may be about to occur.

Perhaps the time is not too far off when, even in rooms like these, the old signals will lose their currency, when an impenetrable, masculine fluency may not be enough to signal value. In some near future, perhaps, these women will not wait politely until the so-called expert is out of range before dismissing him with their eyes, and I will not wait before stating that nothing he has said has any scientific merit. That future is not here yet, but one can catch a whiff of it, even in these rooms with hermetically sealed windows and circulated air.

In the meantime, the women from the marketing firm and I get to work; we lurch, explore, and backtrack; tentatively, disfluently, we connect our minds and we make our way together through the accumulated muck of our knowledge.

Pleasure hunts

I

A memory from childhood: My father prepares to read to his children. He looks at each of us significantly, in turn, as he does when he raises a glass of wine just before making a toast of special importance. He opens the book, touches his finger to his tongue, leafs to the first page. Opens his lips with the lightest of smacks.

Fills his lungs with new air.

A pool of expectation spreads, as I wait for the first word to drop in and wave its ripples toward the edges of my mind.

This memory of my father announced itself when an adult version of me leafed to the first page of Bohumil Hrabal's *Too Loud a Solitude*, translated from Czech by Michael Henry Heim. I found these words: "When I read, I don't really read; I pop a beautiful sentence into my mouth and suck it like a fruit drop, or I sip it like a liqueur until the thought dissolves in me like alcohol, infusing brain and heart and coursing on through the veins to the root of each blood vessel."

I don't recall my father reading to us in any language other than Czech.

I don't recall much of what it was he read to us, but I do remember he embodied Hrabal's words in such a way that I can never read that opening passage without seeing my father and his gestures, hearing the small sound that accompanied the parting of his lips in preparation.

I don't always read as if sipping a liqueur or sucking on a sweet. Most of the time, I simply read.

Most of the time, reading is more like smearing peanut butter over toast and eating it standing up while gathering the objects I need for a day at work, more like the serviceable supper plunked down in the middle of the table, ladled out from the pot in which it was cooked. Nourishing, necessary, consumed without ceremony.

I believe I've spent more hours reading than in any other single activity. If I were forced, I might guess that over the span of my life so far the number of pages I have turned over and read approaches ten million.

When I'm not reading, I'm mostly either speaking or listening to someone speak. Some of my hours are spent writing down—and then reconsidering, and reconsidering again—words that I have herded into sentences. When I appear to be speechless, busy with cooking or gardening, I am probably still immersed in language; I am likely listening to myself speak in my mind, or reconstructing the words that someone else has spoken or written.

Even in sleep: when I sleep, I dream, and in my dreams people are speaking or I am speaking.

Language clogs my life the way an accumulation of junk fills a hoarder's apartment. Survival without it—*all* of it—seems implausible.

What have I gained after tens of thousands of hours spent reading (not to mention the hours spent producing or hearing or dreaming speech)? I've accrued vast statistical bank accounts of language. Aggregates of verbal expectations, cataloged by genre, time, place, and speaker/author. Robust estimates of the probabilities of certain structures. Hyperefficient procedures for extracting information.

Among these tens of thousands of hours, is it possible to estimate the sum total of moments of language pleasure, their frequency and duration?

About the efficient extraction of information, we language scientists know a good deal: we have models that distill the nature of the information sealed within language; we have theories of its anatomies and mechanics; we have experimental methods that divulge how the mind unfolds the syntax of a sentence, how a person overlays the unseen sound waves of speech onto a solid thing in the seen world, how two interlocutors synchronize their separate and overlapping mental models, how all of this becomes automatized and routinized like a language machine purring along without incident.

About the shudderings of pleasure that language incites, we know far less.

I should say, rather, that what we scientists know so little about is how to *explain* pleasure—the how, when, and why of language bristling its electricity along the curvature of a trembling spine.

Language scientists, I suspect, are no less likely than anyone to shudder.

Try to rank the beauty of the following words: "drunken," "liminal," "withstand," "tremulous," "crock," "zoo."

Recruit several friends into the exercise. Your agreement may surprise you.

Try, if you can, to explain what makes a word beautiful. Never mind what is or is not happening along your spine right now. Focus on the word as object: What properties does it have that amplify the likelihood that a member of the population at large will shiver with pleasure?

And loathing. Many people also agree on the ugliness of words. Some words that amplify the likelihood of a loathing event are "moist," "luggage," "phlegm," "ointment," "pulchritude."

The enterprise of quantifying beauty must come with its own pleasures, because it has been known to seduce scholars.

The linguist David Crystal has tabulated elements of sound that contribute to the beauty of an English word: among other findings, the sounds *l* and *m* appear often in beautiful words, whereas *t* and *d*, while exceedingly common among words at large, are found less often in gorgeous words; words of three or more syllables (especially if the first bears the strongest accent) have a lovelier melody than short, abrupt words; in a pretty word that is multisyllabic, the first vowel is likely to be one in which the tongue is extended toward the front of the mouth (*a, e, i*), with vowels pronounced by retracting the tongue to the back (*o, u*) occurring only later in the word— very rarely is the reverse pattern (as it occurs in my first name, Julie) observed among the lexical beauties.

Even more ambitiously, Arthur Jacobs, a scholar of computational stylistics, used machine-learning algorithms and a database of more than a billion German words to devise a method for measuring beauty. He discovered that eight features, when properly combined, can predict pleasure, as experienced by a random sample of speakers of German: "If a German word features an optimal length (in this corpus: about 12 letters), a specific combination of sonorous syllables, semantic associations with words like ANMUT (grace) or FREUDE (joy) and is rather surprising, it has an increased likelihood of being classified as beautiful."

Do gorgeous English words also sound mellifluous to speakers of German, Yoruba, or Malayalam? (Notice the loveliness of that last word: "Malayalam." Such a stark contrast with a word such as "German," let alone "French.")

And if they do, what would we make of this?

Not to be outdone, the artists Vitaly Komar and Alexander Melamid commissioned professional polling companies to study how people determine beauty in visual art. Using a survey composed of 102 questions, they tabulated the features of beautiful paintings, as judged by a random sampling of the citizens of eleven different countries (the United States, Russia, Kenya, Iceland, China, Ukraine, Finland, Turkey, Denmark, China, France).

These polls allowed Komar and Melamid to extrapolate the results, with a statistical accuracy of ±3.2 percent with 95 percent confidence, to a population of approximately two billion people.

The artists were astonished to find remarkable agreement. Around the world, average tastes in art diverged very little, with Kenyans claiming to love paintings much like the ones favored by Icelanders. The most beautiful color is blue. The best-loved compositions are landscapes, either modern or traditional in style, with blended colors that depict water, an open sky, green vegetation, animals roaming over rolling hills, humans in repose.

Recurring, widespread pleasures call for explanation. Some have suggested that beauty is evolution's handmaiden; its pleasures lure us toward substances, activities, and places that improve our chances of survival and/or reproduction. We are drawn to Komar and Melamid's scenic paintings, this story goes, because they represent places where an abundance of water and food can be found.

According to the cognitive scientist Steven Pinker, the pleasure we derive from art is the result of the artist's deliberate manipulation of our evolutionary drives. It is like strawberry cheesecake, which we love not because we've evolved a taste for it but because it has been designed to evoke substances useful for our survival. Cheesecake taps into useful pleasures, offering "trickles of enjoyment from the sweet taste of ripe fruit, the creamy mouth feel of fats and oils from nuts and meat, and the coolness of fresh water. Cheesecake packs

a sensual wallop unlike anything in the natural world because it is a brew of megadoses of agreeable stimuli which we
concocted for the express purpose of pressing our pleasure
buttons."

As for the pleasure buttons pressed by a word such as "Malayalam," I confess I am at a loss. I have no doubt it contains
megadoses of agreeable stimuli, but how these evoke substances or activities useful to our survival and/or reproduction, I cannot easily imagine.

The artists Komar and Melamid have their own ideas about
the allure of the blue landscape. In an interview, Alexander
Melamid offered this: "So I'm wondering, maybe the blue
landscape is genetically imprinted in us, that it's the paradise
within, that we came from the blue landscape and we want
it. Maybe paradise is not something that is awaiting us; it is
already inside of us, and the point is how to figure it out, how
to discover it, how to get it out."

II

A character in Donna Tartt's novel *The Goldfinch* remarks,
"You can have a lifetime of perfectly sincere museum-going
where you traipse around enjoying everything and then go out
and have some lunch. But . . . if a painting really works down
in your heart and changes the way you see, and think, and

feel, you don't think, 'oh, I love this picture because it's universal.' 'I love this painting because it speaks to all mankind.' That's not the reason anyone loves a piece of art. It's a secret whisper. . . . An individual heart-shock. . . . Yours, yours. I was painted for you."

My sister claims to derive no pleasure from poetry. I am skeptical. I send her "The Cinnamon Peeler" by Michael Ondaatje, one of the most seductive, lyrical poems I know. Surely it is, by any objective or universal measure, beautiful.

"And?" I inquire. "Nothing," she writes.

Where do you locate a failure of pleasure? Some hypotheses related to my sister's poetic anhedonia:

1. She suffers from a disconnection between certain perceptual regions of the brain and its reward centers, whether due to injury, interference, or personal history. In other words, there is no neural path from language to joy.

2. My sister has not inherited a predisposition to "aesthetic chill"—a quantifiable tendency to be awestruck and to shudder in the presence of beauty, shown to have a genetic component and to be absent in roughly half the general population.

3. A lifetime of consuming language as if it were a hasty

meal eaten over the sink has predisposed her to habits of mind that, while supremely efficient for her daily purposes, are ill-suited for poetry.

4. By virtue of her younger age, my sister was not present at the times when my father still read to us, did not observe his rituals of preparation, did not learn how to set the mind in readiness for the sacrament of language.

&

Language feeling, it turns out, is entangled with the life one lives in a language.

M. J. Fitzgerald, an American writer who spent her childhood in Italy, writes, "The word *candy* does nothing to my taste buds, whereas the word *caramella* brings instantly back the sweet crunch of the teeth through the shell, softened by sucking for as long as possible, to the soft center." Colors, she claims, have a different quality in Italian than they do in English; the sea's "intensity of blue can only be contained in the Italian word *azzurro*. The word *blue*, an anodyne descriptive term, does not convey that childhood sea, but *azzurro* brings it all back with a violence in memory that invariably hits me like a punch in the stomach."

&

Many multilingual speakers describe their second or third language as utilitarian, drained of the intense feeling that suffuses their mother tongue. Filthy words do not shock the nerves. Tender words cannot instantly soothe. The sounds of words merely *point* to meanings; they are not saturated with them down to their bones.

Some researchers claim that when deliberating in a second language, people make judgments dispassionately, less tainted by the biases and emotions that creep into their mother tongue. A later language offers the purity of abstraction.

This does not surprise me. When we are children, our minds have not yet migrated away from our bodies. We think and learn through our eyes, muscles, skin. Our organs boil with rage; our hair is ravenous for a parent's tender caress. Words of betrayal can flay the skin straight off the body.

When language enters a creature such as this, it cannot hold itself apart. The sounds of a word make a direct line to sensation; the swells and dips of sentences become the music of hunger and its fulfillment, the plaintive melodies of loss—its tightening sting, its gradual dissipation.

In adulthood, some people find pleasure in the origami art of folded sentences.

Maryanne Wolf, a neuroscientist who studies reading, plucks her favorite sentence from George Eliot's novel *Middlemarch*—a sentence whose cognitive demands on the reader, she acknowledges, are "substantial." It goes like this:

> How was it that in the weeks since her marriage Doro-
> thea had not distinctly observed but felt with a stifling
> depression that the large vistas and wide fresh air which
> she had dreamed of finding in her husband's mind were
> replaced by anterooms and winding passages which
> seemed to lead nowhither?

How else but through its winding syntax, asks Wolf, could
Eliot have simulated the tightening claustrophobia one might
feel upon discovering the limits of a husband's meandering,
aimless, going-nowhere intellect?

The author André Aciman thrills to the syntax of Proust. The
Proustian sentence, he writes, operates on three levels. It begins with "an insight or idea that needs to be elaborated upon
and examined and that sets the course."

It ends with "a burst of revelation, a short, almost lapidary
dart that uncovers something altogether surprising and un-
foreseen and unsaddles every expectation the reader might
have had."

In the middle, "Proust allows the sentence to tarry and swell
with intercalated material that proceeds ever so cautiously,
sometimes forced to fork and to fork again while opening up
subsidiary parenthetical clauses along the way, until, after
much deliberation, unannounced, having acquired enough
air and ballast along the way, the sentence suddenly un-

leashes the closing [revelation]. Proust's sentence needs this middle zone. Like a huge wave, it needs to swell and build momentum—sometimes with totally negligible material—before finally crashing against the shoreline."

English professors these days complain that their students find no joy in the syntax of George Eliot or Marcel Proust or Henry James.

When it comes to the art of folded sentences, a widespread anhedonia has set in.

Or perhaps it is, after all, a failure of information extraction.

English professors may not realize that when their students claim to find Proust's sentences incomprehensible, they are perhaps speaking literally and are not merely put off by the whiff of an unfamiliar past.

Apparently, we do not all speak the same English language, even if we are born to it. Among native English speakers, the ability to parse intricate sentences varies considerably—a fact that is as surprising, perhaps, as the convergent love of blue landscapes. Researchers found that many English speakers failed to understand sentences such as "The girl was the one the man fed"; "Every box has a pencil in it"; "The sailor was fed by the plumber." Even fewer could cope with "Paul noticed that the fact that the room was tidy surprised Shona"; "John will be hard to get his wife to vouch for."

They did not test the sentences of Marcel Proust.

If language is a genetic gift, do our own random mutations fence off syntactic paradise, partitioning it into private acreages? Do we inherit a fondness or loathing for certain sentences, the way we carry genes that cause us to desire or despise cilantro?

Unlikely.

The pleasures of syntax spring not from instinct but from the life one has lived in it. Fluency at the margins of syntax, it seems, depends partly on how much one has read. Some scholars think that the very presence of certain linguistic structures within a language—elaborately looped phrases, clauses nested inside others—are the result of literacy spreading within the culture.

Maybe it's only possible to respond with enjoyment to Henry James after reading millions of pages of increasingly complex language. Perhaps the vast statistical bank accounts of language, the hyperefficient procedures of information extraction, the repetitions of parsing, are the soil from which such pleasures can sprout.

Syntax is a coherence that emerges through practice. Regular use sharpens its details. Without it, the most sublime, sculpted sentences are nothing more than indistinct lumps of mud.

⌒

No one ever spontaneously utters a Jamesian sentence, presumably not even Henry James. It is strenuous enough to parse one, let alone compose it, impossible to assemble it on the fly.

Is this not a part of its pleasure when reading it? To climb, sweaty and panting, to the peak of the sentence, and discover that the summit affords a view one never imagined from below. And then the realization that this view, this climb, this melding of effort and perspective was made for you—only for you, only for this windswept moment when your breath fails you—by a mind even more athletic and nimble than yours.

⌒

Many writers these days advocate for prose that has the qualities of plain speech. Avoid passives, they say. Do not be so ostentatious; there is no need to stack clauses into precarious towers. Keep to words within easy reach.

Simple prose has its own beauty, like a crystalline lake with a glass-smooth surface. It offers rest and long drinks of cool water. It's possible to gaze into its clear depths and see straight down to the rocks at the bottom, almost close enough to touch.

But I mourn a little for those who are lulled into sitting by the lake forever. If they avoid the strain of clambering over rocks and up slopes (or if they have little experience at reading the complex terrain), will their legs weaken, unable to carry them to the wilder landscapes? Will they never learn to leap over the gaps between relative clauses or find the faint trail meandering through inverted phrases, appositives, and modifiers? I imagine them eventually growing restless by the shore, bored by the gentle lapping of water but unable to ascend to the heart shocks waiting for them along windy ridges and rugged peaks.

III

My eye is trained, after millions of pages of reading, to recognize words without engaging the mouth, to read at the speed of sight, not at the languid speed of sound or its choreographies of lips, palate, tongue.

But when it's pleasure I'm after, I slow down. I pay attention to the mouth movements evoked by visual symbols. I enunciate each word in my mind. I find someone to read aloud to.

Beautiful words cause my saliva to run. I suck on them like fruit drops.

I feel pangs of remorse whenever I use the word "speech" to mean something larger. I often stretch its meaning to refer to any language, whether spoken or signed, that lives away from the page and labors under the yoke of real time. Such language need not emanate from the mouth. Linguists acknowledge that when ears or tongues cannot easily take part in language, it readily migrates to the hands. In fact, some believe that this is where language was first born, prior to speech.

Sign languages exist all over the world, each as distinct from the other as the world's spoken languages, but they have long been misunderstood to be simple gestures lacking a grammar. Yet these languages spring from the same human urges; they too have worked out how to create symbols out of bodily movements, how to string these symbols together to convey relationships among them, and how to do all this under the tyrannies of time.

Almost everything I have written in this book about speech is true of sign as well.

So why do I persist in using the exclusionary word "speech" to mean both "sign" and "speech," using it when what I'm really referring to is this: *the practical solution to the problem of pressing thought into movements the body can perform and perceive under the strictures of time*?

I confess it comes down to my own pleasure.

My private history of language resides in my body. It is flagrantly oral. All of its pleasures have come to me through the

movements of mouth and tongue and from the mind's reconstruction of such gestures, derived from the waves of sound
lapping against my ears.

Oral language has tuned my attention to what is happening
in my mouth, ever since I lay as an infant in my crib playing with my vocal apparatus, patiently re-creating the sounds
made by the speaking beings around me. I played at degrees
of lip-rounding. I raised or lowered the tongue, pulled it toward the back of my mouth, or extended it forward. I pushed
air out through narrow channels into turbulences of sound or
stopped air short with lips or tongue or let it flow unimpeded
while I performed experiments in shaping the resonant cavity
through which the flow of air passed.

All of this is to say that for me there is no language pleasure
without mouthfeel.

I use the word "speech" to try to contain this pleasure.

Even during sex, when language dissolves into a darker liquid, my mouth needs to be involved. My mouth has held years
and years of language pleasure. It has served as the primary
organ of connection. It believes it is urgently needed to articulate the pleasures of love, even here, in this wordless place,
this place that is all body, body, no abstraction.

If I had lived out my language history in sign rather than speech, where in my body would pleasure be concentrated?

Would my brain expropriate neural tracts from other senses, heightening attention to the postures of palms and fingers, the flow of manual movement from one precise point in space to another? All of this I would have practiced in my crib as I babbled with my fingers, fusing language with handfeel.

Would a beautiful word make my fingertips tingle, the tendons of my wrist snap to attention?

Would I love more tenderly and precisely with my hands and less with my mouth?

☙

I catch a glimmer of what I am missing when I watch a performance of the haiku-like poem "Hands" by Clayton Valli. The poem begins by asking, "What are hands?" Throughout the poem, the same five-fingered handshape dances through the signs that pose the question and give the answer: "what," "hands," "snow falling," "flowers blooming," "wheat swaying," "leaves floating," "all of this," "poetry," "expression." That it is a dance is evident—how the signs themselves embody the natural world and its motion and rhythm, how the hands move in symmetry and balance. Hands that move for pleasure, hands of a lover.

☙

I send my sister a poem by Leonard Cohen. She still claims to feel nothing.

"It's funny," she says, "because when I hear that same poem as a song, I'm really into it. Something about the music makes the words come alive."

He knew what he was doing, Leonard Cohen. He had the cure for my sister's poetic anhedonia.

&

The thing about music is that it cannot exist apart from pleasure. Unlike words, it doesn't stand in for anything outside itself, cannot be severed from bodily experience. It can't have its meaning extracted like ore and processed into something that exists only because it is useful. In this sense, it seems to be the opposite of language, that hyperefficient delivery system for parcels of knowledge: how to organize a mastodon-hunting party, how to build a nuclear reactor.

And yet Charles Darwin himself speculated that language's origins were related to birdsong, which, as far as we can tell, does not refer to abstractions outside itself any more than Mozart's Clarinet Concerto in A Major.

Perhaps our language anhedonia comes from the divorce between language and music. In becoming enthralled with language's usefulness, perhaps we have forgotten the paradise curled within, forgotten that we long to release it.

Leonard Cohen's songs remarry language and music. No one would hum "Suzanne" with the words stripped out. Most of Cohen's melodies do not catch in the mind like the themes of Dvořák or tunes by the Beatles. The beauty of his songs, one has to admit, would shrivel without language.

For Cohen, the music is an instruction. Like my father's rituals as he prepared to read, like Bohumil Hrabal's opening sentences, music is the cue that orients the language mind to pleasure. It says, "Open. This will be beautiful."

His music also does this: it sets the tempo, hitches language to a time signature.

When it is read at the speed of sight, a poem risks disembodiment. At speeds much faster than spoken language—at two hundred, three hundred, four hundred words per minute or more—it is possible to recognize words, compute grammatical relations, assemble schemas of meaning. But to bring language down from the stratosphere of pure thought and settle it back into the body—this requires a measure of slowness.

Like ripples moving from the center of the mind to its edges, it takes time to open the senses, one by one; to wallow in mouthfeel; to wait for the crispness of visual details to slide into focus; to allow hunger and loss to amplify each other in their echoes of call-and-response.

When Cohen sings, languorously, "It's four in the morning, the end of December," he is a metronome setting the pace for my hyperefficient sister. At the tempo of his voice, it's possible to hear the mournful echo of "four" in "morning" and "end" in "December" and feel how their common sounds and pitches bind these words together like fate. At this pace now, she can make out Cohen, his collar standing in defense against the New York winter and its tunneling winds, follow him with her eyes as he trudges down Clinton Street, past the saxophone player pouring his heart out like a thin smoke that is soon blown away.

Now she has descended from ethereal abstraction. She is anchored in body, body, the shivering and ravenous body.

I wonder if my sister would be more receptive to the pleasures of poetry if she had grown up in a Deaf family. Sign languages resist disembodiment, it seems to me, in ways that other languages do not. Most signing exchanges, even those dislocated in time and space, occur without written symbols acting as errand boy between body and meaning. (A SignWriting alphabet exists, but it is not the easiest or most common way to preserve sign.) Even when watching a poem captured on video, the viewer's attention is fixed on the body of the performer. As the Deaf poet Paul Scott has observed, hearing people can take a book from a shelf and read it, but "for Deaf people, I am the book." The viewer of the poet-book, unlike my reading sister, cannot hurry language beyond the limits of pleasure; she is bound to the time signature the performer has chosen.

Vision is the dominant sense for us humans, a fact that hobbles spoken language. It is far easier for signs than it is for sounds to plunge us into a sensory experience of our world: the ASL sign for "paint" involves two fingers brushing up and down the palm of the other hand; to sign "cat," one would pinch the length of an imaginary whisker to one side of the face.

Still, it is the nature of all language to aspire to abstraction; signers, too, use poetry to return to sensation.

"Art-sign" is the term coined by linguists to refer to a style of signing that sets the aesthetic above the utilitarian. They observed the distinction when they gave Bernard Bragg, a Deaf signer, the task of first translating a poem by e. e. cummings into common, everyday sign, and then working it over into a literary translation meant to arouse pleasure. When speaking in art-sign, Bragg used language that drew attention to itself and the body that makes it. He chose signs that repeated handshapes or movement paths, much as a hearing poet might make use of assonance and alliteration. He altered signs so that they involved both hands moving in unison or opposition, and created recurring patterns of movement.

He tightened the transitions between signs, leaving no un-
necessary slack. He exaggerated those aspects of signs that
mirrored the sensory world; the sign for "summer," which
involves a bent index finger brushing against the forehead,
might be lengthened and slightly reshaped to evoke the wip-
ing of sweat off an overheated forehead.

These are the first four lines of the poem translated by Bragg:

> since feeling is first
> who pays any attention
> to the syntax of things
> will never wholly kiss you

There are some writers—Joseph Conrad, Vladimir Nabokov,
Aleksandar Hemon, among many others—who, by virtue of
historical accidents and ruptures, found that language for
them is cut in two: there is the embodied language of childhood and its unruly passions, and then a clean, austere language learned later in life. The greatest obstacle for these
writers is not so much that they have to master subtleties
of vocabulary and syntax that elude even many native-born
speakers. It's that they must learn, somehow, to simulate feeling in a language in which they have not felt enough.

In her memoir *Lost in Translation*, Eva Hoffman describes
learning English as an adolescent, dismayed to find its words

bleached of emotion and drained of life. It was not until well
into adulthood, after having read perhaps millions of pages
in the English language, after having become an instructor
of literature, that she was able to find English words, "as in
childhood, beautiful things." This moment arrived while she
was teaching a poem by T. S. Eliot.

"Over the years," she writes, "I've read so many explications
of these stanzas that I can analyze them in half a dozen ingenious ways. But now, suddenly I'm attuned, through some
mysterious faculty of the mental ear, to their inner sense;
I hear the understated melancholy of that refrain, the civi-
lized restraint of the rhythms reining back the more hilly
swells of emotion, the self-reflective, moody resignation of
the melody. . . . I read, tasting the sounds on the tongue,
hearing the phrases somewhere between tongue and mind.
Bingo, I think, this is it, the extra, the attribute of language
over and above function and criticism. I'm back within the
music of the language, and Eliot's words descend on me with
a sort of grace."

IV

My family and I walk in a sculpture park, where we come
across a granite woman sleeping on a slab of rock beneath
birch and oak. In a clearing, ravens gather, swinging open
their wings of burnished bronze. An obelisk rises toward
the leafy canopy, obeying the vertical lines of surrounding
trees.

These sculptures mimic the forms of nature, but we look at them differently. They pulse with an invisible sentience. We note the contrasts between where the granite has been polished smooth and where it has been left wild and rough, and we read intent. We watch the sunlight catch on bronzed wings, and we see a human plan.

The natural setting is lovely, but it is these intentional forms that leap into our vision, as if the distance between our eyes and these shapes had shrunk or dissolved, as if we had opened the doors in the center of our foreheads and welcomed them inside.

At some point, we come across a dry creek bed in the park. Still attuned to the minds of makers, we are shocked by its beauty; we point out how the tumble of rocks flashes sunlight back at us, making a frothing white against the brooding shade of its banks, exactly as if someone had composed the scene to simulate a churn of liquid and light embraced by dark quietude. In that moment, we see art where there is none—a warm, sentient breath held within the random spill of stones on dry soil.

I have a sense, suddenly, of what it would be like to walk through the world with a belief that God had made it, that he had arranged the trees and rocks just so, in anticipation of our human eyes, in order to make pleasure jump within our bodies.

When talk of the omnipotent Artist enters into the discussion, it's a sign that the word "pleasure" is too mild for whatever is going on. Now we are no longer talking about fruit drops and liqueurs dissolving into the bloodstream; we are talking about being remade in someone else's image. There are times when a poem or a song or a sculpture is a burning bush. *You must change your life.*

"In the upper reaches of pleasure and on the boundary of fear is a little-studied emotion," write Dacher Keltner and Jonathan Haidt, pioneers in the scientific investigation of awe.

The science of awe is even younger, even more fumbling, than the science of ordinary pleasure. As with pleasure, though, there is little doubt that humans have been trembling with awe since time immemorial.

Why wait so long to take a stab at explaining transcendence, to draw up its taxonomies and investigate its sources?

Do we avert our gaze out of instinct for self-preservation? Having already killed God, science had not yet dismantled awe. But whether awe can survive without mystery is doubtful. Also doubtful: whether humanity can survive without awe.

We have been warned since Eden of the perils of too much knowledge.

Albert Einstein wrote, "The most beautiful experience we can have is the mysterious. It is the fundamental emotion which stands at the cradle of true art and true science."

And yet he had no qualms about pitching his own mind head-long in the direction of knowledge. What consoled him was the belief that mystery was endlessly vast; all the best human minds striving to the edges of their lifetimes could hope to comprehend only the tiniest portion of it.

Here is a partial list of things known to elicit a sense of awe in humans:

> seeing Earth from outer space
> music that causes piloerection (raised goose bumps over
>   the skin)
> witnessing the birth of a child
> a view of snowy mountain peaks
> athletic feats that defy belief
> slow-motion videos of intricate patterns in liquid,
>   invisible to the naked eye
> the nearness of a famous or powerful person
> a tour through an elegant mathematical proof
> volcanoes, tornadoes

poetry (for some)

gazing up from the forest floor at eucalyptus trees

being present at someone's death

dance, performed with simultaneous passion and
    control

a leader spilling charisma into a crowd

religious rituals

watching the Twin Towers crumble in the attacks of
    September 11

exquisite paintings or sculptures

the unrelenting blood-beat of powwow drums

stepping into the hush of a cathedral

a new scientific theory unspooled

There are some features that are commonly found in awe-inducing stimuli: a sense of spatial vastness or power; exceptional human qualities or achievements; informational complexity; intense beauty.

There are, however, cross-cultural differences (for example, American respondents were found to stand in greater awe of human accomplishments than their Chinese counterparts) as well as considerable individual variation, currently under investigation.

One way of describing such experiences is to say that they are too large to be contained within the existing borders of a single consciousness. Awe dissolves the membrane enclosing the quivering ego. The self spills out onto the sidewalk, easy and ecstatic prey to rearrangement.

Nor can such experiences be contained within the boundaries of words, and the best poems are the ones that know this.

Rumi (translated by Coleman Barks):

> *This is how it always is*
> *when I finish a poem.*
>
> *A great silence overcomes me,*
> *and I wonder why I ever thought*
> *to use language.*

Note that for Rumi the great silence comes after he *finishes* a poem. It is, in fact, to language that he turned to express the divine, and also the ineffability of the divine. As Maria Popova writes in her blog, *The Marginalian*, "Poetry serves the same function as prayer: to give shape and voice to our unspoken and often unspeakable hopes, fears, and inner tremblings—the tenderest substance of our lives, to be held between the palms and passed from hand to compassionate hand."

In his gorgeous book *The Tree of Meaning*, writer Robert Bringhurst adds, "If something is ineffable, that means it cannot be said. But what cannot be said can sometimes be heard. . . .

Language is a self-transcending mechanism. It tries, and lets us try, to say what it can't. The survival of poetry depends on the failure of language."

Perhaps this is why the early church forbade the playing of instrumental music. To use music as an aid, to help language venture near the unsayable (as Leonard Cohen did), was a sacred thing. But music set apart from the sung prayers of the human voice was deemed merely sensual, perhaps obscenely so. Saint Jerome wrote that maidens should not even know what a lyre or a flute was, let alone how to use one.

A puzzle for neuroscience: how to explain the fact that in a brain where change accrues in increments, through the slow and steady drip of experience, awe can pack a wallop of transformation, changing the entire course of one's life?

Needless to say, there is great interest in harnessing this power for remaking. We long for nothing so much as to burst out of the prison of our own selves. Psilocybin is a therapeutically promising accelerant of awe. So is technology: one study showed that immersion in virtual reality environments of breathtaking scenery yielded a subjective awe rating of 79.7 (on a scale of 10 to 100) and provoked piloerection in almost half the participants.

These incursions into knowledge have not yet dispelled all mystery.

What is the reaction between stimulus and brain that creates the big bang of awe, thrusting consciousness outward?

Eva Hoffman read the poems of T. S. Eliot many times—why did grace descend upon her that day and none prior?

Is the state of grace even something one can reach for? Maybe there are certain feelings—like the squirming that comes from being tickled—that you can't induce in yourself.

In her essay "Seeing," Anne Dillard writes of spending countless hours around her home near Tinker Creek, walking and looking. Her close attention to the natural world yields pleasures that are numerous and daily. But then there is this:

> One day I was walking along Tinker Creek thinking of nothing at all and I saw the tree with the lights in it. I saw the backyard cedar where the mourning doves roost charged and transfigured, each cell buzzing with flame. I stood on the grass with the lights in it, grass that was wholly fire, utterly focused and utterly dreamed. It was less like seeing than being for the first time seen, knocked breathless by a powerful glance. The flood of fire abated, but I'm still spending the power. Gradually, the lights went out in the cedar, the colors died, the cells unflamed and disappeared. I was still ringing. I had been my whole life a bell, and never knew it until at that moment I was lifted and struck. I have since only very

rarely seen the tree with the lights in it. The vision comes and goes, mostly goes, but I live for it, for the moment when the mountains open and a new light roars in spate through the crack, and the mountains slam.

Dillard, Rumi, my father, and all the other mystics agree: You can't hunt grace down. You can only show up and be ready. You pay attention the way you pay a tithe. You traipse through the museum. You walk the creek, day after day. You turn the pages. Perhaps they number in the millions. You fill your lungs with new air.

You wait for the first word to drop into the pool of your waiting mind.

PART III

&

Loss

Missing words

There it is: the moment when I find myself thigh-deep in the squelch of memory, feet held fast, thrashing about for the word that eludes me. No amount of effort enables me to take a step forward, back, to the side, anywhere I might gain a fresh perspective from which to spot the missing word. I'm stuck. In the blank space where the word should appear, a vision of my linguistic future begins to gather like a thunderhead on a summer day. I imagine an inevitable decline, sloped cruelly away from the apex of my verbal powers and bottoming out in a reversion to dumbness.

And still, that damned word nowhere to be found.

Not that this is the first time I've misplaced a word. Far from it. But certain troubling correlations have begun to co-alesce: the ache in the hip and stiffness of knee upon get-ting out of bed, the sudden revelation that reading glasses are useful, the growing effort of preparing a complicated dinner while chatting with the guests. All these petty weaknesses have, in this specific moment, decided to band together and bully me into submission, into conceding that I am staring at the downward path toward my own diminishment.

And that missing word? In hiding, too cowardly to come to my rescue.

Making matters worse is my fiftieth birthday lying in wait. From those who've gone before me, I know to brace myself. I've been warned that, much as I might strain to believe that a number is just a number, I will feel its significance in all of the less gullible cells of my body. I've been told that reaching this number will be like crossing an international border; once on the other side, I will be in a different country, among women whose currency has collapsed and will never recover. The language spoken there is resignation—at times, charmingly inflected with the lilt of humor and irony, but always tightly organized around a semantics of irrelevance, impotence, and decline. An entire lexicon in which to become lost.

But in fact, none of this occurs on my fiftieth birthday. On that day, I happen to be visiting a summer program related to Indigenous languages. For once, I'm one of the few White people in the room. As I exchange life stories with the participants, who come from various First Nations and northern regions of Canada, I keep hearing mentions of elders—of grandmothers and grandfathers and aunties who steadied or redirected life trajectories, who serve as the stars by which others navigate, who are the first to be consulted on matters of importance.

On that day, I have an experience similar to ones I've had several times since, upon encountering an Indigenous perspective. It is as if the world were suddenly inverted, pulled like a sleeve inside out. The fixed elements of the landscape, previously rooted and immobile, begin to waver and shimmer, their reality in doubt. An unfamiliar scenery claims its place.

No wave of despondency breaks over my head the day I turn fifty. Instead, I'm given the gift of altered vision—of a viewpoint from which aging is not a series of inevitable losses, starting small and becoming larger, but a steady accrual of abundance. Becoming very old does not mean lingering in the dim twilight of irrelevance; it is to become an ever more valuable vault stuffed with experience and knowledge.

What does it mean to lose something? It means, simply, that you no longer have something you once had. But the noun "loss" carries added significance, a plaintive moan as an undertone: it means that what you once had but no longer possess was a thing of value, something to be mourned. Not everything lost is a loss—one can be happy to lose a baby tooth, false friends, a crippling inhibition. Of a bad habit or an unhelpful attitude, a friend will advise, "You might want to lose that."

By the time we are in the so-called prime of life, we have lost many, many things. Our bodies have lost the power to heal a broken bone within days. We are no longer able to learn a new language as if we were born into it. We have lost our willingness to throw ourselves to the floor in a fit of temper, and we have lost our porousness to awe and to the experience of time as spacious—as it used to be in those three interminable weeks before Christmas or the luxurious spread of summer holidays when viewed from the threshold of the last day of school.

And yet, even though we look back at our early selves with a rueful nostalgia, we do not, on the whole, think of childhood as a period defined by loss. We see it instead as a period of becoming, a long approach to what will eventually become the true shape of a person. It is a time characterized not by diminishment but by a series of trades. Like baby teeth, certain traits are exchanged for ones that are stronger, more important, or more efficient, overall a good bargain.

At six months of age, an infant can perceive the subtle differences that distinguish the sounds of any language. A six-month-old raised in an English-speaking family can easily hear that a regular *d* is different from its retroflex version, made with the tongue curled back—a contrast that is important in Punjabi, but not in the child's mother tongue. A Japanese child of the same age has no trouble perceiving the distinction between *r* and *l*, an ability no longer shared by either of his parents, who hear both as variants of the same sound. By their first birthdays, however, both infants will have become less sensitive to these distinctions of sound. This is viewed not as a deficit but as growth, a side effect of learning; over time, the child learns which sound contrasts are meaningful in the mother tongue and learns to elevate these while ignoring others. The loss of attunement to the sounds of other languages is a sign of progress in one's own.

How telling, then, that we view a middle-aged person's hunt for the elusive word entirely through the prism of decline and diminishment, never through a lens of transformation or learning. When words go missing, one is apt to think of them as lost, as carelessly dropped through the holes in memory's pockets. We take the futile searches for words to be symptoms of a lexicon that is contracting. But as with Western versus Indigenous views of aging, this perspective can easily be turned inside out.

There is little doubt that as a person ages, words go missing more often, in those moments that language scientists prosaically call tip-of-the-tongue experiences, and that new words are harder to retain. The older person's lapses can be demonstrated in a laboratory version of a competition between young and old: both are given a new set of names to learn and recall, and the young emerge victorious, able to recall a greater percentage of names. But what looks like decline may simply be a side effect of learning. For a young person, the laboratory task is akin to having someone bring a few new books into their apartment, spare in furniture and belongings, and being asked to locate the newly acquired items. For an older person, it's like bringing the same books into a house in which they have lived for forty years: the new books are absorbed into overstuffed shelves, littered about on the ample furniture, and stacked onto piles teetering on the desk, dining room table, and sideboard. Is it any wonder that engulfed in such abundance, the older person will take longer to retrieve a specific item or come up empty-handed or with an armload of substitutions for the requested book?

Astute scientists have asked: If a sixty-year-old can recall only 90 percent of the thousand names she knows, while a sixteen-year-old can recall 98 percent of the hundred names she knows, whose memory is more powerful? What if the purported symptoms of a contracting lexicon are really signs of one that is expanding? Indeed, closer scientific scrutiny reveals that far from shedding words, we hoard them over a lifetime. Unless a person is afflicted by brain disease, her vocabulary continues to grow into old age, becoming a magnificent warehouse of words in which anyone might lose themselves.

∽

What is undeniably lost in the transition from youth to older age is speed. A person my age can only stare in dismay at the towers of evidence that document how, over the course of a lifetime, one becomes slower and slower at performing even the simplest of mental operations. In that regard, I am apparently well into a downward slide that began in my twenties and will continue in a more or less linear fashion until the end of my life.

A mental slowdown, warn researchers, is no trivial matter. It's not as if one can get by simply performing the same computations as a young college graduate but taking more time to complete them, the way a student with a disability might petition for special accommodation when taking an exam. Often, we are not granted the luxury of extra time. Our cognitive lives are lived in the unrelenting flow of real time. Information reaches the senses at certain speeds and must be interpreted then and there. Moreover, a cognitive task may require the precise orchestration of several steps, each under specific time constraints; as with a tight assembly line, a jam early in the production chain can upend the entire system. Even ordinary activities, such as mentally tallying the cost of grocery items or producing and understanding a sentence, demand that certain operations be completed in a timely fashion, before the products of others on which they're reliant melt away in memory. (To add two figures, for example, one might add the tens, then the ones, then merge the two together, but quickly, before the outputs of the earlier calculations vanish.) When one is attempting complex intellectual maneuvers that are time sensitive, to slow down is to risk crashing the system.

Language offers a stark demonstration of time's refusal to accommodate the disability of slowness. Consider the work of listening to a long and looping sentence, in which a web of actions and relationships has been strung out over multiple clauses. Understanding it is like a relay race, with separate computations making up each segment of the race. Acoustic signals must be matched to words stored in memory, which, once retrieved, serve as batons to be passed on and assembled into the latticework of syntactic structure, which in turn must be passed on so that its full meaning can be deciphered. But over the span of every segment, the baton has a time limit; it can survive in memory for only a short time before it dissipates into smoky wisps of nothingness. And the sentence has so many parts to process and assemble into complicated structures, all of which takes time. If the baton is not passed on before it dissolves, the next segment of the race can never be started. Run a sluggish race and you risk being left searching around in bewilderment for the missing baton while the rest of the sentence roars past in a blur of motion.

Given that aging brings with it a merciless slowing of our ability to perform the most basic of mental functions, language should fold into a heap like a house of cards. I should be bracing myself for an imminent collapse of linguistic competence. And yet here I am, old enough for arthritis to have settled into my knees, but reaching more eagerly than ever for books that contain dense and difficult prose. If I've flagged in my ability to gather my thoughts into speech, no one has remarked upon it, nor do I feel any less invigorated after a five-hour conversation over dinner with friends than I did in my twenties.

In fact, people far older than I continue to be strangely effective, not just at uttering and understanding sentences, but even at rocket science—or, for that matter, developing software, translating literature, projecting economic down-turns, diagnosing illnesses based on a rambling patient history, building new theories of nuclear thermodynamics, and so on. One great puzzle for scientists has been why, given the indisputable evidence of degraded performance on simple tests in the lab, older people do so well on dazzlingly complex activities out in the world.

The Indigenous friends who helped me celebrate my fifti-eth birthday found the answer to this question fairly obvious: elders contain an abundance of knowledge that young people lack. As in childhood, aging is not so much a string of losses as a series of trades, a growing into a somewhat different ver-sion of the self than one was at a younger age. Nimbleness and speed—so essential when one knows next to nothing—give way to skill and wisdom. Elders, who have already me-tabolized a lifetime's worth of experiences, have less need for raw computational power with which to efficiently digest new information.

Western scientists are gradually coming to acknowledge

the nature of the trade. Even for language, over which time is such an unyielding master, it is becoming clear that experience is an antidote to the slowing that comes with age. In every leg of the race that must be run in order to understand a sentence, an accumulation of language offers an advantage. Words that have been encountered many times in the past are recognized more quickly than words one has rarely heard or read. The same is true for the structures of sentences, with common phrasings read and understood more quickly than infrequent ones. And it is no less true for sentences that express familiar ideas and events over ones that express novel or surprising ones: the sentence "The dog bit the man" is computed more quickly than "The man bit the dog."

We can hardly avoid accumulating more language as we age; with rare exception, we do not live any part of our lives outside language. And so we come to hoard knowledge not only of words but also of phrases, of the infinite possibilities for composing sentences and the nuances of meaning they might express. By the time we are old, we have spent so much time roaming over the landscape of language we know it like the back of our hand. This is likely why, in laboratory tests, researchers need to crank up the speed or complexity of speech to extreme levels before finding any serious shortcomings due to age, even though older people can be depressingly slow on tasks that require much less intensive computation than the work of comprehending a sentence.

A word such as "portent" may be new to a twenty-year-old, but I have already encountered it many times—even if I sometimes have trouble locating it in my cluttered storage room the precise moment I want to use it. I am familiar with the word's habits and habitats. I know the peers that make up its entourage and the syntactic structures that serve as its watering holes. I am intimate with its gestures, facial expressions, and connotations, with its overtones and undertones, and I know how its demeanor can change in the setting of this sentence or that one.

When I am pitted against the lithe young person, the language race is not as unfair as it seems. My opponent may run like the wind, but I know the terrain; for each leg of the race I find the shortest path.

In the windowless air of a laboratory, the changes that come with age easily take on the appearance of loss. But the more the laboratory resembles the world outside, the less one sees something to mourn. The gulf in performance between young and old is widest when the task in question is "pure"—that is, when the experiment tries to isolate a mental function by stripping away any source of possibly contaminating influence, such as prior knowledge or practice with the task.

On the face of it, this is sound methodology. Even a fourth grader knows that when one sets up a race, it is sloppy to allow the competitors to run races of different lengths, or to have some wearing strappy sandals while others race in high-performance running shoes. If the hypothesis of interest is, for example, that older brains compute less quickly than younger brains, or that they are less efficient at shifting attention from one task to another, or that they retain new material less securely, it is good practice to remove any variables that might either mask or amplify the true effects of age on the mental faculty of interest. In fairness, it is a method that has yielded important insights into which functions are most fragile as we age. But the austerity of such experimental design demands that older subjects leave their greatest talents at the laboratory door. When experience is let into the room, age no longer looks so debilitating.

For instance, one study revealed that older people were even better than young people at remembering whether particular words were ones they had seen earlier in the experiment, but their advantage melted away when the words to be remembered were presented as orphaned items in a list, rather than taking their rightful place in full sentences. Another study tasked participants of various ages with memorizing a list of grocery items and their prices, and found that the older subjects floundered in comparison with the young—but only if the prices assigned to the items were random. When they more reasonably reflected the prices one would find in the aisles of an actual grocery store, the memories of the old were as sharp as those of the young.

Some researchers have suggested that one of the most visible "impairments" of age is the difficulty of learning new information that contradicts what is already known: older subjects are especially poor at remembering altered versions of familiar fairy tales, or memorizing novel spellings of known words or incorrect mathematical equations such as $4 \times 6 = 22$. (When I encountered this last example, I confess I immediately thought of George Orwell's protagonist in *1984*, who heroically resists the totalitarian lie that $2 + 2 = 3$. It is little wonder, perhaps, that certain movements, from the Khmer Rouge to the Soviet regimes, have vigorously recruited and educated the young. To reeducate the old, presumably, involves more costly and brutal efforts.)

And still, we are conditioned to believe that the secret to aging well is to resemble, for as long as possible, a young person. Old people are told to solve crossword puzzles, take up sudoku, sit at the computer to suffer through brain-training "workouts" of dubious value—all in the hope of slowing the downward slide of those mental functions that have been proven in the lab to deteriorate with age. But rather than focus on averting the losses of age, why aren't we determined to cultivate its gains? If age transforms you into someone whose mental power is determined by past knowledge more than by raw computational power—with the former having a far longer shelf life than the latter—a more productive goal would be to stockpile as much experience as you can, of as high a quality as possible, for as long as possible. If you are to become a person who can't help but drag their entire history into every intellectual task, your precious hours are best spent discerning what is true and insightful, in reading widely and deeply, in stuffing your vault with diverse and nuanced experiences that can inform everything you learn and read and think about thereafter. You might also spend time in your mental warehouse putting its contents in order.

I had never *aspired* to be an old person until I spent my fiftieth birthday among my Indigenous friends. (At best, I would wryly remind myself of that familiar quip that growing old is better than the alternative—something that I think many young people truly find hard to believe.) But their obvious esteem for their elders inverted my thinking and fired up my ambition. To be an elder, I learned, it is not enough to be old. One must have filled oneself with valuable experiences.

It seems right, at this time of my life, that I have removed myself from the enclosed spaces of my lab and have turned my efforts toward the work of writing. Into the open air of the empty page, I can drag in all of my past—my discoveries from inside the lab, all that I have read, and all of the pockets of my life into which language has ever squeezed itself. There is no need to be vexed about my lack of speed. Writing a book is inherently slow, archaeological work, more searching and sifting than computing. And I've learned to embrace the fact that writing is much like that maddening attempt to retrieve an elusive word: I know it is there, I can see its silhouette in my mind, but that last step of *uttering* it, of clothing it in its acoustic details, feels like an enormous effort bogged down by the distraction of other words that jostle for attention, by false starts and sidetracks and dead ends. It is a tip-of-the-tongue experience that lasts for hundreds of pages.

A question has nagged at me since my fiftieth birthday celebration: What does it say about a culture that it views aging as a parade of losses, when what is lost with age is most apparent in the artificial tasks of the lab rather than in open-ended work that reflects the richness of a human life? A tacit appraisal underlies the shift from the verb "lost" to the noun "loss." It's hard to avoid the conclusion that contemporary Western society reserves its highest esteem for work that resembles an experiment in a lab: stripped of context or an abundance of knowledge, single-mindedly steered toward a clear and simple goal, with speed as the primary measure of worth.

Our lives have been so carved up into modules that we succumb to a sterile form of accounting. What is most easily measured is what is most highly valued. How quickly a word is read is more important than the subtle fireworks it sets off in the mind, the web of meanings in which it's embedded. How quickly a product is turned out and how much profit it generates matter more than how it enriches or impoverishes lives. Even our universities have taken up the habit of counting publications and citations as the primary metric of worth, bewildered as to how to measure insight. We have come to value work in which the bulk of one's experiences are left at the door.

Implicit, too, is the belief that the past does not much inform the present or future—that in fact it is desirable for the present to disrupt the past, to sever itself from it. In such a world, what good does it do to hoard a warehouse full of experiences? All of these are merely tchotchkes, unwanted heirlooms, impediments to moving at a moment's notice into a discontinuous future. The minimalism of youth is what will allow you to travel lightly and easily.

About 120 miles from where I live is the remarkable historical site of Head-Smashed-In Buffalo Jump. Here, a multitude of Indigenous people used to gather from over vast distances to funnel herds of buffalo into a natural depression and over the edge of a cliff, exploiting the nuances of terrain, the habits and instincts of the buffalo, and their own ingenuity to coordinate what might well have been the largest hunts in human history. Hunts at this precise location can be traced back about six thousand years, and they continued almost without interruption until European settlers emptied the plains of buffalo in the mid-nineteenth century, through the disruptive technology of the rifle and discontinuous habits of mind. Visiting this site fills me with an awe that borders on the sacred. Far older than the pyramids at Giza, in my view it is a cultural site of equal importance. And it is not lost on me that unlike the pyramids, the buffalo jump would still be in active use, much as it was for six thousand years, were it not for the intervention of a culture that placed far less value on the knowledge of its elders.

I make a pilgrimage to this site with increasing frequency as our disruptive technologies move ever faster and break ever more things. Not content to use up the buffalo, we are on the verge of using up our language, feeding it to simulated minds that are disembodied from human lives. The consequences have become impossible to predict. Detached as we are from old knowledge, we risk turning our present moment into a future monument to the past.

I have a friend who lives in Canada's North and devotes her life to preserving her mother tongue of Tłįchǫ; due to historical disruption, all of its words are in danger of going missing, not so much from the minds of the elders as from the minds of the young. Occasionally, in her work as a radio host, she comes across the dilemma of how to refer to a concept that did not exist in traditional Tłıchǫ society and hence has no name. An English speaker might simply appropriate a word from another language ("karaoke") or coin a fresh one ("blog"). My friend tells me that in such instances the elders of her community must be consulted. It is of great importance, she says, that whatever new words are absorbed into the Tłıchǫ language are ones that do not seem alien to the elders. (When a Tłıchǫ term for the AIDS virus was first introduced, for example, the rough translation for the new word was "disease-with-no-cure.") Words must enter the language in such a way as to render generations comprehensible to each other.

There is nothing like the threat of extinction of one's language (and the knowledge that is entwined with it) to make a person feel the urgency of maintaining links to older minds. My Tłıchǫ friend has seen up close the effects of cataclysmic change, how it severs one generation from the next and leaves the young adrift, searching for words and meanings they may not even know they lack. For her, there is no exuberance in turning one's back on the accumulated wisdom of elders.

As our society grapples with the upheavals of technology, it strikes me that the practice described by my friend—to accept innovation, but in a way that is harmonious with the existing lexicon—is a useful one. There is talk now of putting the brakes on our technological disruptions. The brakes that come from a lifetime of knowledge are not a bad place to start. We may believe we can contain and harvest knowledge using artificial minds, but an aggregated language is not the same thing as a language lived amid the crackling particularities of a real life. Rather than rushing blindly toward innovation for its own sake, perhaps we should convene a council of elders and listen closely to what we risk losing and how much change a human life can absorb before it loses coherence. What would it be like, I wonder, if in staring down the existential questions of our age, we drew on the intellectual capacities of the full range of the human life span? If we understood the slowness of age not merely as senescence but as the heft of experience? It seems to me that if our generations continue to become more and more incomprehensible to each other, discontinuity will become its own self-fulfilling prophecy, scattering all our words to the winds.

Limits

It has become nearly impossible to have a meal in a restaurant with friends. If we can hear each other at all, over the racket from the open kitchen and the turbulence of music and voices careening off hard surfaces and colliding with each other, it is with such great effort that no mental juice is left to consider what someone has just said or what you will say in return. In a group of any size, you are doomed to converse only with the person immediately adjacent. Impossible to hang back and witness, from across the table, an argument being spun like a glittering web between two people, and impossible to extract yourself from a conversation that has run itself into the ground in order to join a more promising one. Even in a near-empty dining room, music muddles the sounds of speech. When you ask the server to turn it down, this person—who will cheerfully agree to serve the *poulet aux poires* without the pears or to substitute olives for capers in your salad—informs you that this is beyond their powers. The volume of the music, they claim, is preprogrammed into the sound system. It is dawning on me that this is a deliberate policy of segregation. I look around and see hardly a person over sixty, very few over fifty. I'd heard of a device designed to repel very young people from shopping malls and parking lots by emitting a high-pitched sound imperceptible to their elders—a weapon that turns their acuity of hearing against them. Evidently, it is possible to weaponize, just as effectively, the perceptual decline that comes with age. Like the unruly teenagers, I now belong to an unwelcome demographic. The teens create a disturbance with their chaos and underdeveloped restraint. We who have crested middle age disturb with our visible signs of decay; we are stark reminders to the young of the transience of vigor and beauty. More and more, we stay at home, leaving the dining establishments to those with more capacious energies and appetites.

It is often said that everyone is at best temporarily able-bodied and that to live long is to join the ranks of the disabled. How true this is of our ability to perceive the sounds of speech. A simple auditory test, measuring the ability to hear pure tones at various frequencies, exposes hearing loss among more than two-thirds of Americans older than seventy. But long before this, many people strain to hear one another in noisy rooms or when several people talk at once. Before our ears fail us, our brains begin to have trouble peeling the sounds of speech away from sticky background noise or disentangling the strand of one speaker's voice from a thick cord of many. This work calls for attention to be bestowed upon certain auditory cues while a cacophony of others are discounted, and *ignoring* information, it turns out, is particularly difficult for older brains.

Even worse, as we get older, our ability to process information quickly begins to falter. And while the many gifts of age can often compensate for slowness, speech poses a special challenge: the acoustic information that separates one speech sound from another may come down to a hair's breadth of time. Two- or three-hundredths of a second, in the space between the release of the lips and the vibration of the vowel, distinguish the words "bet" and "pet." In running speech when consonants at the ends of words are often swallowed, a sliver of vowel length sets "weed" apart from "wheat." Such temporal details are blurred by the aging brain; when researchers blur them artificially in the lab and present the resulting speech to young ears, they fare no better than their elders. Unfortunately, residing as it does in the brain and not the ears, slowed processing of speech is not a disability that hearing aids can remedy, a fact that may not be appreciated by younger family members who fail to understand their relatives' lukewarm enthusiasm for the devices.

Live long enough, and the weaknesses of the ear and brain accumulate. A gradual withdrawal begins: first the avoidance of dinners out, then the early departures from loud family gatherings, then the sputtering out of conversations. The flow of language reduces to a trickle. We do not live easily like this, deprived of the nourishment that runs between humans in the form of language; among other consequences, hearing problems put us at greater risk for dementia, with isolation the suspected culprit.

And yet it is not the loss of hearing itself that is so disabling, particularly now that we live in a world where our survival rarely depends upon being able to hear a faint rustle in the leaves behind us. It is language that is crucial to our survival. We can manage without sound quite well; we might miss it no more than we long for the pleasures of echolocation were it not for the fact that so many of us rely on sound as the medium by which language travels.

In graduate school, where a number of my fellow students were Deaf, I first became aware that lack of hearing did not have to entail isolation. With the help of interpreters, these students gave cogent classroom presentations and embroiled themselves in intellectual discussions and hallway gossip. I quickly learned the basics of these cross-cultural interactions: I learned it was rude to keep your eyes fixed on the interpreter rather than the Deaf person with whom you were actually conversing. I learned to give presentations that could readily be transformed into sign. (Avoid racing through technical terms, which need to be fingerspelled, and do not substitute gestures for speech behind the back of your interpreter.) These adaptations were no more difficult than incorporating Slovenian-speaking students into our classes.

There were times when a signed language seemed preferable to a voiced one, and I thought how much better it would be if hearing people were all raised bilingual, each of us able to both speak and sign, as is the case in some communities around the world with high rates of congenital deafness. At loud parties, my hearing peers and I shouted curt sentences into each other's ears, our fragmented exchanges patched together with much shrugging and nodding and pointless

smiling. Meanwhile, the Deaf students were signing in elo-
quent streams to each other from opposite ends of the room,
hands fluttering and heads thrown back in laughter.

These days I wonder why, given how quickly the sounds
of speech become elusive in our later years, our society has
failed to embrace the teaching of signed languages to more
children at school. Learning French or Spanish adds richness
to life, no doubt, and may be essential in some cases, but
it does not offer insurance against a future in which speech
becomes incomprehensible, nor does it help the hearing child
enter the increasingly silent world of her grandmother.

One of the Deaf students in our graduate program married a young hearing woman who had been raised in a Deaf
family. Their vows are captured in the most beautiful wedding
photo I have ever seen: the bride, her eyes brimming with
love, visually frozen in the act of signing "yes." Several years
later, when they were expecting a child, the father expressed
the hope that his daughter would be born unable to hear.
I was startled, but only for a moment. I realized he wanted
what any father did: he wished for his child to be plunged
fully into the culture from which he himself drew so much
love and nourishment, rather than to sit perched at the edge
of it. He wished for her to be immersed in the same river of
sign in which he swam, this abundance, this mother's milk of
his own language.

Most of the world in which we live is imperceptible to us. As
the science writer Ed Yong notes, "Every animal is enclosed

within its own sensory bubble, perceiving but a tiny sliver of an immense world." The German word *Umwelt* refers to this sensory bubble, the totality of what a creature can experience through its apparatus of body and brain. Within these limits, miracles of perception occur. Bees can't see red, but can detect a flower's come-hither ultraviolet, invisible to us. Dogs bumble around in near blindness, but use scent to map out events of the past; I can do so only after a fresh snow, when the tracks that creatures have left behind become visible to me. Peer into the *Umwelt* of an animal, and you become aware of trade-offs; where perception has closed off some links between the mind and the world, it has opened up others.

"The Umwelt concept can feel constrictive," writes Yong, "because it implies that every creature is trapped within the house of its senses. But to me, the idea is wonderfully expansive. It tells us that all is not as it seems and that everything we experience is but a filtered version of what we *could* experience." It is perhaps no coincidence, he suggests, that many who study animal perception are perceptually "disordered"; those who experience the world differently can easily imagine alternative *Umwelten*.

To be stripped of a sense that is available to the majority of humans, then, is to enter one of these alternative *Umwelten*, to become a creature with a slightly different sensory repertoire. Of the blindness that descended upon him in old age, Jorge Luis Borges wrote that it "has not been for me a total misfortune; it should not be seen in a pathetic way. It should be seen as a way of life: one of the styles of living." A muting of one sense often leads to the sharpening of another. In a piece called "Hearing Essay," the musician Evelyn Glennie describes how deafness expanded her ways of hearing. Hearing is, in fact, merely a specialized form of touch, the detection of vibrations in the air through the ears. As her own hearing dulled, Glennie learned to feel vibrations more fully in her body: low frequencies in her legs and feet and high frequencies in her face and neck. She discovered she could even hear through sight: seeing the vibrations of a drum or leaves moving in the wind created an impression of sound in her mind.

Language has no trouble thriving within an alternative *Umwelt*. Its life force is potent enough to not depend upon a single sense, and it readily finds its way into any sensory link available, opening a new route whenever one is closed: we use voice if we can hear; visual sign if we can see but do not hear; touch if we neither see nor hear. These languages adapt themselves to the sensory bubble in which their speakers live. Each *Umwelt* presents its own constraints and possibilities, limits and openings that shape the contours of the language that thrives within it.

Visual sign languages such as ASL feel the pressure of time even more acutely than spoken languages; where the movements of lips, tongue, palate, and vocal folds can be executed within the thinnest shavings of time, hands are much slower articulators. But the added dimension of visual space creates certain opportunities not available to spoken language. Where speech is confined to a sequential flow of sound projected out of the vocal tract, sign languages exuberantly use several body parts simultaneously—separate hands, torso, lips, eyebrows—to layer meanings into small temporal spaces.

Raising the eyebrows while signing a sentence in ASL transforms it into a yes/no question; scrunching them downward turns it into a query as to why.

Freed from the linearity of speech, a sign language can use space as a canvas on which to elaborate meaning. An ASL speaker uses the area around the body to keep track of the various characters that populate a story, bypassing the ambiguous and fraught pronouns of a language like English. In the various spoken languages I know, I need to first settle on the appropriate gender of pronoun and then register whether that pronoun might be misinterpreted by my interlocutor as referring to someone else ("Sam says he loves her . . . Bernice, I mean, not Eloise"). A speaker of ASL assigns a location to each person mentioned and then uses it to refer to them, an elegant system of pronouns that avoids all confusion or gender politics. These locations can then be merged with verbs to indicate who did what to whom: to convey that Sam insulted Bernice, you would begin the sign for "insult" at the Sam location and complete it at the Bernice location; if Sam were the target of Bernice's insults, the movement would be reversed, all without the need for trailing together separate signs for subject, verb, object.

Even when cut off from both sight and sound, language still finds a way, pouring itself into the crevices of shared perception. The story of Helen Keller receiving the fingerspelled version of "w-a-t-e-r" into her hand is well-known, and her teacher is thought of as the heroine who brought language to the poor deaf and blind child. But the form of language Helen received, entirely parasitic on English, bears no resemblance to the kind of language that emerges most naturally among people who inhabit the same perceptual universe of sightless, soundless touch. Imagine learning Arabic by having each of its words spelled aloud to you, in the Arabic names for its alphabetic characters—the word for "book" (*kitaab*) comes to you as *kaaf-taa'-alif-baa'*—and you begin to approximate Helen's initiation into communal language.

What style of language arises among DeafBlind people who are free to shape language in accordance with their shared *Umwelt*? One solution, known as Protactile language, has emerged within American communities of people who were born deaf, learned ASL as children, and then gradually lost their sight. Although ASL was the starting point for the members of this linguistic group, the language they now use has morphed into something very different. In a visual sign language, one forms words by shaping the hands in very precise ways and moving them in the space around one's body. The details of handshape and location are paramount, but for someone who cannot see, and who might try to discern ASL by placing their hands in the air and trying to *feel* the signs as they're being produced, a great deal of information is lost. I imagine that trying to feel ASL might be similar to a Deaf person trying to read lips: only a fraction of the movements involved in speech are visible to the eye (try visually distinguishing between the words "big" and "pick," for example), and the lip-reader is forced to play a game of rapid-fire guesswork.

In Protactile, signs do not float in the air around the speaker's body, but are uttered against the space of the listener's body;

they incorporate the listener's hands, arms, thighs, torso, and face. One of the listener's hands is continuously tethered to the back of one of the speaker's hands, detecting the shapes and movements this hand makes. But the speaker also uses both hands to make contact with the listener's body, and meaning is assigned to specific movements at specific locations. ASL signs may be borrowed if they are easily felt, but are otherwise modified or replaced. For example, where ASL relies heavily on the details of handshape, Protactile uses ingredients that play to the sense of touch. Through tapping or the manner of movement against the listener's skin (such as a walking motion of the fingers or a smooth line traced) or the degree of pressure exerted, it takes advantage of the skin as a perceptual organ, an ingredient entirely missing from ASL. To create complex meanings, the speaker may even involve the listener in a collaborative act of articulation: she may shape the listener's hand into the sign for tree (arm raised at the elbow, with the five fingers splayed out), and then, with her own fingers, describe, for example, a cat climbing the trunk of the tree, nestling in its branches, and so on.

Given the immensity of perceptual space, it should be possible for all creatures to coexist within our separate slivers of this immense world, but we have a way of forgetting that our sensory bubbles are not universal. And so the *Umwelt* of some determines the sensory universe for all creatures, often to their peril: our human desire to see in the dark leads us to flood the night with the glare of light, which lures birds off their migratory routes and insects to a fatal exhaustion beneath streetlamps; our tolerance for traffic noise drowns out the sounds of certain predators, leaving their prey vulnerable to attack. From within the enclosures of our sensory bubbles, we crowd out creatures whose perceptual capacities diverge from ours.

It is the same among humans. We fail to consider or cannot imagine the *Umwelt* of those who occupy different perceptual bubbles. We forget, for example, that the *Umwelt* of the elderly is different from that of the young. As a result, the world is built for the sensory universe of the builders. I have lost track of the number of seniors' residences I have visited in which the dining room is a noisy, open, reverberating space that stymies conversation. And although every person endowed with both sight and hearing could easily learn a sign language, the majority have long insisted that those who are born deaf adapt themselves to the *Umwelt* of the hearing, as if a language in a different modality might somehow leave a person slightly less human—only partially languaged—rather than merely possessing a different style of language.

We neglect the fact that anyone's senses, including our own, capture mere shards of reality. Or as Ed Yong puts it, "Every Umwelt is limited; it just doesn't feel that way. Each one feels all-encompassing to those who experience it. Our Umwelt is all we know, and so we easily mistake it for all there is to know. This is an illusion that every creature shares."

And so, a paradox: to escape the limits of your senses, try locking yourself inside a smaller *Umwelt*. Once you shake off the illusion of all-encompassing perception, it becomes apparent how you have settled into routines, repeatedly trudging down the same narrow paths and leaving vast territories of your *Umwelt* unexplored. Blocking off these paths is a kind of forced freedom; now you have no choice but to make your way through the fields that remain open.

The writer Jhumpa Lahiri set aside her facility with English to write in Italian, a language she knew imperfectly. Her decision was met with some bafflement: *Why write in a foreign tongue?* To trade a language she had mastered for another in which she was hobbled was an odd choice for a writer, all the more because she laid no claim to Italian heritage, nor had any practical or professional incentives to do so.

For Lahiri, writing in Italian was a way of simulating blindness, a practice that illuminated language in a new way, much as Borges's literal blindness did for him. In her book *Translating Myself and Others*, Lahiri writes, "By now, I can see in Italian, but only partially. I still grope around in semi-obscurity." This groping, she claims, leads to a heightened care with language. More vigilance and agility are required of her. In English, she is also blind, "only in reverse. Familiarity, dexterity, and ease with a language can confer another form of blindness. One tends to feel safe, and thus more passive, perhaps even lazy. I can write in English without straining, as I must in Italian, without having to examine and double-check almost every word."

Learning a new language in adulthood is a humbling business in which one rams into limits at every turn. Lahiri describes the frustrations she felt upon learning Italian relatively late in life: "For decades, ever since I immersed myself in the language, ever since I fell in love with it, I've struggled to open a series of doors. Each one leads me to another. The more I confront them, the more I pass through them, the more others appear, needing to be opened, to be overcome." She points out, however, that a door has a dual nature: it is at once a barrier and a point of entry, an invitation. What lies on the other side is not yet known. "I don't wish to live, or write, in a world without doors," she concludes. "An unconditional opening, without complications or obstacles, doesn't stimulate me. Such a landscape, without closed spaces, without secrets, without the presence of the unknown, would have no significance or enchantment for me."

Lahiri's self-inflicted limitations are merely an extreme form of the kinds of constraints artists have long imposed on themselves as a way to spur creativity. We tend to think of art as something that thrives in unlimited freedom. Maybe this is because limitlessness is what we feel when we take in art. Hearing a song or a story might wrench open the chest cavity until we seem to have no body at all, no ribs to confine the largeness of feeling. And so we create false images of artists, portraying them as mere wires for transmitting this energy— the genius who attacks a blank canvas and hours later emerges panting and paint-spattered to stare at his masterpiece, the writer whose floor is littered with manuscript pages after one perfect, feverish night of scribbling. But art is made under every constraint imaginable: within the limits of one's talent and powers of concentration, on scraps of time stolen from employers or family members, under the load of worries about

how to pay for the kid's braces or who will take Mom to chemotherapy. In her book *On Freedom*, Maggie Nelson reveals
that writing "feels like a forced, daily encounter with limits."
Much of the time, making art is like "sanding aluminum for
eight hours and breathing in toxic dust, wondering why you're
not hanging out with your family or binge-watching Netflix
or visiting your sick mother."

Perhaps art is at its essence the articulation of being
human, with all its constraints. And so, artists gravitate to
limits, accepting the strictures of a quatrain or triptych or concerto. Or, they invent new hindrances, having learned that
in the feeling of freedom there is no discovery; in freedom,
we fall into the familiar ways of seeing and moving, and for
this nobody needs art. It is only when the usual becomes
impossible—as when sight dims or a comfortable language
is set aside—that an artist can experiment with unknown
gradations of expression.

It may be that human inventiveness itself is spurred on
by limitations. I find it telling that the innovations of sign
languages and tactile languages were not made by those who
had the capacity to see or hear. There is nothing to prevent
this; hearing children readily learn ASL, for example, when
that is the family language, so the ability to hear is clearly not
an impediment to learning or using a sign language. But sign
languages (of which as many as three hundred are thought
to be in use in the world today) were not invented by clever
hearing people, even though this was in principle possible.
Rather, these languages were born within communities of
Deaf people for whom the usual method of communication

was impossible. The young Nicaraguan Sign Language, for instance, arose in the 1980s when dozens of children, previously stranded in hearing communities that did not sign, were gathered into a national school for the Deaf, where all the latest pedagogical methods were aimed at teaching them spoken Spanish. The children did not succeed much in learning Spanish, but uneducated and linguistically deprived as they were, they did manage to combine their rudimentary and private systems of gestures into a richly textured common language. Similarly, the Protactile language was not brought to life by sighted ASL speakers, even though they were perfectly able to feel its signs on their skin.

Again and again, constraints that on the surface seem as if they would surely imprison human creativity have instead been found to liberate it. For some, physical incarceration with its attendant boredom is the ultimate mind killer. In a famous study, a team of psychologists sent people alone into an empty room for fifteen minutes, with nothing but a machine that delivered electric shock: many of their subjects—a solid majority of the men and a fair proportion of the women—chose to shock themselves into pain rather than merely sit there with nothing but their own thoughts to stimulate them. In light of this study, imprisonment seems the cruelest of penalties, and it should surprise no one that jails continually erupt in violence, a jolt of pain being one cure for the intolerable emptiness of boredom. Nonetheless, for centuries monks have simulated the conditions of incarceration, willingly spending much of their lives alone in a cell. In the desert of the solitary mind, some are able to locate an underground spring. While in prison, Nelson Mandela and Václav Havel cultivated a moral resolve that, upon their release, helped them to lead their nations into a new era. Much of the world's transformative writing has occurred within prison walls: Sir Thomas Malory's *Le Morte d'Arthur*; Marco Polo's *Travels*; Miguel de Cervantes; Oscar Wilde; Dostoevsky. Deprived even of pen and paper, Mahmoud Dowlatabadi composed the five-hundred-page *Missing Soluch* in his head, fixing it in ink only once freed.

Over the course of an eleven-year incarceration at the hands of the Italian Fascist government, Antonio Gramsci produced his most influential writings (*Prison Notebooks*), thereby undermining the goals of his imprisonment as stated by the prosecutor at his trial—to "stop his brain from functioning for the next twenty years." Rather than having the intended effect of numbing his mind, perhaps his lengthy prison term created the very conditions needed for the patient labor of writing. As Maggie Nelson notes, "Patient labor differs from moments of liberation or itinerant moments of freedom in that it *goes on*. Because it goes on, it has more space and time for striated, even contradictory sensations, such as boredom and excitement, hope and despair, purpose and purposelessness, emancipation and constraint, feeling good and feeling otherwise. These vacillations can make it difficult to recognize our patient labor as a practice of freedom in and of itself. 'Art is like having a nail file and being in prison and trying to get out,' says British artist Sarah Lucas."

The incarcerated Gramsci proved to be a consummate practitioner of freedom. Jhumpa Lahiri writes that he "contradicted his confinement through language, resisting it always by communicating and with the staggering amount of scholarly writing he produced. His febrile intellectual activity while in captivity, and the scope of his thought, can best be described in Italian with the privative *sconfinato*: literally, lacking confines, or boundless."

My mother is losing her hearing. As treatment for severe Ménière's disease, she has endured a labyrinthectomy, the surgical removal of the organs of the inner ear, a procedure that has left her completely deaf in one ear. Now she is progressively losing her hearing in the other. The unraveling of threads to others has begun. Interactions with store clerks and medical personnel are riddled with miscomprehensions, and dinners with more than one person leave her struggling to collect scraps of conversation and piece them together; words aimed into her fully deafened ear bypass her entirely. Other ailments of age reel her in close to home, keep her from venturing into unknown places.

If we're to believe the artists who find inspiration in constraint, the shrinking world of the aged has its own gifts to offer. In an interview she gave shortly after winning the Nobel Prize in Literature at the age of seventy-seven, the poet Louise Glück remarked, "One of the few good things to say about old age is that you have a new experience. Diminishment is not everybody's most anticipated joy, but there is news in this situation. And that, for a poet or writer, is invaluable. . . . And though it's grim and unpleasant and bodes ill, it's still, from the point of view of the artist, exciting and new."

My mother is not an artist. I doubt she is stimulated by the novelty of the aging experience. Still, I feel we are missing something, my siblings and I, when, aware of the risks that accompany hearing loss, we urge her to preserve function for as long as possible, beg her to get fitted for a new hearing aid, plead with her to wear it often to avoid atrophy in the auditory regions of her brain, encourage her to adapt to new technologies. She is not always patient with these conversations. In one such talk, I point to the dwindling of her social world and the loss of former enjoyments. She exclaims, "But many of the things I used to enjoy just don't interest me anymore!" It dawns on me that we have been insisting on springing her from the prison of her *Umwelt* rather than learning how to join her there.

An animal's *Umwelt*, notes Ed Yong, is tuned to its most essential needs. A tick, whose entire purpose is to drink mammalian blood, senses only body heat, the scent of butyric acid emanating from skin, and the texture of hair. Birds (whose songs my mother can no longer hear) have more complicated needs. As with humans, their survival depends upon the communicative threads that link them to each other. Even more than human speech, birdsong moves in fast time, containing subtle information within the thinnest of temporal slices. Unlike humans, many birds suffer no hearing loss at all with age, able to regenerate the tiny hairs of the inner ear that we humans sacrifice over time.

Nonetheless, a bird's communicative needs may change

from season to season, and so may its hearing. In the autumn, Carolina chickadees congregate in flocks, calling to each other with their *chick-a-dee-dee* cries, which contain intricacies too rapid for humans to detect. But in the spring, individual birds separate from the flock, find mates, and devote themselves to family. The courtship songs of the male are temporally simpler than the social chatter of the flock; to seduce their mates, the most desirable males sing notes that are pure and true and at exactly the right intervals of pitch. The springtime hearing of these birds is now tuned to love, trading the speed of their hyper-sociable autumn hearing for the ability to discern exact pitch.

Perhaps this is a hint that human needs also change over the seasons of a life. Though trapped in bodies that are prone to pain and disability, the old, whether artists or not, tend to be happier than the young or middle-aged; a number of studies find that contentment expands at precisely the time of life when limits impose the strictest constraints—a startling fact, in a culture that equates happiness with limitlessness. The psychologist Laura Carstensen has found that as the enclosure of a life changes shape, so do a person's desires. The thrill of meeting an attractive stranger or a revered author becomes less compelling with age, and the pleasure of a daughter's visit or tea with a dear friend intensifies. Older people have a greater talent for savoring the small joys of the present moment than the young, who always keep one eye fixed on the horizon yet to be attained, driven by the hunger to explore and accomplish. With age, perception becomes tuned to happiness: in the psychologist's lab, older people remember pleasant words and images more accurately than noxious ones, expending more vigorous brain energy on the former. Among the young, acuity for unhappiness is high. It is as if the senses that detect unpleasantness become dulled with age, as if there were less room—or need—for unhappiness in a contracting *Umwelt*.

Unlike the seasonal changes in hearing acuity among birds, which are driven by changes in sex hormones during breeding season, this very human shift is neither cyclical nor biological. Rather, it appears to be linked to human mortality—that is, to the human perception of time as linear and bounded by death. Carstensen reports that when the young are asked to imagine that they have only a short time left to live, their responses resemble those of the old. Conversely, when the old are asked to imagine a medical breakthrough that will add twenty years to their life, their eyes shift toward the horizon and they abandon the joys of the present. This is the essential tragedy of being human: our capacity for happiness is greatest when we sense death's walls closing in, but given half a chance, we will forsake happiness in exchange for a future.

If we paid closer attention to the actual needs of the elderly, would we find that they are, after all, not so misaligned with their perceptual faculties at this stage of life? In older age, perhaps a person has less need to venture out into crowded spaces and a greater need to draw close to a chosen few; what becomes important is not the chatter of new acquaintances in new places, but having slow and satisfying conversations in intimate settings. Eventually, as hearing loss deepens and the elderly person becomes ever more reliant on seeing lips and tongue moving in time with speech, perhaps this too reflects the greatest longings at this season of life: to sit opposite just one person at a time, close enough to clearly see their face, speaking together in a quiet room, and sifting through a life's accumulation of experiences.

When I ask my mother what gives her life meaning now, she tells me of the monastic joys of reading and contemplation, the deep rewards of a stillness that makes room for her spirituality. She has become like the Desert Fathers, the hermit monks of the third and fourth centuries, who, alienated by the cacophony of the urban world and its endless turmoil, withdrew into the silence of desolate landscapes in order to cultivate a lush interiority. She talks about tuning her perception to the presence of God.

I realize I need to rethink what our future intimacy might look like. Neither of us is likely to become fluent in ASL, but I can imagine the mastery of new forms of expressiveness under constraint if I can resist the urge to keep her anchored in my own *Umwelt* and retreading our familiar paths of communication. All I need to do is open the door to her perceptual bubble and be fully present there. Like someone learning the art of speaking against skin, I may discover a form of language I'd never imagined.

Perhaps our future conversations will be less like the excursion of essay and more like the intensity of haiku. Each word will be weighted with our shared experiences, the sparseness of language making room for all its resonances.

Perhaps I too will discover new powers of perception; maybe I will learn to sit with her in her quiet world and use my eyes to hear, as she does, the stirring of the wind in the leaves, the way it whips through the tall grasses, feel the low rumble of love between us, listen for the soundlessness of the divine.

Silence

—⁀—

I harbor a secret medical fear, amplified by family history, of the Worst Thing That Could Happen, the one loss I'm not sure I could bear. Perhaps everyone has such a fear—dementia, quadriplegia, schizophrenia; there is no shortage of candidates. For me the insurmountable terror is the prospect of a stroke that would leave me aphasic. Language-broken. It is one thing, as far as I'm concerned, to lose your hearing or your voice. I can imagine adapting to language that bypasses speech. But aphasia reaches into the chambers of the brain where meaning is forged, where the nebulous vapors of thought are gathered into the shape of language, or where incoming words—those arbitrary symbols we've collectively agreed to honor as meaningful—bloom into ideas, images, sensations. To be deprived of these capacities would be nothing less than a Kafkaesque nightmare, waking up one day to find myself changed into a member of a separate species—perhaps a raven or an octopus, a creature of undeniable intelligence but lacking (as far as we know) the human talent for passing thought back and forth, one mind to another.

All it would take to trigger this metamorphosis is for a

tiny clot to form somewhere in my body, travel through my blood vessels into my brain, and wedge itself into a narrowing artery, blocking the flow of blood. Thus deprived of oxygen, brain cells would suffocate and begin to die off in minutes. If death were to fan out and spread like a silent gas leak over certain neural regions in my left hemisphere, I might find that I am, in the span of instants, unable to speak, even though the mouth and tongue can perform all other functions. I imagine the horror of discovering that a foot-trampled path leading from thought to word has suddenly been cut in two by an impassable canyon, of looking around and finding that the rolling hills of language over which I've wandered all my life have morphed into a lurid landscape of fissures, deserts, and steep gullies rattling with loose rock. Suffocate other tracts of neurons, and I might find myself releasing long ribbons of speech that no one else agrees to honor as meaningful, a mooring line that finds nowhere to land. I might be incapable of writing my own name or I might stare at text, only to find that it has detached itself from meaning and sound. I might even wake up to find that the inner voice of my own mind has deserted me, the voice that accompanies me even in solitude and silence, collecting my fragments of experience and knitting them into a story that links my present self to my past and my future. If I am unlucky enough, if neural death spreads out over acreages of brain tissue, all of these things may happen to me at once, as they did to the writer Paul West, who, before his stroke, had authored more than fifty books and taught literature at Pennsylvania State University.

Apparently, no other disease, including Alzheimer's or

cancer, drains a life as efficiently as aphasia, at least as measured by standard "quality of life" scales. Among its many
victims, West stands out as a person singled out for an inordinately cruel loss; the obliteration of his language faculties was
so total (resulting in a diagnosis of global aphasia), and the self
at which it struck was so entirely constructed of language—
and so little else—that to read his story is to stir the embers
of my worst fears. In the words of Diane Ackerman, his wife
and a fellow writer, prior to his stroke West had been someone
who "had a draper's touch for the unfolding fabric of a sentence, and he collected words like rare buttons." Shortly after
his stroke, he was assessed by a speech and language patholo-
gist who offered the following prognosis for his long-term recovery: with luck, he might be able to communicate his basic
wants and needs "verbally or in gestures or maybe using a
communication board, with about 80 percent accuracy." How,
wondered Ackerman, could a communicative life restricted
to basic needs ever be enough for the "word-besotted" couple
they had been, a couple who had fallen in love with language
and over language, the fabric of whose entire relationship was
richly embroidered with words, who expressed their affection
for each other with verbal sparring, private idioms, and mutual delight at the mouthfeel of words like "mollusk." How, she
wondered, "could Paul's immense cosmos of words shrink to
the size of a communication board overnight"?

And this was the *long-term* hope. In the days after the
lightning bolt of his stroke, all efforts at communication came
out in the form of a single nonsensical syllable: "mem". The
assault on his brain had left him with this one pitiful token

that stood in for everything he could possibly want to say. *Mem, mem, mem.* As Ackerman writes in her memoir of his illness, "He groaned it, he whispered it, he uttered it civilly as a greeting, he barked it in anger, he solicited help with it, and finally in frustration, when none of that worked, he sat upright in bed and spat it out as a curse."

In my version of the nightmare, language collapses on itself in precisely this manner, like a star imploding at the end of its life, and I become like Paul West, or like the famous patient of the famous nineteenth-century doctor Paul Broca, for whom a variety of aphasia has been named. This patient, the victim of a neurological assault at a mere thirty years of age, suddenly found himself unable to articulate anything but a few swear words and the syllable "tan," produced repetitively and with great urgency. His name was Louis Victor Leborgne, but he was known in the hospital as Tan, in acknowledgment of his erasure, of the fact that his entire essence had been melted down, cooled, and poured into a single, meaningless syllable.

I admit that my fears are an exaggeration. The desperate affliction I've just painted is, in reality, not very likely to descend upon me, at least not permanently, even if I were to suffer a massive stroke. The reduction of a person to a solitary syllable rarely persists; with time, as the inflamed brain cools down, surviving neurons announce their presence, like dazed people rousing themselves and calling out from under the rubble once the earthquake has stopped heaving. Moreover, we now know that language does not huddle within a single region of the brain, making it vulnerable to a targeted attack; it lives as a meandering set of paths and connections that sprawl over vast neural territories, linking together the many different functions that we try to contain within the single word "language." If one pathway is destroyed, a detour can often be found, or a new path is eventually tamped down with repeated crossings. Those whose minds hold multiple languages may find that one or more of them remain fairly unscathed; I have done well to hoard languages throughout my lifetime.

With resolute and repetitive therapy, some meaningful recovery—or re-creation—of lost language is to be expected for most stroke patients. Even Paul West far exceeded his tentative prognosis, after five years of what amounted to roughly twenty to thirty hours of language rehabilitation per week. Despite his ravaged left hemisphere, he was able not only to make his basic needs known but also to use language like a toy, to make jokes, converse—though haltingly—with friends over lunch, and express his affection for his wife in the form of wildly inventive pet names, among them Betelgeuse of Bright Inquiry, Dream Hobbit, Lovely Ampersand of the Morning. It certainly helped that as a fellow word juggler she was able to follow his looping and nonlinear flights of speech and that both she and Paul derived some delight from the jarring word combinations that are prone to leaping from the mouths of aphasics.

It's likely that West's stockpile of language, amassed over a lifetime, is precisely what allowed him to recover as well as he did, despite suffering brain damage so extensive that one doctor who viewed his scans several years after the stroke assumed he was looking at the brain of a patient reduced to a vegetative state of consciousness. West had never been content to keep to the well-traveled routes of language laid down in his early life; his drive to explore the remote regions of language took him far into the backcountry, where, through his peregrinations, his boots packed down a crisscrossing network of tracks. These tracks served him well once the main roads were washed out. Still, the words he proffered were not always recognized by those with more humble vocabularies. Ackerman recounts a session during which a therapist encouraged West to learn to distinguish between real words and the meaningless sounds that often tumbled from his lips. She showed West a picture of a famous painting by Raphael, asking him to identify what he saw in the image. "Cherubim," he replied. Gently, the therapist corrected him: "An-gels. These are an-gels." On another occasion, West was unable to dredge up the word "check" when he wanted to inquire whether a payment had arrived from a publisher. Instead, he asked his wife, "Has that . . . double-barreled entity sent their . . . hmm . . . their . . . *spondulicks*?" Stumped, she asked, "What's a spondulicks?" He asserted that it was a British term for money. Incredulous, Ackerman rushed to a dictionary, only to discover that he was indeed correct.

Eventually, West was able to produce several more books, working laboriously with the help of an assistant during the two or three hours in the middle of the day when language was least slippery. His first post-stroke book was a memoir, dictated with dogged effort, in which he related his experience of aphasia. Even after painstaking revisions during which he applied his intellect like a centrifugal force to separate sense from nonsense, his language retains a slight seasickness that only serves to heighten the vividness with which he describes his linguistic injury. Of the first weeks after his stroke, he writes, "There was a bewildering assortment of false starts and incomplete sentences for the mind only. I no sooner thought of something to say to myself than I forgot it, and I was lucky to get beyond the second or third imagined word. Of course no one in his right mind overheard any of this, the dumb speaking to the silent in a reverse image, so no one was upset. But if this happens 50 or 60 times, one wants a little revenge of some sort." And then, of the reassuring return of inner speech, which anchored him to language as he began to make his way back to speaking again: "The second day in the rehab unit I heard the voice of pellucid, articulate reason droning on in the absence of any sound and I knew at once that I was going to be all right even then, in spite of the evil-seeming things that had been happening to me. I mean that though I hadn't tried to speak yet and the whole world was some kind of abstract fanfare waiting to be fed on or off, I would be all right because I could still think language even though it led to an immensely private universe decorated with the full panoply of speech."

All of this is to say that I shouldn't catastrophize. If I were to be at the receiving end of the Worst Thing, I might be language hobbled, it is true, limping along with painful effort where I once scampered freely. No doubt I would grieve for my former verbose self, as would those who love me (or so I assume, though one can never be sure). My professional life would possibly be over, and my social world might shrink down to those few souls patient enough to endure my lurching disfluencies and opacities of meaning. But in truth, I would hardly be exiled from the human race, rendered octopus-like.

Why, then, do I spend so much time ruminating on this hypothetical calamity, trying to envision a life in which I'm completely stripped of language? I suspect it's because the loss of language approximates, if only asymptotically, that final silence, the permanent extinction of the self. It's no accident that the gift of language sits alongside our other uniquely human endowment: the awareness of our own mortality, blinking constantly like a warning light on the dashboard. Hannah Arendt argued that we humans are burdened by mortality because we see our lives as separate from the rest of our species and from the rest of nature; we fixate on our individual lives, spooled out in linear time with a clear beginning and a defined end, set apart from the cyclical nature of the universe. Language, that medium by which we narrate our separate, linear lives, is quite possibly the source of our mortality, in Arendt's sense of the word. Language thickens the self, peels it further apart from the world in which we are embedded— the world from which our particles derive and to which they will return.

I think it's the loss of the inner voice, even more than the ability to communicate with others, that I fear the most. When I imagine the absence of language, I envision the extinction of my life's plot, of the ability to observe myself as if I were an omniscient narrator. Without this private voice, it's hard to imagine having a detailed sense of my human, mortal self, complete with its knowledge of impending death. Would I be willing to give up language in exchange for the dimming of that blinking light? It seems that I would not. Verbal creature that I am, when I'm faced with the incomprehensible prospect of my own nonexistence, my instinct is to use language to simulate it. I suspect that my morbid projections of life as an aphasic are my mind's attempts to imagine my own absence, before my genetic predispositions rise up and deprive me of the ability to rehearse my own death.

My father died unrehearsed, unlike his own father, who suffered a stroke in his forties and lingered on for a few more years, severely disabled, until a more powerful stroke ended his life. Or rather, not knowing the contents of my father's mind while he was alive, I should say that I had not rehearsed for my father's death. It was at the stunned end of a tender and sorrowful phone call from my mother that I learned he had died without warning in his sleep. His absence detonated in my head as if a patch of my own neurons had been wiped out. Where his voice should have been there was a bewildering silence. It was a silence that spread; he had been one of the only people in my life with whom I spoke Czech, and with his death this language—the only one I had ever heard (and begun to primitively love) while still in the womb, and the only language in which my father had ever been fully articulate— became very quiet for a long time.

This was the nature of grief for me: a heavy and disorderly muteness. I muddled through my days with the vague sense that there were words I was meant to find, but having no idea of where to begin looking for them. Other family members reported some of those comforting experiences that are common after the death of a loved one: feeling his physical presence as if he were sitting right next to them, visitations in dreams, even the sound of his voice. But for me there was only a dumb nothingness. I barely seemed to recall what he looked like, let alone what he sounded like.

"May his memory be a blessing" are the Jewish words of solace after a death. But my memories of my father were like the elusive sentences in Paul West's aphasic mind, breaking apart after the first two or three words. They were unfinished memories was the trouble, stories interrupted midstream. My father died at precisely the phase in my life when the distance between us was the greatest—at a remove from the intimacies of childhood but at a time when I was still in the hot, judgmental flush of earlier adulthood, not yet having resolved my own disillusionments. We were at the height of our misunderstandings of each other. There was the sense that at some point in the future we might work through these. At the time he died, he had been in the midst of a years-long campaign to persuade me to come visit him in the Czech Republic, where he'd returned to live a number of years earlier. But caught in what felt like the urgent linear movement of my separate life, I procrastinated. After his death, it was the conversations we'd not yet had that made the silence so deafening.

But the dead have a way of not staying silent forever, even my abruptly extinguished father. As when the swelling of the brain settles after a stroke and words tentatively resurface,

after some time memories of my father began to spontaneously materialize. One day I was placing cut flowers into a
vase in my usual fastidious manner: arranging, surveying,
snipping a quarter inch from the stem of one flower so that
it stood at just the right height to set off another, surveying
again, shuffling stems here and there, and then setting the
angle of the vase precisely so that its most pleasing composition would be seen as one entered the room. I remembered
just then a moment from my adolescence when my father had
observed me arranging wildflowers in a similar manner. He'd
remarked that maybe I'd enjoy a job in a flower shop making
floral arrangements, because I seemed to have an eye for it. At
the time, I'd peevishly shrugged off his remark, adding it to
my file of evidence that he failed to take my intellect seriously
and that he harbored overly modest aspirations for my future.
But as this memory resurfaced, I heard his words differently. It
occurred to me that he was noticing something *specific* about
me, a detail that set me apart from my numerous siblings (I'd
often had the impression that my parents viewed us as an
undifferentiated mass of children). Perhaps this detail caught
his attention because it bore a resemblance to details woven
into himself that he, in turn, had inherited from his mother.

I'm sure that in my younger years I'd often misread my
father's attempts at connection as subtle disparagement. Much
as I'd suspected him of seeing me only as a blurry shape
throughout much of my youth, it's obvious to me now that
my own vision of him was hazy. Maybe this is how it always
is with parents and children: you need to become separate
enough from each other, accurately discerning where you

end and the other person begins, in order to be able to see the details that are particular to that other. It's only with the appropriate degree of individuation, or so our contemporary Western wisdom would have us believe, that we can stop hearing each other merely as the muffled reverberations of our own emotions and anxieties. As I've grown older and the narrative I've constructed of my own life has gained some depth and subtlety, my father's particular details have come into sharper focus for me. In these recovered and revised memories, he has emerged as warm and companionable. These days I rarely set flowers into a vase without replaying his words and sensing that we're linked in our absorption of the limitless aesthetic possibilities of peonies or columbines, together tilting our heads to assess the results of my fussing with flowers.

His returned presence has come as a great relief, as though I were rehabilitating an essential function of my own brain. In truth, the notion that our selves are enclosed within our own bodies and that our lives are individual strands is a fiction, or at best an oversimplification. It is like the early theories of the brain, which held that language was contained more or less entirely within the brain regions named after Drs. Broca and Wernicke, who first observed that lesions within these areas coincided with certain aphasias. Our selves, much like our brains, are tangles of connections. Just as language reaches far beyond Broca's and Wernicke's areas, laying down pathways that link far-flung tracts of neural tissue, so do we, from within our own skin enclosures, set down our tracks in the minds of others. We think our brains are ours alone, but each time we talk with one another, we synchronize brain states:

If I tell you a story, the patterns of brain activity that arise as I choose my words are closely replicated in your brain as you listen. If we speak often or with intense emotion, the synchrony becomes etched within us; our neurons become prone to firing in similar patterns.

These incursions into other minds become the routes by which the dead remain articulate. Like language that is taken up by alternate pathways in the brain of a stroke patient, the surviving neurons take up the functions of those no longer alive. At funerals, we feel compelled to hear stories about the dead from those who remain living; we need these as evidence that the soul of the deceased has succeeded in dispersing itself.

As comforting as all this is, I can still be bludgeoned by remorse at the thought that my father might have remained unaware, at the end of his life, of the extent of his dispersal into me—indeed, of the ways in which our minds would become ever more synchronized after his death. It pains me that I can't send into his mind my own maturing reflections about our relationship, or memories of how, after his death, I did travel to his homeland, spent time in his village with his family, renewed my proficiency in his mother tongue. I regret that he will never know that my own grief at his death was the catalyst for a book I wrote about the pain of language loss and the joys of recovering it.

A few years ago, I was traveling in the Czech Republic with my siblings on a pilgrimage of sorts to the important familial sites. As we stood at my father's grave site in a churchyard in southern Moravia, it occurred to me that my father, while still alive, had believed that his own consciousness would persist after his death. But synchrony failed me there. I couldn't muster for myself the belief that he could see us at his grave, lighting the candles and laying down the flowers, let alone know what we were remembering and feeling.

Later, I sat in the village *hospoda* with my younger brother Vac, reminiscing over beer and *guláš*. Unlike me, Vac had taken our father up on one of his invitations to visit him in Moravia, and during that time they had managed to clear some stubborn blockages in their relationship. I have a photograph of the two of them that someone took on that visit, their heads leaning in toward each other as they converse.

"The trouble is not just that he died too young, but that he died when *I* was still too young," I lamented. "I wish he'd lived long enough for *me* to live longer. I understand so much more now. We would have so much to talk about if he were still alive."

My brother took a moment to consider this. "I have a feeling," he told me, "that *he* had lived long enough to have a sense of how things would end up between the two of you."

I had to grant that this was probably true. Vac, after all, was the one who'd put in the time; he had a better sense of my father's mind in the years close to his death. In any case, my brother wasn't one to tell a falsehood in order to lessen someone's pain. I then thought of my own children, who were just entering adulthood. What loose ends might they be left with if I were to unexpectedly die? It occurred to me that I should take some measures to try to spare them the kind of bitter remorse I still felt about my father. I made Vac promise that if I were to die abruptly, he would find ways to explain to my children that I had understood something of how a child's relationship with a parent can continue to evolve, deepen, and even repair, long after the parent's death.

My brother Vac will never explain anything to my children after my death. Instead, he was the one to die, of pancreatic cancer, soon after the trip we took together to the Czech Republic.

We spoke often during the five months between his diagnosis, just after his fiftieth birthday, and his death. In rambling, near-daily phone calls, we retraced some of our old conversational routes, about relationships with family members, our ethical and religious beliefs, the things in life that gave us pleasure and the things that did not. More than ever, he was preoccupied with the topic of love, holding up proof of its abundance in his life as if planning a documentary film and gathering reels of footage. In his younger days he had struggled against a headwind of frustrated goals and thwarted expectations, but in the last decade of his life, having put right his most important relationships and living exactly as he wished to, he'd achieved that rarest of states in life: serenity. Now he seemed to be pruning himself of any remaining causes for discontentment.

Nonetheless, as his treatment and his body began to fail, he withdrew from everyone, as if not speaking to anybody at all would postpone the inevitable slide into final inarticulateness. He'd given me access to his electronic medical records, and from across the country I watched in alarm as the test results for his kidney and liver function took a sharp turn for the worse. And yet, when our older brother drove the six hours from Toronto to Montreal, to help him write out his will as they'd planned a few weeks prior, Vac turned him away, claiming it was not yet time to worry about such things.

By the time I flew in from Calgary, and Vac's best friend, Oliver, drove in from northern Quebec, my brother was so determined to recuse himself from the world that we almost had to break his door down before he would let us in. We found a man who was obviously dying: rail thin, jaundiced, barely able to stand. When we drove him to his scheduled chemotherapy treatment at the hospital that week, having loaded him into the car with enormous difficulty, I was not surprised to hear that his treatment was being terminated. The prescribed dose of therapeutic poison risked immediately shutting down his failing liver.

How long? my brother wanted to know. The oncologist told him up to two months. I thought, this poor man does not have two months left, noting how the doctor's estimate of my brother's remaining life span was introduced by the evasive words "up to," in the same way the phrase is used in ads that overpromise the results of a weight loss program.

But for my brother, the proximity of death, inaccurately represented though it was, loosened something in him. There was no longer any reason to hide from the world as if the reality of his impending death would fail to materialize so long as his condition remained unwitnessed. On the day of his death sentence, when Oliver and I brought him back to his apartment, he asked us to stay. He requested an enormous hot dog and wolfed it down with a gusto bordering on mania, as if it were his last meal (which it very nearly turned out to be). He and Oliver smoked while I drank some of Vac's excellent Colombian rum, and we talked for hours with an ease and freedom that shocked me. Each time I suggested we leave him to rest, thinking he was beginning to tire, he would reel us back in for more stories and jokes. He especially seemed to revel in Oliver's low-quality puns, giggling at every feeble attempt at wordplay. Later, Oliver and I would remember it as one of the most wonderful days either of us had ever shared with Vac.

He so wanted to continue living. Somerset Maugham wrote that "the great tragedy of life is not that men perish, but that they cease to love," a line that Julian Barnes, in his book-length rumination on mortality, reads as "a lament for the loss of the ability to feel, first about your friends, then about yourself, and finally even about your own extinction." Which is better, asks Barnes, to "die wrenched away from those you have long loved or would you rather die when your emotional life has run its course, when you gaze out at the world with indifference, both towards others and towards yourself"? My brother was nowhere near done with love. Death came for him not at a time of indifference but at the apex of his happiness. He was less like Maugham and more like Samuel LeBaron, who in his own book about death wrote, "Pretend if you like that death will never come. Your mother calls you to come have dinner, take a bath, and get ready for sleep. You want to believe that bedtime is for the other kids. If you keep on playing, the afternoon will never end."

On the evening of what would be the third-to-last day of

his life, unable to eat and struggling even to swallow water, Vac asked me, "I can't remember, did the doctor say two months or four months?" Knowing full well how misleading I was being in that moment, I told him, as gently as I could: "Two months."

Each death is different, reflecting not only its medical particulars but also the many permutations by which a self can insinuate its way into others. If you are extremely lucky, you may at some point witness a death that lessens your fear of your own. This was Vac's parting gift to those of us who were near him in his last days: he showed us how it was done.

We think of those who tend to the dying as doing just that: as *tending* to the dying, as if the responsibility of care flowed in one direction only, with the person who is firmly planted on this side of mortality providing the services and comforts that will ease the sick person's journey over the threshold. But in my final week with Vac, I realized that the dying person has certain gifts to offer, even a responsibility to those he has caused to love him: it is his task to prepare them for his death, to help them endure life without him. After all, he will be dead. It is the others who will need intensive rehabilitation afterward. They will have to eventually shake off the torpor of grief and fire up the neural remnants of the person who has been extinguished. The work of the dying person is to reinforce, as much as possible, those faint tracks he has laid down in other minds, to send as much of himself as he can into these beloved minds, for them to do with what they need to do so that they (and he) can go on living after his death.

There are times in a life when neural connections are eagerly made. In a child's first few years, more than one million new synaptic connections take place every second, in a furious proliferation of axons and dendrites that seek each other out as if driven together by a fierce hunger. Within the neural circuits that enable language, this connective frenzy peaks in middle childhood, then drops off sharply, which is likely why a language learned after puberty always remains somewhat alien in the mind it inhabits. Certain conditions can accelerate new connections; it has been discovered, for example, that infants more readily learn the sounds of a new language when they are in the physical presence of the person uttering them than when they observe a video recording of the same person uttering the same sounds.

Surely something similar is true for the parts of the self that cross from one mind to another. I suspect there are critical periods during which there is a surge in connections between two minds, that there are times and circumstances when our brains are especially receptive to synchronizing with each other. I am sure that the days leading up to death are among them.

Language began to leave Vac near the end. Speaking became too strenuous, though for some time he could still follow conversations around him. When my siblings and I joked with each other about our mother's propensity to supply us with far too much food, he chuckled and nodded knowingly, having been the chief recipient of her excessive food love for the five months of his illness. As the hours went on, he began to weave in and out of our shared physical reality, slipping into versions that ran in parallel, at times merging them with ours. His words often had the resonance of other dimensions, and his sense of time bent in ways that diverged from our experience of it. Then came long periods when no language at all passed between us.

And yet blending selves had never been so easy. When I sat next to him on his bed, having poured myself a drink of his rum (which he could no longer swallow), I held the glass up for him to sniff. He inhaled deeply, pulling into himself all the good things the world still had in store for both of us. Each time I took a sip, he gave a small sigh of pleasure, as though he had a direct line to the sensation of the liquor's warmth spreading in my throat. I, in turn, had a direct line to the way in which he locked onto the pure beauty of the moment, everything else fading away.

We were porous to each other despite the absence of language—or perhaps because of it. It occurred to me to wonder whether Vac was in a state akin to the mystical experience that the neuroscientist Jill Bolte Taylor has described in her account of her own stroke: When an artery ruptured, spilling blood into Broca's and Wernicke's areas, silence cloaked her brain. But far from being thrown into the desperate panic that I've long imagined would grip me under such circumstances, she writes of her relief at the muting of her continuous brain chatter. As her mind quieted, she found herself detached from her autobiographical memories and floating free from any concerns about the future, losing all awareness, in fact, of any division of time into past, present, and future. All of this provoked "an expanding sense of grace," she writes. "I sensed the composition of my being as that of a fluid rather than that of a solid. I no longer perceived myself as a whole object separate from everything. Instead, I now blended in with the space and flow around me." Cut free from the sense that she was a solid being, an entity with borders that separated her from the rest of the universe, she claims it became impossible to conceive of personal loss, whether through heartache, injury, or even death.

Whatever was going on in Vac's brain in those last wordless days, he was busy diffusing himself beyond his own membranes. I spent long stretches of time propping him up from behind as we sat on his bed, in an effort to ease the fierce attacks of acid reflux that would come over him. As I held his wrecked body, the slow rise and fall of our chests moved in unison. On each exhale, he released particles of himself; on each inhale, I breathed them in. They traveled through my bloodstream, pushed themselves into the ends of my fingertips, wound their way through the synaptic tangles of my brain. Every breath existed in perfect isolation, suspended in an eternal present. And as I sensed language withdraw from my brother, I could feel my own memories of him crystallizing within me in the form of words—as if it were up to me not only to drink for him now but to hold together the linear thread of his separate life.

The moment of his death took place some hours after I left him for the night in Oliver's care. I didn't sleep; the wind howled through the cracks in my windows, and all night I thought, that is death coming for Vac. And then came Oliver's call.

When I returned to his room just after dawn, I found Vac in his bed, sitting up and leaning forward in the posture that had best seemed to ease his pain. His eyes were open and he wore a soft expression on his face, as if he were taking a very long time to consider something I had just said.

Sadness would come later, but in the days after Vac's death we felt no sense of loss. We were filled up, full of Vac, brimming with gratitude for the way he had streamed himself into us.

A week later, Oliver and I sat down together to record several hours of audio in which we narrated his last days. We felt compelled to immortalize the beautiful details of his death: How right after he heard that his chemotherapy was being withdrawn, he told the nurse about the day one August when we had climbed Mount Temple and sat in unblemished peace at the summit, gazing at the world spread beneath us. (Just before he described them to the nurse, those very same images had been flitting through my own mind.) How his musical ear never erred, even as death brushed up against him: how he'd criticized my attempts at singing while I washed the dishes, and how he'd been openly annoyed at Oliver's choice of deathbed music. His joy at hearing that all five of his siblings were boarding flights or climbing into vehicles to come see him. The way he declined a dose of morphine, as if, in those last hours, he wanted to remain lucid in the company of his loved ones. How his five-toed cat kept vigil next to his hip.

All these details existed in what had felt, at the time, like a present tense that extended in all directions. But Oliver and I knew that we needed some way to carry them forward into the future. Together we tried to gather these experiences, which had spilled outside the boundaries of language, and pack them into the only containers we had for preserving them. It was an impossible task, like trying to capture the sunlight of summer and the scent of fresh grass and strawberries and the sound of bees gorging themselves, and press all of it into jars of pickles and jams to be stored on a shelf.

I am still caught in linear time myself. And so I have listened to these recordings many times, and it has been one way to keep alive all the synaptic connections between my brother's life and mine that formed in the crucible of those expanded moments near the end of his life.

Here is the jar that I've opened most often: in the hours before dawn, as the stillness of night shifted toward the sounds of morning, garbage trucks clattering and traffic beginning to rev up its omnipresent daytime hum, Oliver had the sense that Vac would rather not spend another day in his body. He began to recite the evidence of Vac's successful diffusion into other minds. For several hours, he narrated every shared memory he could think of, from the day they first met in junior high school to the moment at hand. When he got to the end, he started all over again.

Was Vac able to travel with Oliver through the lines of these stories, in those final moments before he surrendered his last remnant of language and the last of his own, separate human life? It doesn't matter. In the end, Vac knew that all of language could be melted down, cooled, and poured into a single syllable: "love." In response to Oliver's recitations, he offered up the word, repeated over and over again. "Love. Love. Love." Oliver sent it back to him: "Love. Yeah, Vac, love." And Vac responded, "Love. Love."

This is all I need. This is how Vac left me with everything I needed to face my life without him, with everything I need each day to withstand the terrors of linear time, and even with what I would eventually need upon learning, only eighteen months later, of the deadly return of my husband's own previously vanquished cancer, his diagnosis a harbinger of a literally unspeakable loss that would leave my brain feeling as if one of its hemispheres had been removed.

I have this moment in which I'm reminded that all of our words, all of our languages, these splendid palaces that inevitably fall into ruin, exist for only one thing. I have this moment into which my brother's life is compressed, this moment of him and Oliver passing the word "love" back and forth between them, until there is nothing more to be said and Vac steers his small boat into the great silence.

Notes

These notes do not pretend to offer an exhaustive overview of relevant research, nor are they meant to document the sources for every assertion I've made that leans on the work of others. Rather, they are intended as an invitation to the curious—a portal through which one might enter and begin an exploration of the vast body of research on language or make a deeper connection to the works I have cited. In this spirit, I've done my best to select writing that is as accessible as possible to the nonspecialist reader. The works listed here should be reasonably available to those without access to an academic library (Google Scholar is a useful tool for locating most of these writings). Moreover, I've tried to avoid writing that is so technical as to be discouraging to a general reader, though some disorientation is to be expected upon entering an unfamiliar approach to language.

I hope the reader will take these sources as openings to further exploration and never the last word on a subject, which no scientist or scholar should ever claim to have. If a subject fascinates, I encourage the reader to follow the through line of the research by examining some of the work that is cited in the writings I've listed below and by searching for work that picks up the thread from there.

Before meaning

5 *[An infant's] mind flares with recognition when it hears the language that flowed outside the flesh walls that cradled it.*
Newborns prefer listening to their mother tongue over other languages, as discovered by the following seminal studies:

Jacques Mehler, Peter Jusczyk, Ghislaine Lambertz, Nilofar Halsted, Josiane Bertoncini, and Claudine Amiel-Tison. (1988). A precursor of language acquisition in young infants. *Cognition*, 29(2), 143–178.

Christine Moon, Robin Panneton Cooper, and William P. Fifer. (1993). Two-day-olds prefer their native language. *Infant Behavior and Development*, 16(4), 495–500.

These studies show that by the time they are born, infants have learned enough to be able to distinguish the language spoken around them from other languages. Since not all of the qualities of speech can pass through the tissues and fluids that enclose a fetus, what can newborns have already learned about their language? To simulate what the fetus might be hearing in utero, speech scientists run speech through a low-pass filter that distorts acoustic information at the higher frequencies of speech. This makes it impossible to distinguish the details of one consonant from another, for example, but it preserves the rhythmic character of speech, its typical melodies, and the general structure of its syllables (all of which together are called a language's prosodic characteristics). When newborn babies hear the filtered speech of several different unfamiliar languages, they distinguish between languages with different prosodic organizations, but not between different languages that have similar prosodic properties, as shown by the following study, giving us a sense of how they might be hearing and responding to languages in utero:

Thierry Nazzi, Josiane Bertoncini, and Jacques Mehler. (1998). Language discrimination by newborns: Toward an understanding of the role of rhythm. *Journal of Experimental Psychology: Human Perception and Performance*, 24(3), 756–766.

9 *Order begins at the pulsing center of language, as if a fetus were somehow conditioned, by nearness to its mother's heart, to seek out the regularity of rhythm that propels speech forward.*
The sound of its mother's heartbeat and voice may prompt the development of a fetus's auditory system, according to the following study of infants born very prematurely (between twenty-five and thirty-two weeks of gestation). In this study, some infants heard recordings of their mother's heartbeat and voice (through a low-pass filter, to mimic what a fetus might hear in utero), whereas others heard only ambient hospital sounds. After a month, preemies who'd been exposed to sounds of the mother's voice and heartbeat had better-developed auditory regions in the brain. The authors suggest that the presence of these sounds may help prepare the fetal brain for language learning:

Alexandra R. Webb, Howard T. Heller, Carol B. Benson, and Amir Lahav. (2015). Mother's voice and heartbeat sounds elicit auditory plasticity in the human brain before full gestation. *Proceedings of the National Academy of Sciences, 112*(10), 3152–3157.

11 *But how do these infants intuit the shapes of words, immersed as they are in language in its liquid form?*

The great majority of words spoken to an infant are not uttered in isolation, with silence clearly marking their boundaries; instead, they are uttered within a river of speech, and the child must somehow determine where each word ends and another begins—an exercise that will be familiar to anyone who's ever been plunged into an environment in which conversation swirls in an unknown language. The following study was the first among many to demonstrate that babies can break speech down into coherent "units" based solely on the statistical fact that syllables within units (words) are more likely to occur side by side than syllables that originate from different words. In this study, Jenny Saffran and her colleagues found that infants began to learn the invented "words" of a fabricated language after only three minutes of continuous speech.

Jenny Saffran, Richard Aslin, and Elissa Newport. (1996). Statistical learning by 8-month-old infants. *Science, 274*(5294), 1926–1928.

Adults can intuit these and other patterns too, but there is some intriguing evidence to suggest that adults may have different strategies from children and babies for learning the patterns of an unfamiliar language, which may explain why adults who begin learning a language late in life rarely achieve the same degree of proficiency as child learners of the same language:

Carla Hudson Kam and Elissa Newport. (2005). Regularizing unpredictable variation: The roles of adult and child learners in language formation and change. *Language Learning and Development, 1*(2), 151–195.

12 *[Babies] babble alone in their cribs like ardent believers touched by the gift of tongues, and though their babble has no meaning, it becomes a closer and closer imitation of the structured sounds of the mother tongue.*

A baby's babbling reflects the sound patterns of its mother tongue. Researchers now think that the long period of nonsensical babbling that most infants go through is a form of intensive vocal practice. As the following study suggests, it seems that babies spend many hours learning to match up the speech sounds they hear with the movements of their mouth, tongue, and lips—a hint that the vocal skills needed for language are not instinctive but quite difficult and need to be learned:

D. Kimbrough Oller, Leslie Wieman, William Doyle, and Carol Ross. (1976). Infant babbling and speech. *Journal of Child Language*, 3(1), 1–11.

Practice is needed for sign languages as well; babies born into Deaf families babble with their hands if they're exposed to a sign language, producing hand movements that are noticeably different from those made by infants who are not exposed to sign language. They do this of their own initiative, without prompting from adults. The following paper documents the differences between the hand movements of Deaf and hearing babies:

Laura Ann Petitto and Paula Marentette. (1991). Babbling in the manual mode: Evidence for the ontogeny of language. *Science*, 251(5000), 1493–1496.

13 *[E]ven the most articulate of apes fail tragically in their efforts to shape the sounds of speech.*
Primates are surprisingly bad mimics of speech. Most of the vocal sounds made by monkeys and apes seem to be instinctive rather than learned. For example, a "switched at birth" experiment between rhesus monkeys and Japanese macaques showed that the adopted animals sounded more like their biological parents than their adoptive ones, a scenario that never happens with humans, who are not biologically destined to speak any particular language:

Michael Owren, Jacquelyn Dieter, Robert Seyfarth, and Dorothy Cheney. (1993). Vocalizations of rhesus (*Macaca mulatta*) and Japanese (*M. fuscata*) macaques cross-fostered between species show evidence of only limited modification. *Developmental Psychobiology*, 26(7), 389–406.

Mammals in general are not good vocal imitators (unlike birds), even when they can readily learn to *distinguish* sounds of speech; your dog may understand many words and commands, but it's unlikely that you've managed to get him to talk back to you. A few mammalian species do show an impressive ability for vocal mimicry, including some of the sounds of speech. But surprisingly, they are not among our closer relatives, or even animals we tend to spend much time around. Good vocal imitators include certain aquatic mammals (such as whales, dolphins, and seals), elephants, and some species of bats, as noted in the following review of animals' vocal learning abilities:

Vincent Janik and Mirjam Knörnschild. (2021). Vocal production learning in mammals revisited. *Philosophical Transactions of the Royal Society B*, 376(1836), 20200244.

13 *[A]mong songbirds, we find our kindred patternmakers and imitators of sound.*

The many parallels between language and birdsong have been well-known for some time; in fact, Charles Darwin himself speculated that birdsong might be an evolutionary precursor of human language:

Charles Darwin. (1871). *The descent of man*. New York: D. Appleton. Available at Project Gutenberg, retrieved Jan. 22, 2023, www.gutenberg.org /ebooks/2300.

A long and detailed summary of the similarities and differences between birdsong and language can be found in this article:

Allison Doupe and Patricia K. Kuhl. (1999). Birdsong and human speech: Common themes and mechanisms. *Annual Review of Neuroscience*, 22(1), 567–631.

17 *"Whenever I read a modern poem, it's like my brother has his foot on the back of my neck in the swimming pool."*

This is a quotation from a teenage student of poetry, reported by Billy Collins in his introduction to the following anthology of poems:

Billy Collins. (Ed.). (2003). *Poetry 180: A turning back to poetry* (pp. xv–xvi). New York: Random House.

17 *These scholars say we are driven to maintain meaning at all costs.*

Uncanny, nonsensical, or existentially threatening experiences provoke attempts to restore a sense of order and meaning, as argued in the following article. These experiences can be profound (meditating on one's impending death) or trivial (watching a Monty Python sketch), according to some researchers, but they share the capacity to trigger an attempt to restore equilibrium in some meaningful way:

Travis Proulx and Steven J. Heine. (2010). The frog in Kierkegaard's beer: Finding meaning in the threat-compensation literature. *Social and Personality Psychology Compass*, 4(10), 889–905.

Minds, meeting and parting

22 *My most important work then was to merge my mind and attention with yours.*

In a lucid and very readable article, Paul Bloom lays out some of the evidence that has convinced psychologists that children do much more than passively register associations between words and things in the world—that they actively generate theories about a speaker's intentions and make inferences about why the speaker used *this* word in *this* particular moment:

Paul Bloom. (2002). Mindreading, communication, and the learning of names for things. *Mind and Language, 17*(1–2), 37–54.

Dare Baldwin is one of the pioneers of research exploring how children learn language by making inferences about the contents of others' minds. This paper with Jodie Baird puts that work in a broader context, showing how mind reading is at the heart of how children and adults alike make sense of the human world:

Dare Baldwin and Jodie Baird. (2001). Discerning intentions in dynamic human action. *Trends in Cognitive Sciences, 5*(4), 171–178.

24 *Language taught us to look closely for such essences.*
        The psychologist Sandy Waxman has an extensive body of work, in collaboration with her many students and colleagues, devoted to exploring how language prompts infants and young children to interrogate their world in focused ways. In the earliest months, the very presence of language (or a language-like signal) tunes attention, and as children become more linguistically sophisticated, they use their knowledge of grammar and syntax to direct their attention more precisely to properties, actions, and categories both coarse and fine. The following paper lays out the details of this scientific program:

Sandra Waxman and Erin Leddon. (2011). Early word learning and conceptual development: Everything had a name, and each name gave birth to a new thought. In Usha Goswami (Ed.), *The Wiley-Blackwell handbook of childhood cognitive development* (pp. 180–208). Malden, Mass.: Wiley-Blackwell.

The effect of infants' early experiences with language upon their thinking is profound and far-reaching. The following paper offers a breezy, bird's-eye tour of some of the research and its implications:

Athena Vouloumanos and Sandra Waxman. (2014). Listen up! Speech is for thinking during infancy. *Trends in Cognitive Sciences, 18*(12), 642–646.

25 *[C]hildren can't enter into meaning unless an opening is provided.*
        By re-creating some of the conditions that confront infants who are

trying to link language to their observations of the world, the following study makes it clear that word learning is no trivial task, given that people often talk about things that are invisible or abstract:

Jane Gillette, Henry Gleitman, Lila Gleitman, and Anne Lederer. (1999). Human simulations of vocabulary learning. *Cognition*, 73(135), 135–176.

In the following detailed study, researchers document the specific behaviors and interactions between parents and children that best support word learning, showing that learning is difficult unless there is a clear alignment in the timing of the uttered word and some physical indication of its meaning:

John Trueswell, Yi Lin, Benjamin Armstrong III, Erica Cartmill, Susan Goldin-Meadow, and Lila Gleitman. (2016). Perceiving referential intent: Dynamics of reference in natural parent–child interactions. *Cognition*, 148, 117–135.

28 *"I left the well-house eager to learn."*
Helen Keller's recollections of her initiation into language are vividly rendered in chapters 2 to 5 of her memoir:

Helen Keller. *The story of my life.* (1903). Available at Project Gutenberg, retrieved Jan. 22, 2023, www.gutenberg.org/cache/epub/2397/pg2397-images.html.

37 *"Everything would be fine if language did not deceive us."*
The lines from Czesław Miłosz are drawn from this:

Czesław Miłosz. (2001). From the rising of the sun (Lillian Vallee, Trans.). In *New and collected poems, 1931–2001* (pp. 284–285). New York: HarperCollins.

37 *As children, we sense that there are risks to merging minds with others.*
Given that the great majority of what humans learn comes from the verbal reports of others rather than what can be seen, heard, or touched directly, scientists are very interested in understanding how we learn to evaluate the knowledge passed on to us by others—what information do we let in, and what do we block? The very beginnings of selective trust have been investigated by scientists who study word learning in infants. The following paper offers a detailed empirical review of the literature, looking closely at the cues that children use to assess the speaker's knowledge and trustworthiness and what happens when such cues conflict with each other. For example, does the child rely on a familiar teacher who has just made

an error in naming an object, or a total stranger who seems to use language accurately? How do children, over the period of their preschool years, during which word learning occurs at an explosive rate, learn to fine-tune their degree of openness to other minds?

David Sobel and Zoe Finiasz. (2020). How children learn from others: An analysis of selective word learning. *Child Development*, 91(6), e1134–e1161.

The following paper takes a more philosophical stance, suggesting that when children evaluate a speaker, they do more than probe the reliability of the speaker's knowledge; they also expect their conversational partners to enter into a mutual pact of trust with them, whose betrayal can have emotional and moral consequences:

Melissa Koenig, Pearl Han Li, and Benjamin McMyler. (2022). Interpersonal trust in children's testimonial learning. *Mind and Language*, 37(5), 955–974.

42 *I have read studies suggesting that entirely different thoughts are summoned when people of liberal and conservative political leanings say the words "right" and "wrong."*
Jonathan Haidt has studied how culture and political orientation can dramatically shape the ways in which people think and talk about moral issues. His book provides a detailed overview of this work, which prompted me to generate my list of words with divergent meanings:

Jonathan Haidt. (2012). *The righteous mind: Why good people are divided by politics and religion*. New York: Vintage.

Feral polyglot

53 *Among these legends is the notion that children who hear multiple languages willy-nilly are unable to distinguish between them.*
An enormous body of research counters the many myths and misconceptions about raising children in more than one language. Most of this work is written with other researchers as the intended audience, but below are some resources for those who are unfamiliar with the research but are looking for reliable information about bilingualism or multilingualism. The following article answers questions that may come to mind for many parents or educators:

Krista Byers-Heinlein and Casey Lew-Williams. (2013). Bilingualism in the early years: What the science says. *LEARNing Landscapes*, 7(1), 95–112.

This article considers the science of bilingualism as it relates to the varied and complex realities that face many families who might wish to raise a bilingual child:

Laia Fibla, Jessica E. Kosie, Ruth Kircher, Casey Lew-Williams, and Krista Byers-Heinlein. (2022). Bilingual language development in infancy: What can we do to support bilingual families? *Policy Insights from the Behavioral and Brain Sciences*, 9(1), 35–43.

The following article considers research on the outcomes of bilingual education and dispels concerns that such education may disadvantage children who are educated in two languages:

Ellen Bialystok. (2018). Bilingual education for young children: Review of the effects and consequences. *International Journal of Bilingual Education and Bilingualism*, 21(6), 666–679.

A treasure trove of insights about bilingualism can be found on the *Psychology Today* blog maintained by François Grosjean between 2010 and 2021. Grosjean is a renowned figure in the field of bilingualism, and his blog also includes guest posts by other experts:

www.psychologytoday.com/ca/blog/life-bilingual.

58 *It is as if children think that the language one speaks is immutable, the very stuff of which one is made.*
Katherine Kinzler is a leading figure when it comes to studying the social categories that children and adults construct on the basis of language. Her article below offers an expansive and readable summary of this fascinating field and a lucid discussion of its implications. It is chock-full of studies revealing how sensitive both children and adults are to language as a marker of identity, ranging from children's beliefs about the immutability of language to adults' persistent biases regarding accent. It also offers a nuanced view of how one's experiences can influence these responses. For example, she discusses how exposure to linguistic diversity can make a person less rigid about social categories based on language and how Black children know from a younger age than White children that race is less malleable than language.

Katherine D. Kinzler. (2021). Language as a social cue. *Annual Review of Psychology*, 72, 241–264.

For those wishing to delve even deeper, Kinzler has a wonderful book on the same subject:

Katherine D. Kinzler. (2020). *How you say it: Why we judge others by the way they talk—and the costs of this hidden bias.* Boston: Mariner Books.

60 *More and more, the child begins to emulate those who speak the more valued language and edges away from the language of her own parents.*
      The shift away from a minority family language in favor of the dominant language in a society is widespread and not limited to North America. It leads to ruptures between generations in immigrant and Indigenous families and, in the case of small or vulnerable languages, can result in the eventual extinction of the ancestral tongue. I've written a book exploring such language loss, drawing on my own experiences and the memoirs of other writers, as well as on scholarly research related to the cognitive and social aspects of bilingualism:

Julie Sedivy. (2021). *Memory speaks: On losing and reclaiming language and self.* Boston: Harvard University Press.

60 *It is true that knowing only one language comes with a certain efficiency in using it.*
      There is a good deal of evidence that some aspects of language use are slightly more sluggish for bilingual people than for monolingual people. But the details, as always, are complicated, because the term "bilingualism" encompasses many different language histories and situations. The following article offers a detailed review of some of this literature, highlighting a number of factors that determine how strongly two languages within a single brain interfere with each other:

François Grosjean. (2018). Spoken word recognition. In François Grosjean and Krista Byers-Heinlein (Eds.), *The listening bilingual: Speech perception, comprehension, and bilingualism* (pp. 65–85). Hoboken, N.J.: John Wiley & Sons.

61 *It is also true that the presence of a second language very subtly alters the shape of the first one that took up residence in the same mind.*
      It's well-known that a first language influences how people speak a new language they are learning; this is why we can distinguish the accents of people whose first language differs. Much less obvious is that a new language can change the way people pronounce the sounds of their native tongue, often after very little exposure to the new language. The following paper is somewhat dry, but it offers a very thorough review of this intriguing line of research:

Natalia Kartushina, Ulrich H. Frauenfelder, and Narly Golestani. (2016). How and when does the second language influence the production of native speech sounds: A literature review. *Language Learning*, *66*(S2), 155–186.

A second language can also redraw the boundaries of word meanings in the first. This paper shows how learning the Russian words for beverage containers (a task that took a mere twenty minutes) affected how native English speakers then named containers in their own language; for example, their criteria for what distinguishes a glass versus a cup shifted in the direction of the Russian categories:

Barbara C. Malt, Rachel L. Jobe, Ping Li, Aneta Pavlenko, and Eef Ameel. (2016). What constrains simultaneous mastery of first and second language word use? *International Journal of Bilingualism*, *20*(6), 684–699.

61 *A brain's allegiance to a single language is a form of selective hearing.*
Over the course of the first year of life, babies raised in monolingual families learn to attend to the sounds of their own language and disregard the fine details of the sounds of other languages. This phenomenon is known as perceptual narrowing. The following article compares monolingual infants to bilingual babies and finds that children who are raised in two languages maintain a greater openness to the sounds of other languages:

Krista Byers-Heinlein and Christopher T. Fennell. (2014). Perceptual narrowing in the context of increased variation: Insights from bilingual infants. *Developmental Psychobiology*, *56*(2), 274–291.

This study explored how exposing toddlers to multiple accents made it easier for them to understand words in a new accent they had never heard before:

Christine E. Potter and Jenny R. Saffran. (2017). Exposure to multiple accents supports infants' understanding of novel accents. *Cognition*, *166*, 67–72.

Prosthesis

69 Puhpowee *is the unseen, animating force that inhabits the natural world.*
A discussion of the Potawatomi concept of *Puhpowee* appears in Robin Wall Kimmerer's beautiful essay, which is not about reading but about the equally fascinating subject of the grammar of animacy in Potawatomi and many other Indigenous languages:

Robin Wall Kimmerer. (2013). Learning the grammar of animacy. In *Braiding sweetgrass: Indigenous wisdom, scientific knowledge, and the teachings of plants.* Minneapolis: Milkweed Editions.

70 *Among scientists who study reading, there is agreement that such laborious, explicit teaching is necessary.*
    There has been much less agreement among educators about the benefits of deliberate teaching of the correspondence between letters and sounds, leading to what have become known as the reading wars, with fierce debates in pedagogical circles about the best methods for teaching children to read. However, there is growing evidence, now increasingly recognized among educators, that children do much better at learning to read when the curriculum includes a phonics-based component that highlights the relationships between individual letters and sounds. The following article lays out the scientific case for phonics; it also discusses many of the skills that go into reading, beyond basic word decoding:

Anne Castles, Kathleen Rastle, and Kate Nation. (2018). Ending the reading wars: Reading acquisition from novice to expert. *Psychological Science in the Public Interest, 19*(1), 5–51.

    The psychologist Mark Seidenberg's book offers a wide-ranging exploration of reading, from the history of writing, to the psychology and neuroscience of reading, to pedagogy and public policy:

Mark Seidenberg. (2017). *Language at the speed of sight: How we read, why so many can't, and what can be done about it.* New York: Basic Books.

70 *The number of children who learn to read without much help from adults is exceedingly small.*
    A tiny proportion of children (by some estimates no more than 1 percent) appear to learn to read with little to no formal instruction. This article summarizes what is known about such children:

Lynn A. Olson, James R. Evans, and Wade T. Keckler. (2006). Precocious readers: Past, present, and future. *Journal for the Education of the Gifted, 30*(2), 205–235.

70 *There is much about reading that is unnatural, that pushes against our senses.*
    Learning to read involves a transformation in how we process information, both visual and auditory. This somewhat dense article gives the reader

a brief tour of the scientific literature—including research that shows which cognitive processes do *not* seem to depend on literacy:

Régine Kolinsky. (2015). How learning to read influences language and cognition. In Alexander Pollatsek and Rebecca Treiman (Eds.), *The Oxford handbook of reading* (pp. 377–393). Oxford: Oxford University Press.

74 *[O]bjects he described as "skeleton-shaped, bloodless, ghostly apparitions."*
This quotation from Horace Mann appeared in the seventh of eight annual reports he produced as secretary of the Massachusetts Board of Education. All of the reports can be found here:

babel.hathitrust.org/cgi/pt?id=hvd.hxq9wu&view=1up&seq=7.

Crevasses

82 *Philosophers tell us that much of the meaning that appears to come from language is in fact imagined.*
There is an entire subfield of linguistics (called pragmatics) devoted to the study of meaning that can't be pinned directly onto linguistic objects, that relies instead on the listener reconstructing the speaker's intended meaning on the basis of the context in which the language has been used. This article offers a sweeping historical overview of some of the major developments in the study of pragmatics:

Geoffrey Leech and Jenny Thomas. (2002). Language, meaning, and context: Pragmatics. In N. E. Collinge (Ed.), *An encyclopedia of language* (pp. 105–124). London: Routledge.

84 *What we think has been said is merely our theory of what the speaker surely must have meant by using the words she did.*
In the following paper, which is one of the most frequently cited articles in the study of language, the philosopher Herbert P. Grice laid out his painstaking account of how to separate *what is said* from *what is meant*, and why it is so easy to conflate the two:

Herbert P. Grice. (1975). Logic and conversation. In Peter Cole and Jerry L. Morgan (Eds.), *Syntax and semantics 3: Speech acts* (pp. 41–58). New York: Academic Press.

87 *The Japanese are known for their penchant for obliqueness.*
The anthropologist Edward T. Hall is often cited for his distinction

between "high-context" and "low-context" cultures; the former are cultures in which communication puts less weight on the linguistic content of a message and greater weight on the contextual assumptions shared by the speaker and the hearer, whereas the latter are cultures that favor explicitness in the linguistic message. Hall identified Japan as a particularly strong example of a "high-context" culture. His observations, which have provided much fodder for cross-cultural training sessions in business programs, can be found here:

Edward T. Hall. (1976). *Beyond culture.* Garden City, N.Y.: Anchor Press/ Doubleday.

Anna Wierzbicka is widely known for her work in cross-cultural linguistics. In the article below, she analyzes culturally specific communication patterns in terms of implicit scripts that guide speakers' linguistic choices and behavior. For example, Japanese cultural scripts might include the following guidelines:

- It is good not to say everything that I think.
- Often it is good not to say anything to other people.
- When I want someone to know what I think/feel, I don't have to say it; I can do something else.
- It is good if I can know what another person thinks/feels/wants; this person doesn't have to say anything.

In contrast, Anglo-American scripts might include the following:

- It is good to say to someone what I think/feel.
- It is good to say to others, "I want you to tell me what you think/feel."

Anna Wierzbicka. (1994). "Cultural scripts": A semantic approach to cultural analysis and cross-cultural communication. In Lawrence F. Bouton and Yamuna Kachru (Eds.), *Pragmatics and language learning* (pp. 1–24). Urbana: University of Illinois.

Cultural comparisons of communication patterns may indeed capture some meaningful distinctions, but they also risk obscuring the tremendous variation in communication styles that exist *within* a culture. Within all cultures, people choose a different style of communication depending on, among other things, the status of the hearer and the speaker, the specific subculture(s) to which they belong, and even the nature of the message to be delivered. The following article argues for the importance of considering such nuances:

Kristin Rygg. (2015). Japanese and Norwegian metapragmatic perceptions of contextual factors in intercultural business communication. *Journal of Intercultural Communication, 38.*

90 *Children are chaotic imaginers of meaning, because their theories of reasonable speakers and possible ways of saying are still poorly formed.*
    From a very young age, children show that they understand the importance of being attuned to context in order to understand a speaker's intended meaning, but they are less sophisticated and more prone to making egocentric mistakes than adults are. A review of the relevant literature can be found here:

Myrto Grigoroglou and Anna Papafragou. (2017). Acquisition of pragmatics. In R. Clark and M. Aronoff (Eds.), *Oxford research encyclopedia of linguistics.* Online edition: Oxford University Press.

95 *Some time ago, I read an essay in which the author described the experiences she and other women had with unwanted sex involving men. These episodes were described as failures of language.*
    In this personal essay, the author Susan Dominus articulates why verbal directness can be so difficult in certain sexual situations:

Susan Dominus. (2014). Getting to "no." *The New York Times,* Dec. 11. www .nytimes.com/2014/12/07/magazine/getting-to-no.html.

97 *[A] German study found similar lapses of communicative clarity among physicians and nurses.*
    The results of this study can be found here:

Michael St. Pierre, Axel Scholler, Dieter Strembski, and Georg Breuer. (2012). "Blind obedience" and "blind trust": A simulator study on factors influencing the willingness of residents and nurses to "speak up" and to challenge authority when safety is at stake. *Der Anästhesist, 61,* 857–866.

97 *Researchers who study communication styles find that obliqueness can be predicted in specific situations.*
    For an enjoyable (and often humorous) discussion of when and why people opt for indirectness, read chapter 8 ("Games People Play") of this book:

Steven Pinker. (2007). *The stuff of thought: Language as a window into human nature*. London: Penguin Books.

98 *A much-cited article introduces Western readers to sixteen ways in which a Japanese person might refuse a request without saying "no."*
The article in question is this:

Keiko Ueda. (1974). Sixteen ways to avoid saying "no" in Japan. In John C. Condon and Mitsuko Saito (Eds.), *Intercultural encounters with Japan* (pp. 185–192). Tokyo: Simul Press.

99 *[W]hen rejecting a sexual advance, both Japanese and American college students said they preferred to deliver a soft and oblique refusal rather than flat out saying "no."*
These findings are summarized in the following article:

Jamie L. Goldenberg, Elizabeth M. Ginexi, Carol K. Sigelman, and Paul J. Poppen. (1999). Just say no: Japanese and American styles of refusing unwanted sexual advances. *Journal of Applied Social Psychology*, 29(5), 889–902.

99 *"These behaviors," suggests one paper, "are some of the most likely to result in honest disagreements about consent."*
This quotation (along with arguments for how conflicting communication patterns and agendas might lead to "honest disagreements" between men and women) can be found in the article below:

J. Guillermo Villalobos, Deborah Davis, and Richard A. Leo. (2016). His story, her story: Sexual miscommunication, motivated remembering, and intoxication as pathways to honest false testimony regarding sexual consent. In Ros Burnett (Ed.), *Wrongful allegations of sexual and child abuse* (pp. 129–142). Oxford: Oxford University Press.

99 *[O]ther authors object, citing evidence that men are perfectly aware of the subtle means by which seduction is advanced and rebuffed, and at times simply choose to disregard them.*
Some researchers reject the claim that many alleged instances of sexual assault can be attributed to miscommunications or "honest disagreement" between men and women. They point out that women are indirect in their sexual refusals not because they lack clarity or assertiveness or because they have a different conversational "style" from men but simply because people tend to be delicate and indirect when refusing *any* request that puts a person's feelings on the line, whether sexual or otherwise. They argue that both women and men are generally competent at navigating the subtle art of re-

fusal that is part of their culture and that most claims of miscommunication are simply attempts to paper over a blatant disregard for the other person's wishes. This argument can be found in the following articles, among others:

Melanie Beres. (2010). Sexual miscommunication? Untangling assumptions about sexual communication between casual sex partners. *Culture, Health, and Sexuality*, 12(1), 1–14.

Rachael O'Byrne, Mark Rapley, and Susan Hansen. (2006). You couldn't say "no," could you? Young men's understandings of sexual refusal. *Feminism and Psychology*, 16(2), 133–154.

Ginger Tate Clausen. (2020). "Next time" means "no": Sexual consent and the structure of refusals. *Feminist Philosophy Quarterly*, 6(4), Article no. 5.

99 *[M]isunderstanding itself can be monstrous—a moral failure, not merely a sad but blameless accident.*
  The following article offers an especially lucid discussion of communication and sexual consent. The author argues that consent is complicated, that it cannot be reduced to a simple slogan, and that people often do not say what they mean, in sexual situations as in any other. While acknowledging that the complexity of consent has often been used to justify or excuse assault, she maintains that retreating into oversimplification robs us all of the means by which we might "act ethically in the midst of inevitable and unavoidable ambiguity."

Kate Lockwood Harris. (2018). Yes means yes and no means no, but both these mantras need to go: Communication myths in consent education and anti-rape activism. *Journal of Applied Communication Research*, 46(2), 155–178.

The rectilinear movement of time

113 *Saint Augustine ruminated about time and language.*
  I have drawn on the following edition of Augustine's work for his penetrating remarks on time:

Saint Augustine. (2008). Book XI: Time and eternity. In *Confessions* (Henry Chadwick, Trans.) (pp. 221–245). Oxford: Oxford University Press.

116 *[L]anguage, in its everyday use, involves a frantic negotiation between future and past.*
  Discussions of the interplay of memory and prediction in language are distributed over hundreds of scientific papers. A bird's-eye view can be

found in this book, particularly in the chapters titled "Word Recognition," "Understanding Sentence Structure and Meaning," and "Speaking: From Planning to Articulation":

Julie Sedivy. (2020). *Language in mind: An introduction to psycholinguistics* (2nd ed.). New York: Oxford University Press.

125 *In her book* The Human Condition, *Hannah Arendt remarks that humans are the only beings on earth that are mortal.*
    Arendt's remarks can be found in the third chapter of her book ("Eternity Versus Immortality"), on pages 17–21:

Hannah Arendt. (2018). *The human condition* (2nd ed.). Chicago: University of Chicago Press.

126 *"Our existence is but a brief crack of light between two eternities of darkness."*
    This quotation is drawn from the opening lines of Nabokov's memoir:

Vladimir Nabokov. (1967). *Speak, memory: An autobiography revisited.* New York: Vintage.

129 *The problem of speech is that "there is no way to stop sound and have sound," as noted by Walter Ong, who studied the historical shifts from oral to written cultures.*
    Ong's seminal work, first published in 1982, was reissued in a special edition with additional chapters by John Hartley commenting on Ong's legacy:

Walter J. Ong. (2012). *Orality and literacy: 30th anniversary edition.* London: Routledge.

131 *Some scholars have argued that writing has reshaped the syntax of its host languages.*
    A discussion of the ways in which writing might have changed language, along with the excerpts from the Hittite and Akkadian texts, can be found in this expansive survey of the history of language:

Guy Deutscher. (2006). *The unfolding of language.* New York: Henry Holt.

135 *It is not enough time to entwine the mind of the reader with the mind of the writer.*
    Reading researchers have pointed out that *how* one reads a text is at

least as important as what the text is; the same text can recruit different cognitive processes and elicit different brain responses depending on how attentively one reads it. The following article summarizes some results from brain imaging that make this point:

Natalie M. Phillips. (2015). Literary neuroscience and history of mind: An interdisciplinary fMRI study of attention and Jane Austen. In Lisa Zunshine (Ed.), *The Oxford handbook of cognitive literary studies* (pp. 55–81). Oxford: Oxford University Press.

Lisa Zunshine has argued that literary fiction, far from being a cognitive luxury, is one of the best ways of training the mind for complexity and that it should be given at least as much priority as so-called informational texts in education. She makes an impassioned case in the article below, pointing out that literary fiction, more than any other text, is filled with situations in which the reader must work out nested states of mind (for example, Romeo *didn't know* that Juliet merely *wanted* some people to *think* she was dead). These complex structures, which serve to give a work of fiction its dramatic tension, arguably help readers learn how to build elaborate theories of the emotional states and motivations of others.

Lisa Zunshine. (2015). The secret life of fiction. *PMLA, 130*(3), 724–731.

136 *Decades ago, Walter Ong proposed that we were on the cusp of an era of "secondary orality."*
Some thoughts on the development of this new form of orality can be found in a section titled "Post-typography: Electronics," on pages 133–136 of the thirtieth anniversary edition of Ong's classic work:

Walter J. Ong. (2012). *Orality and literacy: 30th anniversary edition.* London: Routledge.

136 *Tom Pettitt has embraced the term "Gutenberg parenthesis."*
The link below offers a thought-provoking lecture by Tom Pettitt on the ways in which the technology of print has frozen and contained language, and on how new digital technologies may be returning us to less static forms of language. Lively commentary and discussion follow the talk. In keeping with the theme of the lecture, it is available in the forms of video, audio podcast, or a written summary:

commforum.mit.edu/the-gutenberg-parenthesis-oral-tradition-and-digital -technologies-29e1a4fde271.

136 *An optimist might speculate that we will come to harvest the best of both written and oral cultures.*

Gretchen McCulloch has written an exuberant book in which she describes the creativity and patterned behavior that are evident in the informal language of the internet. The book should be required reading for digital optimists and pessimists alike:

Gretchen McCulloch. (2019). *Because internet: Understanding the new rules of language.* New York: Riverhead.

137 *There is evidence that people read less deeply on digital devices than on paper.*

There have been many studies addressing whether reading comprehension suffers when people read text on digital devices. This paper offers a comprehensive review of these studies and points out that the disadvantage of reading onscreen rather than on paper has in fact *increased* in recent years, suggesting that so-called digital natives are not better at reading digital text than those who grew up in a world of print:

Pablo Delgado, Cristina Vargas, Rakefet Ackerman, and Ladislao Salmerón. (2018). Don't throw away your printed books: A meta-analysis on the effects of reading media on reading comprehension. *Educational Research Review, 25,* 23–38.

However, the evidence is nuanced, and it's unlikely that reading comprehension is better on paper for all texts or for all readers. The following article finds that when the analysis is limited to narrative texts, there is no disadvantage to reading narrative texts onscreen. It is unclear why this might be the case. It could be that stories are inherently engrossing, so readers generally read them more attentively than expository texts, regardless of the format. Or, it could be that the narrative texts included in this analysis were on the whole less cognitively taxing than the texts studied in other papers. It would not be surprising in the least if there turned out to be a digital disadvantage for denser narrative texts but no such effect for breezier stories.

Annika Schwabe, Fabienne Lind, Lukas Kosch, and Hajo G. Boomgaarden. (2022). No negative effects of reading on screen on comprehension of narrative texts compared to print: A meta-analysis. *Media Psychology, 25*(6), 779–796.

This short paper does not settle the debate, but it offers a rich theoretical framework within which to understand the cognitive work that goes into reading and why the format of text might matter:

Terje Hillesund, Theresa Schilhab, and Anne Mangen. (2022). Text materi-
alities, affordances, and the embodied turn in the study of reading. *Frontiers
in Psychology, 13*, 827058.

137 *Maryanne Wolf invites readers to consider whether [reading in frag-
ments] is becoming the default manner of reading.*
     Wolf articulates her worries about the loss of deep reading in this elo-
quent and informative book. The book is at once a reflection on the ways in
which reading has shaped her own intellect, an exposition of the cognitive
skills needed to do it well, and a prescription for how to raise children to
love text in a distraction-filled digital world:

Maryanne Wolf. (2018). *Reader, come home: The reading brain in a digital world.*
New York: HarperCollins.

     Whether such worries will be borne out by hard evidence remains
to be seen, because there hasn't yet been enough research to offer a clear
picture of how digital environments are affecting our cognitive lives. Some
work, however, does suggest that use of digital devices can have detri-
mental effects on attention and memory. The following paper provides a
review:

Joseph Firth, John Torous, Brendon Stubbs, Josh A. Firth, Genevieve Z.
Steiner, Lee Smith, Mario Alvarez-Jimenez, et al. (2019). The "online brain":
How the internet may be changing our cognition. *World Psychiatry, 18*(2),
119–129.

139 *Many years after I first set eyes on Rembrandt's* Anatomy Lesson, *I
came across a piece of writing by Sarah Kofman about the same painting.*
     Kofman's meditations on Rembrandt's painting can be found in this
thoughtful essay:

Sarah Kofman. (2007). Conjuring death: Remarks on *The Anatomy Lesson of
Doctor Nicolas Tulp* (1632). In *Selected Writings* (pp. 237–241). Stanford, Calif.:
Stanford University Press.

Resolving ambiguities

147 *Geoff Pullum laid out evidence for [language's] inherently ambiguous
nature.*
     Pullum has written many posts about ambiguity for the blog *Language
Log*, all worth reading. The quoted excerpt comes from this:

Geoff Pullum. (2012). Waterstones. *Language Log*, Jan. 15. languagelog.ldc
.upenn.edu/nll/?p=3705.

148 *When language is spoken rather than written, its ambiguous nature is
especially evident.*
  The problem of ambiguity has preoccupied psycholinguists for decades.
My colleagues and I at the University of Rochester were the first to use eye
movements as a method for investigating how people manage to understand
each other despite the ambiguity. Some of that work is summarized here:

Michael K. Tanenhaus, Michael J. Spivey-Knowlton, Kathleen M. Eberhard,
and Julie Sedivy. (1995). Integration of visual and linguistic information in
spoken language comprehension. *Science, 268*(5217), 1632–1634.

150 *Virginia Woolf . . . might not have been as quick as the others to disavow
the stifled meanings.*
  With the combination of precision and exploration that is so charac-
teristic of her work, in this wonderful essay Woolf turns her thoughts to the
layers of ambiguities and associations that are inherent to words:

Virginia Woolf. (2008). Craftsmanship. In *Selected essays* (pp. 85–94). Oxford: Oxford University Press.

155 *[C]hildren are said to be creative in ways that adults are not.*
  The pure and unshackled creativity of a child's mind is somewhat of
a cliché; we often assume that children have not yet been imprisoned by
the rigid patterns of thought that constrain us as adults, after creativity has
allegedly been beaten out of us by authoritarian pedagogical methods or
society at large. But a child may owe her creativity in large part to the fact
that the prefrontal cortex, the mind's control center, is slower to mature
than other brain regions. This article discusses some of the trade-offs inherent to cognitive control and proposes evolutionary reasons for its slow
maturation:

Sharon L. Thompson-Schill, Michael Ramscar, and Evangelia G. Chrysikou.
(2009). Cognition without control: When a little frontal lobe goes a long
way. *Current Directions in Psychological Science, 18*(5), 259–263.

156 *[C]reativity thrives when the mind's director knows when to step in and
lead and when to let the associative fireworks of the brain do their work.*
  It's widely accepted among researchers that creativity involves the interplay between spontaneous and disciplined mental processes. However,

many questions remain about what the optimal mix is, whether both are recruited in equal amounts at various stages of creative work, and whether different types of creative work call on different proportions of each. The articles below summarize the research in this area:

Mathias Benedek and Emanuel Jauk. (2019). Creativity and cognitive control. In James C. Kaufman and Robert J. Sternberg (Eds.), *Cambridge handbook of creativity* (pp. 200–223). Cambridge, U.K.: Cambridge University Press.

Darya L. Zabelina. (2018). Attention and creativity. In Rex E. Jung and Oshin Vartanian (Eds.), *The Cambridge handbook of the neuroscience of creativity* (pp. 161–179). Cambridge, U.K.: Cambridge University Press.

157 *"How does a woman know when a marriage is over? Because of the way her life suddenly shears off in just two directions: past and future."*
These lines are drawn from this book:

Carol Shields. (2008). *The stone diaries: 15th anniversary edition.* New York: Penguin. P. 71.

How to be a success!

166 *When narrative speech is stripped of all disfluencies in the lab, listeners find it more difficult to understand or remember.*
Disfluencies may be involuntary side effects of the temporal challenges of speech, but listeners do not treat them as useless garbage; instead, they put them to good use in their own work of comprehension. In the following study, researchers manipulated speech and found the presence of filled pauses helped listeners retain information that followed in the wake of disfluencies:

Scott H. Fraundorf and Duane G. Watson. (2011). The disfluent discourse: Effects of filled pauses on recall. *Journal of Memory and Language, 65*(2), 161–175.

This paper found that filled pauses helped listeners recognize upcoming words more quickly. Moreover, listeners were sensitive to informational differences between "uhs" versus "ums":

Jean E. Fox Tree. (2001). Listeners' uses of *um* and *uh* in speech comprehension. *Memory and Cognition, 29,* 320–326.

And the following study found that filled pauses allowed listeners to anticipate upcoming complex phrases, thereby easing comprehension:

Michiko Watanabe, Keikichi Hirose, Yasuharu Den, and Nobuaki Mine-matsu. (2008). Filled pauses as cues to the complexity of upcoming phrases for native and non-native listeners. *Speech Communication*, *50*(2), 81–94.

169 *[M]en were more likely than women to use [tag questions] as markers of uncertainty whereas women more often used them to lubricate interactions with a conversational partner.*
   In this article, Janet Holmes takes a detailed look at the conversational functions of elements that are mistakenly assumed to be mere expressions of powerlessness, and finds that the story of language and gender is far more interesting and complicated than commonly believed:

Janet Holmes. (1987). Hedging, fencing, and other conversational gambits: An analysis of gender differences in New Zealand speech. In Anne Pauwels (Ed.), *Women and language in Australian and New Zealand society* (pp. 59–79). Sydney: Australian Professional Publications.

169 *A similar richness of function has been documented for uptalk.*
   A dive into this volume will reveal how much you never knew you didn't know about the phenomenon of uptalk. The author covers its historical origins, its social influences, its presence in other languages, and the collision between how uptalk is discussed in the media and how it is viewed by linguistic experts:

Paul Warren. (2016). *Uptalk: The phenomenon of rising intonation.* Cambridge, U.K.: Cambridge University Press.

170 *Uptalk, like filled pauses, can direct the beam of a listener's attention.*
   Jean Fox Tree has made a career out of bringing what many take to be language's detritus—disfluencies, so-called meaningless words or phrases ("like," "you know"), and listener feedback ("uh-huh," "mmm," "really!")—into the light of day and subjecting it to scientific scrutiny. Here, she and Jack Tomlinson turn their attention to the effects of uptalk on listeners' comprehension:

John M. Tomlinson Jr. and Jean E. Fox Tree. (2011). Listeners' comprehension of uptalk in spontaneous speech. *Cognition*, *119*(1), 58–69.

171 *[T]he same kind of talk can elicit different reactions depending on whether the speaker is male or female.*

A number of studies have observed, in line with complaints commonly voiced by women, that men's linguistic behavior does not come under the same scrutiny. Not all studies find that men and women are subject to different standards, but when there are differences, it is always in the direction of greater constraints on women. The following studies report that women are more penalized than men for using so-called tentative language:

Stephen M. Utych. (2021). Speaking style and candidate evaluations. *Politics, Groups, and Identities, 9*(3), 589–607.

Renata Bongiorno, Paul G. Bain, and Barbara David. (2014). If you're going to be a leader, at least act like it! Prejudice towards women who are tentative in leader roles. *British Journal of Social Psychology, 53*(2), 217–234.

This study found that vocal fry in women's voices hurt their evaluations as job candidates more strongly than it did for men.

Rindy C. Anderson, Casey A. Klofstad, William J. Mayew, and Mohan Venkatachalam. (2014). Vocal fry may undermine the success of young women in the labor market. *PLOS One, 9*(5), e97506.

And lest anyone have the overly rosy view that women are immune to perpetuating these standards, it is worth noting that in some of these studies women were found to be penalized for their speech even more heavily by their fellow women than by men.

171 *[T]entative language rendered a woman less influential in the eyes of other women but more influential in the eyes of men.*
   The article below reports that men and women responded differently to tentative language used by women.

Linda L. Carli. (1990). Gender, language, and influence. *Journal of Personality and Social Psychology, 59*(5), 941–952.

These results are somewhat different from the more recent papers listed above, by Stephen Utych and by Renata Bongiorno and her colleagues, who reported that women were judged harshly by men and women alike for speaking unassertively. The authors of these more recent papers suggest that expectations of women have shifted over time; as it has become more acceptable for women to abandon traditional female roles, they are more broadly expected—by both men and women—to adopt forceful styles of communication. While the passage of time has likely shifted attitudes, I suspect there is still quite a lot of variation across subcultures or even specific situations when it comes to how assertively women are expected to speak, dress, and behave, and that they have not completely escaped judgment for being insufficiently demure. These suspicions are confirmed by a paper published around the same time as the one by Bongiorno and colleagues, showing that women were more successful at salary negotiations if they *avoided* forceful language:

Hannah R. Bowles and Linda Babcock. (2013). How can women escape the compensation negotiation dilemma? Relational accounts are one answer. *Psychology of Women Quarterly*, 37(1), 80–96.

172 *[U]ptalk, a stereotypical marker of powerlessness, patterned differently for male and female contestants on the* Jeopardy! *game show.*
     These intriguing results are reported in the following article:

Thomas J. Linneman. (2013). Gender in Jeopardy! Intonation variation on a television game show. *Gender and Society*, 27(1), 82–105.

174 *Much depends upon who is speaking, and when, and where, and upon who is watching.*
     This chapter focuses on gender and language, but the linguistic issues surrounding race, ethnicity, and class are even more complex, with well-documented evidence that certain groups, more than others, are judged harshly for their manner of speaking. Excellent books on the topic include the following:

Katherine D. Kinzler. (2021). *How you say it: Why we judge others by the way they talk—and the costs of this hidden bias.* Boston: Mariner Books.

Rosina Lippi-Green. (2012). *English with an accent: Language, ideology, and discrimination in the United States* (2nd ed.). London: Routledge.

Pleasure hunts

177 *"When I read, I don't really read; I pop a beautiful sentence into my mouth and suck it like a fruit drop."*
     These lines are from the opening paragraph of Hrabal's novel:

Bohumil Hrabal. (1990). *Too loud a solitude* (Michael Henry Heim, Trans.). San Diego: Harcourt.

181 *David Crystal has tabulated elements of sound that contribute to the beauty of an English word.*
Crystal's conclusions are summarized here:

David Crystal. (1995). Phonaesthetically speaking. *English Today, 11*(2), 8–12.

182 *Even more ambitiously, Arthur Jacobs . . . used machine-learning algorithms and a database of more than a billion German words to devise a method for measuring beauty.*
This study is somewhat technical, but illuminating:

Arthur M. Jacobs. (2017). Quantifying the beauty of words: A neurocognitive perspective. *Frontiers in Human Neuroscience, 11*, 622.

182 *Vitaly Komar and Alexander Melamid commissioned professional polling companies to study how people determine beauty in visual art.*
This intriguing and often contrarian book is part scientific report, part exploration of the meaning of art in a commodified world:

JoAnn Wypijewski. (Ed.). (1997). *Painting by numbers: Komar and Melamid's scientific guide to art.* New York: Farrar, Straus and Giroux.

184 *[Cheesecake offers] "trickles of enjoyment from the sweet taste of ripe fruit, the creamy mouth feel of fats and oils from nuts and meat, and the coolness of fresh water."*
Steven Pinker's analogy of art as cheesecake can be found here:

Steven Pinker. (1997). *How the mind works.* New York: Norton. Pp. 524–525.

184 *"So I'm wondering, maybe the blue landscape is genetically imprinted in us, that it's the paradise within."*
These remarks by Alexander Melamid appear on page 13 of *Painting by Numbers*, ed. JoAnn Wypijewski.

184 *"You can have a lifetime of perfectly sincere museum-going where you traipse around enjoying everything and then go out and have some lunch."*
The quoted lines are taken from Donna Tartt's novel:

Donna Tartt. *The goldfinch.* New York: Little, Brown.

185 *I send her "The Cinnamon Peeler" by Michael Ondaatje, one of the most seductive, lyrical poems I know.*

This sure test for poetic anhedonia can be found, among other equally diagnostic poems, in Ondaatje's collection:

Michael Ondaatje. (1984). *Secular love*. New York: Norton.

185 *My sister has not inherited a predisposition to "aesthetic chill."*
"Aesthetic chill" is a term used by scientists to refer to that intense feeling of pleasure or awe, often accompanied by goose bumps or shivers down the spine, that occurs in the presence of something that is perceived as beautiful. Evidently, we are not all born with the same capacity for aesthetic chill. The genetic basis of this trait is investigated in the following article:

Giacomo Bignardi, Rebecca Chamberlain, Sofieke T. Kevenaar, Zenab Tamimy, and Dorret I. Boomsma. (2022). On the etiology of aesthetic chills: A behavioral genetic study. *Scientific Reports*, *12*(1), 3247.

Along similar lines, this paper explores the considerable variation among people in their aesthetic experiences and concludes that judgments of beauty are closely linked with the ability to feel pleasure; people who have difficulty feeling pleasure struggle to experience beauty:

Aenne A. Brielmann and Denis G. Pelli. (2019). Intense beauty requires intense pleasure. *Frontiers in Psychology*, *10*, 2420.

186 *"The word* candy *does nothing to my taste buds, whereas the word* caramella *brings instantly back the sweet crunch of the teeth through the shell."*
M. J. Fitzgerald's meditations on the sensory richness that comes with a childhood language is one of numerous beautiful essays in the anthology below:

M. J. Fitzgerald. (2004). Limpid, blue, poppy. In Wendy Lesser (Ed.), *The genius of language: Fifteen writers reflect on their mother tongues* (pp. 127–144). New York: Anchor Books.

187 *Some researchers claim that when deliberating in a second language, people make judgments dispassionately, less tainted by the biases and emotions that creep into their mother tongue.*
Though such results are not without controversy, they do seem to fit well with a wide range of observations, both anecdotal (see M. J. Fitzgerald's essay above) and experimental, that a language learned later in life is often less potent than a language learned in childhood. Here is one article that is representative of this research program:

Sayuri Hayakawa, David Tannenbaum, Albert Costa, Joanna D. Corey, and Boaz Keysar. (2017). Thinking more or feeling less? Explaining the foreign-language effect on moral judgment. *Psychological Science*, 28(10), 1387–1397.

187 *Maryanne Wolf, a neuroscientist who studies reading, plucks her favorite sentence from George Eliot's novel* Middlemarch.

The sentence, and Wolf's remarks about it, can be found here:

Maryanne Wolf. (2018). *Reader, come home*. New York: Harper. P. 90.

188 *André Aciman thrills to the syntax of Proust.*

Aciman's commentary on the sentences of Proust are contained in an essay titled "Beethoven's Soufflé in A Minor," in the following collection:

André Aciman. (2021). *Homo irrealis: Essays*. New York: Farrar, Straus and Giroux.

189 *Among native English speakers, the ability to parse intricate sentences varies considerably.*

Ewa Dąbrowska's work has shown that the ability to handle complex syntax varies greatly from one individual to another, even among monolingual speakers. Education and exposure to print play a significant part in one's syntactic repertoire, suggesting that people do not hit a ceiling of language function simply by virtue of being native speakers in a language, but continue to stretch their capabilities if their linguistic diet is rich in complexity. Here are two articles that represent this line of work:

Ewa Dąbrowska. (2012). Different speakers, different grammars: Individual differences in native language attainment. *Linguistic Approaches to Bilingualism*, 2(3), 219–253.

James A. Street and Ewa Dąbrowska. (2010). More individual differences in language attainment: How much do adult native speakers of English know about passives and quantifiers? *Lingua*, 120(8), 2080–2094.

195 *I catch a glimmer of what I am missing when I watch a performance of the haiku-like poem "Hands" by Clayton Valli.*

A performance of the poem by the author can be viewed here:

www.youtube.com/watch?v=r2VNzOns5q0.

My favorite performance of this poem is by Claudia Jimenez, which can be viewed at this link, with subsequent commentary in ASL by the poem's author:

www.youtube.com/watch?v=HdjGBzIGDgE.

My appreciation of the poem, and of ASL poetry in general, deepened upon reading an analysis of the poem's aesthetic elements in this master's thesis by Jessica Cole:

Jessica Cole. (2009). *American Sign Language poetry: Literature in motion*. Master's thesis, University of California, San Diego.

198 *As the Deaf poet Paul Scott has observed, hearing people can take a book from a shelf and read it, but "for Deaf people, I am the book."*
Much like the tradition of spoken word poetry, sign language poetry relies on an immediacy of language. Scott's remarks on his poetic practice, along with insights drawn from interviews with other Deaf poets, can be found here:

Rachel Sutton-Spence and Ronice Müller de Quadros. (2014). "I am the book"—Deaf poets' views on signed poetry. *Journal of Deaf Studies and Deaf Education, 19*(4), 546–558.

199 *"Art-sign" is the term coined by linguists to refer to a style of signing that sets the aesthetic above the utilitarian.*
This eye-opening article by the linguists Edward Klima and Ursula Bellugi offers a detailed look at the aesthetic elements found in signed poetry:

Edward S. Klima and Ursula Bellugi. (1976). Poetry and song in a language without sound. *Cognition, 4*, 45–97.

A later and more comprehensive discussion of sign language poetics appears in this book, which should be required reading in any introductory course on poetry:

Rachel Sutton-Spence, Paddy Ladd, and Gillian Rudd. (2005). *Analysing sign language poetry*. Basingstoke, U.K.: Palgrave Macmillan.

200 *"since feeling is first."*
This poem by e. e. cummings can be found in the following collection, first published in 1926:

e. e. cummings. (2022). *is 5*. Bristol, U.K.: Ragged Hand.

Since cummings was a master of syntactic play, I take his opposition in this poem between "syntax" and "feeling" with a grain of salt.

200 *There are some writers . . . who . . . found that language for them is cut in two: there is the embodied language of childhood and its unruly passions, and then a clean, austere language learned later in life.*
This duality has been explored by numerous writers who have experienced dislocation. I've discussed these experiences, as well as the scientific studies addressing such linguistic cleavages, in more detail in the third chapter of my book *Memory Speaks*:

Julie Sedivy. (2021). *Memory speaks: On losing and reclaiming language and self.* Boston: Harvard University Press.

201 *"I've read so many explications of these stanzas that I can analyze them in half a dozen ingenious ways."*
Eva Hoffman's description of the moment that English became for her a language infused with music can be found here:

Eva Hoffman. (1989). *Lost in translation: A life in a new language.* New York: Penguin. P. 186.

203 *There are times when a poem or a song or a sculpture is a burning bush. You must change your life.*
These lines allude to the poem "Archaïscher Torso Apollos" (Archaic torso of Apollo), in which the poet describes an awestruck encounter with a sculptural work of art. One version of the poem can be found on pages 60–61 of this collection:

Rainer Maria Rilke. (1989). *The selected poetry of Rainer Maria Rilke* (Stephen Mitchell, Trans.). New York: Vintage International.

203 *"In the upper reaches of pleasure and on the boundary of fear is a little-studied emotion."*
This quotation comes from a classic paper by Dacher Keltner and Jonathan Haidt, one of the earliest scientific investigations of awe:

Dacher Keltner and Jonathan Haidt. (2003). Approaching awe, a moral, spiritual, and aesthetic emotion. *Cognition and Emotion, 17*(2), 297–314.

The following article reviews the scientific discussion of awe since the publication of Keltner and Haidt's paper. Although awe can be an intensely positive emotion, it can sometimes have negative overtones as well, colored by fear and a feeling of threat. One of its defining properties is that it enlarges a person's sense of the world, requiring some adjustment of one's frame of understanding. Presumably, it is this reframing that causes people to feel that an event or work of art has permanently changed their life.

Alice Chirico and David B. Yaden. (2018). Awe: A self-transcendent and sometimes transformative emotion. In Heather C. Lench (Ed.), *The function of emotions: When and why emotions help us* (pp. 221–233). New York: Springer.

206 *"This is how it always is / when I finish a poem."*
    The lines from Rumi are the closing lines of a poem titled "A Thirsty Fish," which can be found on pages 19–20 of this volume:

Coleman Barks. (Trans.). (2004). *The essential Rumi: New expanded edition.* New York: HarperOne.

206 *As Maria Popova writes in her blog,* The Marginalian, *"Poetry serves the same function as prayer."*
    The following blog post contains Popova's musings on poetry's attempts to express the unsayable, along with links to other authors who have explored this theme:

Maria Popova. Saying the ineffable: Poetry and the language of silence. *The Marginalian.* www.themarginalian.org/2023/02/18/robert-bringhurst-poetry/.

206 *"If something is ineffable, that means it cannot be said. But what cannot be said can sometimes be heard."*
    Robert Bringhurst's remarks come in the closing pages of his beautiful exploration of language and literature:

Robert Bringhurst. (2006). *The tree of meaning: Language, mind, and ecology.* Berkeley, Calif.: Counterpoint.

207 *Psilocybin is a therapeutically promising accelerant of awe. So is technology.*
    Most transformations of the self are painstakingly slow, requiring an accumulation of experiences over a long period of time, which is what makes awe so fascinating to scientists of the mind; experiences of awe can lead to surprisingly rapid and long-lasting transformations of the self, as biblically captured in Saint Paul's sudden conversion on the road to Damascus.

Yet these experiences are elusive. The following article suggests that psychedelics, which have been shown to spur transformational change in some people's lives, are powerful precisely because of their capacity to induce experiences of awe:

Peter S. Hendricks. (2018). Awe: A putative mechanism underlying the effects of classic psychedelic-assisted psychotherapy. *International Review of Psychiatry, 30*(4), 331–342.

And this paper explores whether simulations in virtual reality can bring experiences of awe within reach of more people who might otherwise not have access to spectacular natural experiences:

Denise Quesnel and Bernhard E. Riecke. (2018). Are you awed yet? How virtual reality gives us awe and goose bumps. *Frontiers in Psychology, 9*, 2158.

208 *"One day I was walking along Tinker Creek thinking of nothing at all and I saw the tree with the lights in it."*
Anne Dillard's luminous description of a transformational moment of grace in the natural world was drawn from this work:

Anne Dillard. (2013) [1974]. Seeing. In *Pilgrim at Tinker Creek* (pp. 16–36). New York: Harper Perennial.

Missing words

216 *At six months of age, an infant can perceive the subtle differences that distinguish the sounds of any language.*
This paper, considered one of the most important in research on language development, was the first to document the narrowing of perceptual abilities in the first year of an infant's life, showing that at a very young age children lose sensitivity to the speech sounds of languages other than their own:

Janet F. Werker and Richard C. Tees. (1984). Cross-language speech perception: Evidence for perceptual reorganization during the first year of life. *Infant Behavior and Development, 7*(1), 49–63.

Perceptual narrowing is not limited to the sounds of speech; it is also evident in sensitivity to the handshapes of sign languages. In the following study, researchers found that at four months of age, babies who lived in an English-only household could distinguish between certain handshapes that appear in ASL, but by fourteen months they had lost this ability. On the other hand, babies being raised in bilingual English-ASL households retained this ability.

Stephanie Baker Palmer, Laurel Fais, Roberta Michnick Golinkoff, and Janet F. Werker. (2012). Perceptual narrowing of linguistic sign occurs in the 1st year of life. *Child Development*, 83(2), 543–553.

217 *[W]hat looks like decline may simply be a side effect of learning.*
      In this article, the author pushes for a reframing of findings that purport to show evidence of declines in memory and language among older people. He argues that studies that fail to statistically take into account how knowledge expands over a lifetime (and hence, the size of the mental storehouse from which information is being retrieved) are methodologically flawed.

Michael Ramscar. (2022). Psycholinguistics and aging. In *Oxford research encyclopedia of linguistics*.

A somewhat different perspective is offered in the article below. The authors agree that older people differ from young people in the sheer quantity of information they have accumulated over time. However, they also argue that due to age-related declines in how well older adults control attention, they are less able to suppress irrelevant information, dragging a clutter of information out of memory and into their attention. This is not without its benefits, the authors point out, but it has costs as well.

Tarek Amer, Jordana S. Wynn, and Lynn Hasher. (2022). Cluttered memory representations shape cognition in old age. *Trends in Cognitive Sciences*, 26(3), 255–267.

218 *What is undeniably lost in the transition from youth to older age is speed.*
      The following article laid the groundwork for decades of scientific discussion that revolved around the slowing of the aging mind. It is somewhat dense and theoretical, but it provides an explicit rationale for the methodologies involved in this line of research.

Timothy A. Salthouse. (1996). The processing-speed theory of adult age differences in cognition. *Psychological Review*, 103(3), 403–428.

220 *One great puzzle . . . has been why, given the indisputable evidence of degraded performance on simple tests in the lab, older people do so well on dazzlingly complex activities out in the world.*

In the following paper, Timothy Salthouse—who spent much of his research career documenting age-related declines—addresses the question of why clear evidence of declining performance on cognitive tests in the lab is not more directly reflected in real-life performance:

Timothy Salthouse. (2012). Consequences of age-related cognitive declines. *Annual Review of Psychology, 63*, 201–226.

221 *[I]t is becoming clear that experience is an antidote to the slowing that comes with age.*
    Working memory—that is, the capacity to hold and manipulate information in short-term memory—is known to be one of the functions that declines with age. It is also known to be important for using and understanding language. However, a wealth of experience with language can compensate for this otherwise significant loss. The study below found that older people who were avid readers performed well at understanding and recalling sentences, even in the face of a clear decline in working memory:

Brennan R. Payne, Xuefei Gao, Soo Rim Noh, Carolyn J. Anderson, and Elizabeth A. L. Stine-Morrow. (2012). The effects of print exposure on sentence processing and memory in older adults: Evidence for efficiency and reserve. *Aging, Neuropsychology, and Cognition, 19*(1–2), 122–149.

222 *[T]he more the laboratory resembles the world outside, the less one sees something to mourn.*
    Several studies have shown that putting a memory task in a realistic context can reduce, eliminate, or even reverse the performance gap between older and younger participants. This applies to memory for words, as found in the study below:

Laura E. Matzen and Aaron S. Benjamin. (2013). Older and wiser: Older adults' episodic word memory benefits from sentence study contexts. *Psychology and Aging, 28*(3), 754–767.

It has also been demonstrated in memory for numbers, as shown here:

Alan D. Castel. (2005). Memory for grocery prices in younger and older adults: The role of schematic support. *Psychology and Aging, 20*(4), 718–721.

224 *But rather than focus on averting the losses of age, why aren't we determined to cultivate its gains?*
    This article takes a holistic view of aging, summarizing the changes

to our brains, cognitive skills, and emotions that occur over a lifetime and arguing that each phase of life comes with its own strengths and weaknesses. When we are young, we are optimized for exploration and discovery; when we are old, we shine at exploiting the experiences we've accumulated.

R. Nathan Spreng and Gary R. Turner. (2021). From exploration to exploitation: A shifting mental mode in late life development. *Trends in Cognitive Sciences*, 25(12), 1058–1071.

Limits

232 *Live long enough, and the weaknesses of the ear and brain accumulate.*
   Hearing loss due to aging is complex and involves multiple causes. The following article is a short and friendly summary of some of the changes in the ear and brain that lead to difficulties in understanding speech:

Samira Anderson, Sandra Gordon-Salant, and Judy R. Dubno. (2018). Hearing and aging effects on speech understanding: Challenges and solutions. *Acoustics Today*, 14(4), 10–18.

A more detailed overview of auditory and cognitive changes over the human life span can be found in this book chapter:

Chad S. Rogers and Jonathan E. Peelle. Interactions between cognition and audition in hearing loss and aging. In Lori L. Holt, Jonathan E. Peelle, Allison B. Coffin, Arthur N. Popper, and Richard R. Fay (Eds.), *Speech perception* (pp. 227–252). Cham, Switzerland: Springer.

234 *As the science writer Ed Yong notes, "Every animal is enclosed within its own sensory bubble, perceiving but a tiny sliver of an immense world."*
   In this magnificent and beautifully written book, Ed Yong takes the reader on a mind-expanding tour of the perceptual capabilities of nonhuman creatures:

Ed Yong. (2022). *An immense world: How animal senses reveal the hidden realms around us.* New York: Random House.

235 *Of the blindness that descended upon him in old age, Jorge Luis Borges wrote that it "has not been for me a total misfortune."*
   Borges's meditative essay "Blindness," translated by Eliot Weinberger, can be found in the following collection:

Jorge Luis Borges. (2009). *Seven nights* (Eliot Weinberger, Trans.). New York: New Directions.

235 *In a piece called "Hearing Essay," the musician Evelyn Glennie describes how deafness expanded her ways of hearing.*
This essay can be found on Glennie's website at the following link:

www.evelyn.co.uk/hearing-essay/.

238 *What style of language arises among DeafBlind people who are free to shape language in accordance with their shared* Umwelt?
Much like the spontaneous growth of new sign languages within communities of Deaf people who don't know any sign language, it is the shared perceptual experience among DeafBlind people that appears to be driving the linguistic innovations of Protactile language. The following online resource, which is presented as a conversation between the expert Protactile speakers John Lee Clark and Jelica Nuccio, offers a fascinating introduction to some of the distinctive properties of this language while also providing a beautiful visual illustration of it, with simultaneous English translation.

John Lee Clark and Jelica B. Nuccio. (2020). Protactile linguistics: Discussing recent research findings. *Journal of American Sign Languages and Literatures*, journalofasl.com/protactile-linguistics/.

241 *"By now, I can see in Italian, but only partially. I still grope around in semi-obscurity."*
In an essay titled "Why Italian?," Jhumpa Lahiri elaborates on her decision to begin writing in Italian, a foreign language she adopted relatively late in life. The essay was originally written in Italian, and translated by Molly L. O'Brien, in collaboration with the author. It can be found in the following collection:

Jhumpa Lahiri. (2022). *Translating myself and others*. Princeton, N.J.: Princeton University Press.

243 *[W]riting "feels like a forced, daily encounter with limits."*
Maggie Nelson explores the relationship of freedom to art in a piece titled "Art Song," in the following volume:

Maggie Nelson. (2021). *On freedom: Four songs of care and constraint*. Minneapolis: Graywolf Press.

244 *The young Nicaraguan Sign Language . . . arose in the 1980s when dozens of children, previously stranded in hearing communities that did not sign, were gathered into a national school for the Deaf.*

It is exceedingly rare that linguists are able to observe the beginnings of an entirely new language. Most commonly, "new" languages arise much as new species do, that is, through a series of very gradual changes that eventually result in enough differences to set them apart from an ancestral language—as happened when, over time, Latin evolved into French, Spanish, and Portuguese. In such cases, the historical connection to the ancestral language is clearly visible in the words and grammar of the younger language. Because all groups of hearing people inherit language from previous generations, the spontaneous birth of an entirely new *spoken* language is never seen. But occasionally, a population of Deaf people springs up quickly enough that a new sign language is created from nothing. In these cases, the language does not originate from an ancestral sign language, nor is it derived from the spoken language that is used in that geographic region. As such, it offers a fascinating look at how, over subsequent generations of speakers, a set of rudimentary signs blooms into a fully elaborated, grammatically complex language. Nicaraguan Sign Language (NSL) is the most heavily documented example of such a language. Its history and development are discussed in the following magazine article:

Susan Meiselas. (1999). A linguistic big bang. *The New York Times Magazine*, Oct. 24. archive.nytimes.com/www.nytimes.com/library/magazine/home/19991024mag-sign-language.html.

NSL is not, however, the only such sign language to emerge in contemporary times. The following book chapter surveys a number of new and emerging sign languages around the world and discusses their typical properties and conditions of birth:

Irit Meir, Wendy Sandler, Carol Padden, and Mark Aronoff. (2010). Emerging sign languages. In *Oxford handbook of Deaf studies, language, and education* 2, 267–280.

244 *In a famous study, a team of psychologists sent people alone into an empty room for fifteen minutes, with nothing but a machine that delivered electric shock.*

Most people do not enjoy "just thinking" and prefer their mental excursions to be anchored to a concrete activity. They will even go to some lengths to avoid the boredom of having nothing to do, as reported in this study:

Timothy D. Wilson, David A. Reinhard, Erin C. Westgate, Daniel T. Gilbert, Nicole Ellerbeck, Cheryl Hahn, Casey L. Brown, and Adi Shaked. (2014). Just think: The challenges of the disengaged mind. *Science, 345*(6192), 75–77.

245 *Over the course of an eleven-year incarceration at the hands of the Italian Fascist government, Antonio Gramsci produced his most influential writings.*
    A brief essay about the life and work of Antonio Gramsci, published online by the *Stanford Encyclopedia of Philosophy,* can be found at the following link:

plato.stanford.edu/entries/gramsci/.

    Jhumpa Lahiri has written an essay about her own engagement with Gramsci's writings, titled "Traduzione (stra)ordinaria/(Extra)ordinary Translation." It can be found in the following collection:

Jhumpa Lahiri. (2022). *Translating myself and others.* Princeton, N.J.: Princeton University Press.

245 *"Patient labor differs from moments of liberation or itinerant moments of freedom in that it goes on."*
    This passage is taken from the essay "Art Song" in the following collection:

Maggie Nelson. (2021). *On freedom: Four songs of care and constraint.* Minneapolis: Graywolf Press.

246 *"One of the few good things to say about old age is that you have a new experience."*
    Louise Glück's remarks on aging are taken from the following interview:

Alexandra Alter. (2020). "I was unprepared": Louise Glück on poetry, aging, and a surprise Nobel Prize. *The New York Times,* Oct. 8. www.nytimes.com/2020/10/08/books/louise-gluck-nobel-prize-literature.html.

247 *[A] bird's communicative needs may change from season to season, and so may its hearing.*
    Ed Yong summarizes the fascinating research on the seasonal changes in birds' auditory perception in the eighth chapter ("All Ears") of his book:

Ed Yong. (2022). An *immense world: How animal senses reveal the hidden realms around us.* New York: Random House.

248 *The psychologist Laura Carstensen has found that as the enclosure of a life changes shape, so do a person's desires.*

The core insight of Laura Carstensen's extensive research program is that our perception of how much time we have left to live affects our goals, desires, and even what we notice or remember. A good entry point into this intriguing line of research is the following overview article:

Laura L. Carstensen. (2021). Socioemotional selectivity theory: The role of perceived endings in human motivation. *Gerontologist, 61*(8), 1188–1196.

Silence

254 *Among its many victims, West stands out as a person singled out for an inordinately cruel loss.*

Diane Ackerman chronicles Paul West's stroke and partial recovery in a moving and scientifically informed memoir:

Diane Ackerman. (2011). *A hundred names for love: A stroke, a marriage, and the language of healing.* New York: Norton.

255 *His name was Louis Victor Leborgne, but he was known in the hospital as Tan.*

Paul Broca wrote a detailed and lucid account of his meetings with Louis Victor Leborgne. A translation can be found here:

Ennis Ata Berker, Ata Husnu Berker, and Aaron Smith. (1986). Translation of Broca's 1865 report: Localization of speech in the third left frontal convolution. *Archives of Neurology, 43*(10), 1065–1072.

Leborgne's brain was preserved after his death and was found to have sustained massive damage to the brain tissues. In fact, modern imaging has found that the damage was considerably more extensive than initially thought by Broca. The anatomically curious can find the results of the imaging here:

Nina F. Dronkers, Odile Plaisant, Marie Therese Iba-Zizen, and Emmanuel A. Cabanis. (2007). Paul Broca's historic cases: High resolution MR imaging of the brains of Leborgne and Lelong. *Brain, 130*(5), 1432–1441.

257 *[West's] first post-stroke book was a memoir, dictated with dogged effort, in which he related his experience of aphasia.*

West's memoir, disorienting as it is, is a lesson in the resilience of language and the human spirit, in addition to being a revelatory reading experience.

Paul West. (2008). *The shadow factory*. Santa Fe, N.M.: Lumen Books.

263 *Our selves, much like our brains, are tangles of connections.*
    In this book, the cognitive scientist Michael Spivey pushes against the notion of the enclosed self, gathering scientific evidence for the complicated interactions that exist between brains, bodies, other beings, and the larger environment in which we live:

Michael J. Spivey. (2020). *Who you are: The science of connectedness*. Cambridge, Mass.: MIT Press.

268 *Somerset Maugham wrote that "the great tragedy of life is not that men perish, but that they cease to love."*
    Julian Barnes's meditations on this quotation from Maugham appear in his memoir:

Julian Barnes. (2009). *Nothing to be frightened of*. New York: Vintage.

268 *"Pretend if you like that death will never come."*
    These lines were drawn from Samuel LeBaron's memoir about mortality and his own impending death:

Samuel LeBaron. (2022). *Ordinary deaths: Stories from memory*. Edmonton: University of Alberta Press.

270 *[I]nfants more readily learn the sounds of a new language when they are in the physical presence of the person uttering them.*
    In this article, the researcher Pat Kuhl argues that speech learning in early life is not just a computational problem to be solved by the infant brain but a process that is dependent on social involvement:

Patricia K. Kuhl. (2007). Is speech learning "gated" by the social brain? *Developmental Science, 10*(1), 110–120.

271 *It occurred to me to wonder whether Vac was in a state akin to the mystical experience that the neuroscientist Jill Bolte Taylor has described in her account of her own stroke.*
    While the loss of the inner voice may be terrifying to some (including myself), Jill Bolte Taylor's eloquent memoir suggests that its quies-

cence offers an escape from mortality. Her book also renders, in exquisite and knowledgeable detail, the subjective experience of a stroke and its aftermath:

Jill Bolte Taylor. (2008). *My stroke of insight: A brain scientist's personal journey.* New York: Penguin.

Acknowledgments

The most emotionally taxing phases of book writing are for me the early stages of the first draft and the final stages of revision; these are the times when the fear of failure roars its loudest. At the beginning, you're not sure if you can write the book you want to write, and at the end you don't know if you've succeeded in writing it. In my work on this book, two great losses accompanied these most difficult stages: the death of my beloved brother Vac overlapped with its beginning, and the death of my husband, Ian, came near its completion. The presence of these men is woven into every page of the book; their departures clarified its themes of time and love.

Vac, thank you for meandering with me through the fields of our childhood memories, for the meanings you extracted from them and shared with me, for the insights around every corner, and for being, more than anyone else in my life, the person who understood what is important and what is not.

Ian, thank you for . . . well, all of it. You literally saved me. The person that I am would not exist had the waters of your self not mingled with my own. Thank you for everything you did that made it possible for me to write, especially those things that really cost you. You have enriched and deepened the meanings of countless words for me, but especially these: "connection," "strength," "trust," "ardor," "seeing," "open."

Many others carried me through all the stages of writing this book with the gifts of their friendship and talents. A special thanks to Sharon Butala, Greg Carnie, Weyman Chan, Jennifer Graham, Jill Graham, Ben Haley, Samuel LeBaron, Berend McKenzie, Sherryl Melnyk, Ann Murphy, Jim Murphy (who also reached the end of his life, leaving me to carry on our conversations), Valeh Hosseinzadeh Nasser, Jana Sedivy. Thank you to my mother, Vera Sedivy, for your intellect and your influence. Thank you to Chigusa Kurumada and Florian Jaeger for the endless support, and for the stimulating talks that awakened my mind when I thought it had gone dead—a number of our discussions have found their way into these pages. Thank you to Michael Spivey for the conversations about life, the mind, and the life of the mind. Thank you to Kate Sedivy-Haley for being the most attentive and analytical reader I know.

I'm grateful to my agent, the late Beth Vesel, who nudged this book into being and who found the best possible home for it. Thank you to Jonathan Galassi for believing it could be written and to Katie Liptak for your warm and perceptive editing.

All of you have contributed to the miracle of this book's existence.